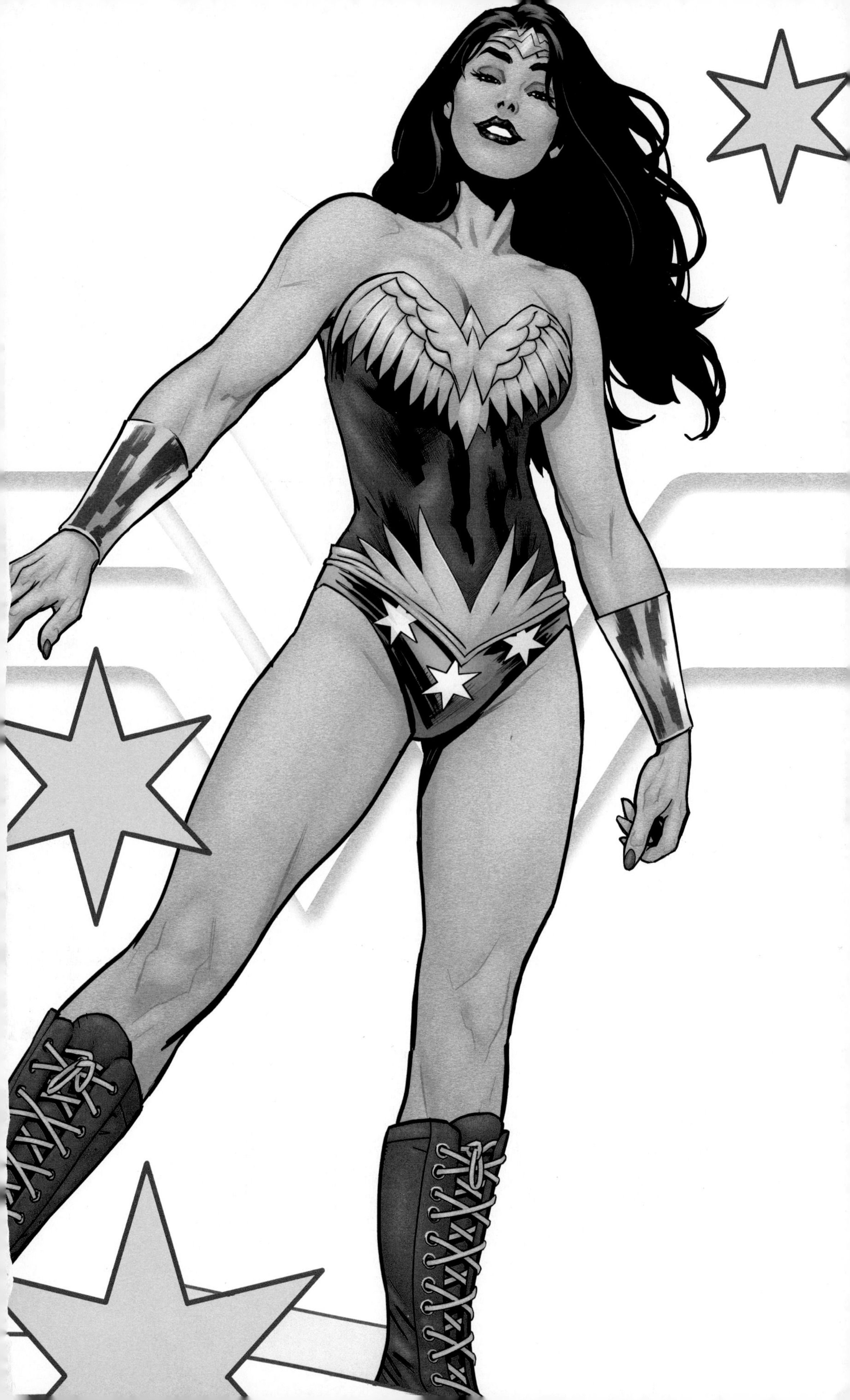

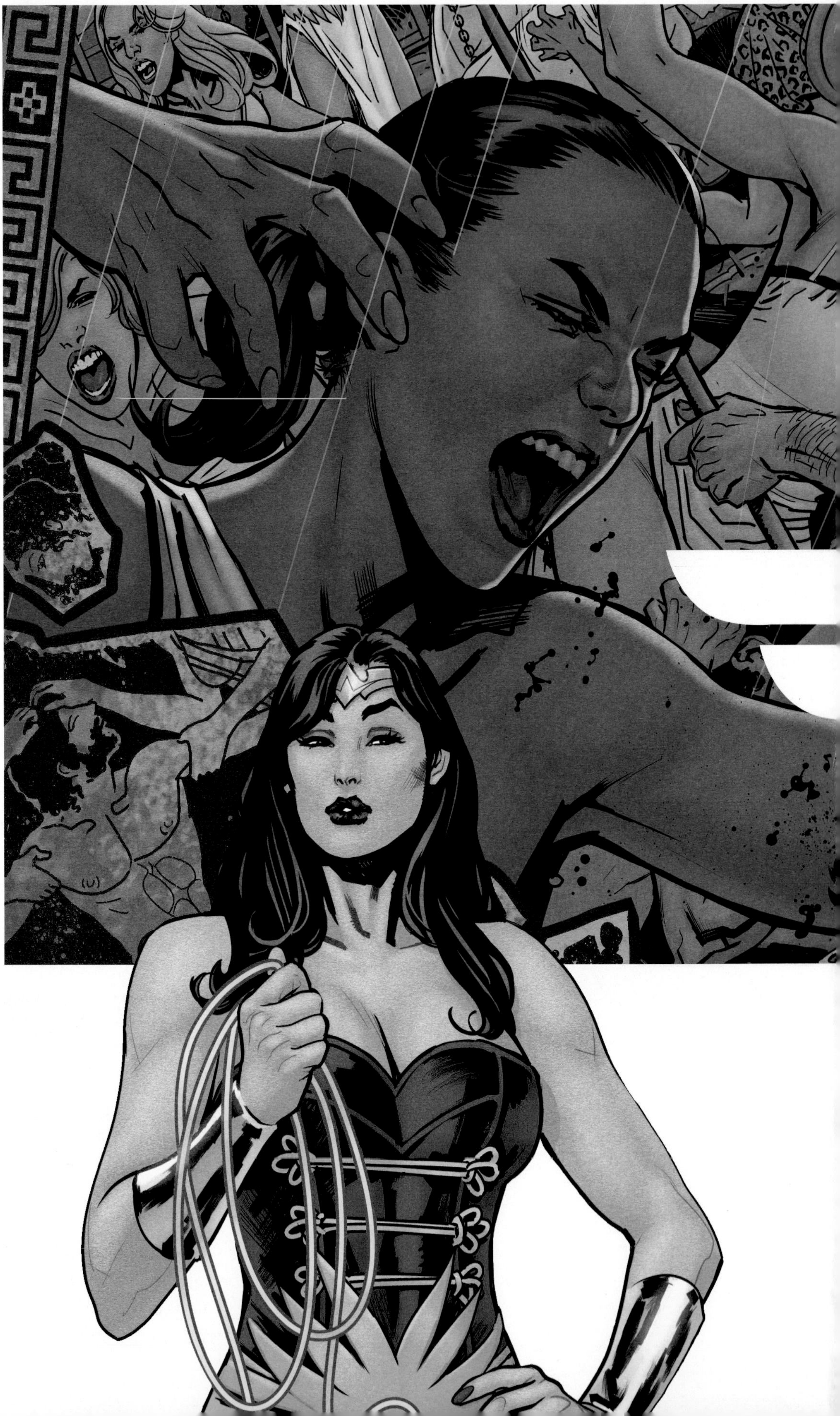

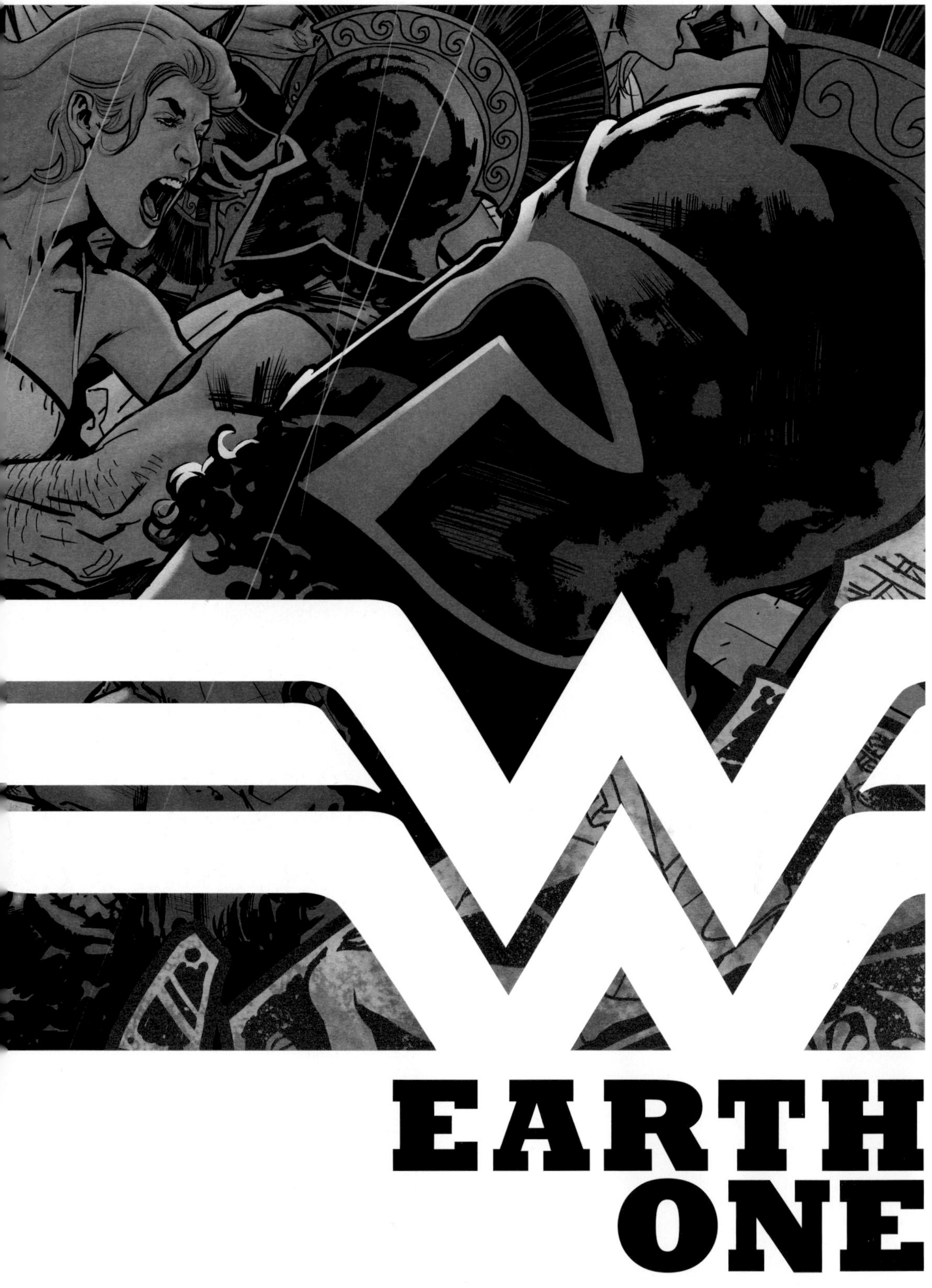

EARTH ONE

Written by Grant Morrison

Art by Yanick Paquette

Colors by Nathan Fairbairn

Letters by Todd Klein

Wonder Woman created by William Moulton Marston.

Eddie Berganza Editor
Andrew Marino Assistant Editor
Steve Cook Design Director – Books
Louis Prandi Publication Design

Bob Harras Senior VP – Editor-in-Chief, DC Comics

Diane Nelson President
Dan DiDio and Jim Lee Co-Publishers
Geoff Johns Chief Creative Officer
Amit Desai Senior VP – Marketing & Global Franchise Management
Nairi Gardiner Senior VP – Finance
Sam Ades VP – Digital Marketing
Bobbie Chase VP – Talent Development
Mark Chiarello Senior VP – Art, Design & Collected Editions
John Cunningham VP – Content Strategy
Anne DePies VP – Strategy Planning & Reporting
Don Falletti VP – Manufacturing Operations
Lawrence Ganem VP – Editorial Administration & Talent Relations
Alison Gill Senior VP – Manufacturing & Operations
Hank Kanalz Senior VP – Editorial Strategy & Administration
Jay Kogan VP – Legal Affairs
Derek Maddalena Senior VP – Sales & Business Development
Jack Mahan VP – Business Affairs
Dan Miron VP – Sales Planning & Trade Development
Nick Napolitano VP – Manufacturing Administration
Carol Roeder VP – Marketing
Eddie Scannell VP – Mass Account & Digital Sales
Courtney Simmons Senior VP – Publicity & Communications
Jim (Ski) Sokolowski VP – Comic Book Specialty & Newsstand Sales
Sandy Yi Senior VP – Global Franchise Management

 WONDER WOMAN: EARTH ONE VOLUME ONE

Published by DC Comics. Copyright © 2016 by DC Comics. All Rights
Reserved. All characters featured in this publication, the distinctive like-
nesses thereof and related elements are trademarks of DC Comics. The
stories, characters and incidents featured in this publication are entirely fic-
tional. DC Comics does not read or accept unsolicited submissions of ideas,
stories or artwork. Printed by RR Donnelley, Salem, VA, USA. 3/4/16
First Printing.

DC Comics, 2900 W. Alameda Ave., Burbank, CA 91505

ISBN: 978-1-4012-2978-8

Library of Congress Cataloging-in-Publication Data is available

DEDICATIONS

"To all the Wonder Women — "
Grant Morrison

"This one is for Diane, my mother, who shares with Wonder Woman more than just the name. Being raised in a feminist household offered me a modern view of the world, allowing me to define my relation to women in a fulfilling, egalitarian way and to find my own path to manhood Merci, Diane."
Yanick Paquette

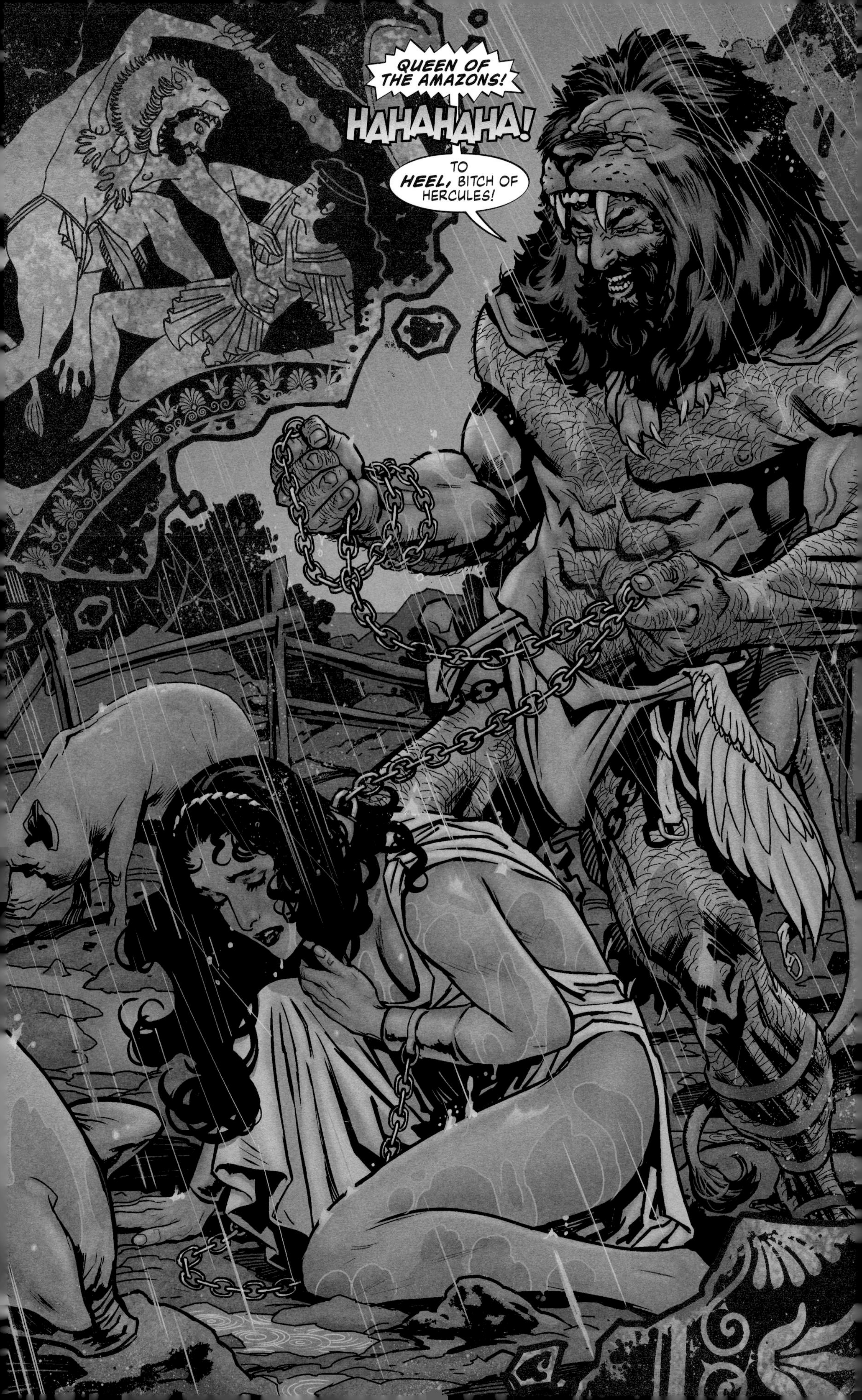
QUEEN OF THE AMAZONS!
HAHAHAHA!
TO HEEL, BITCH OF HERCULES!

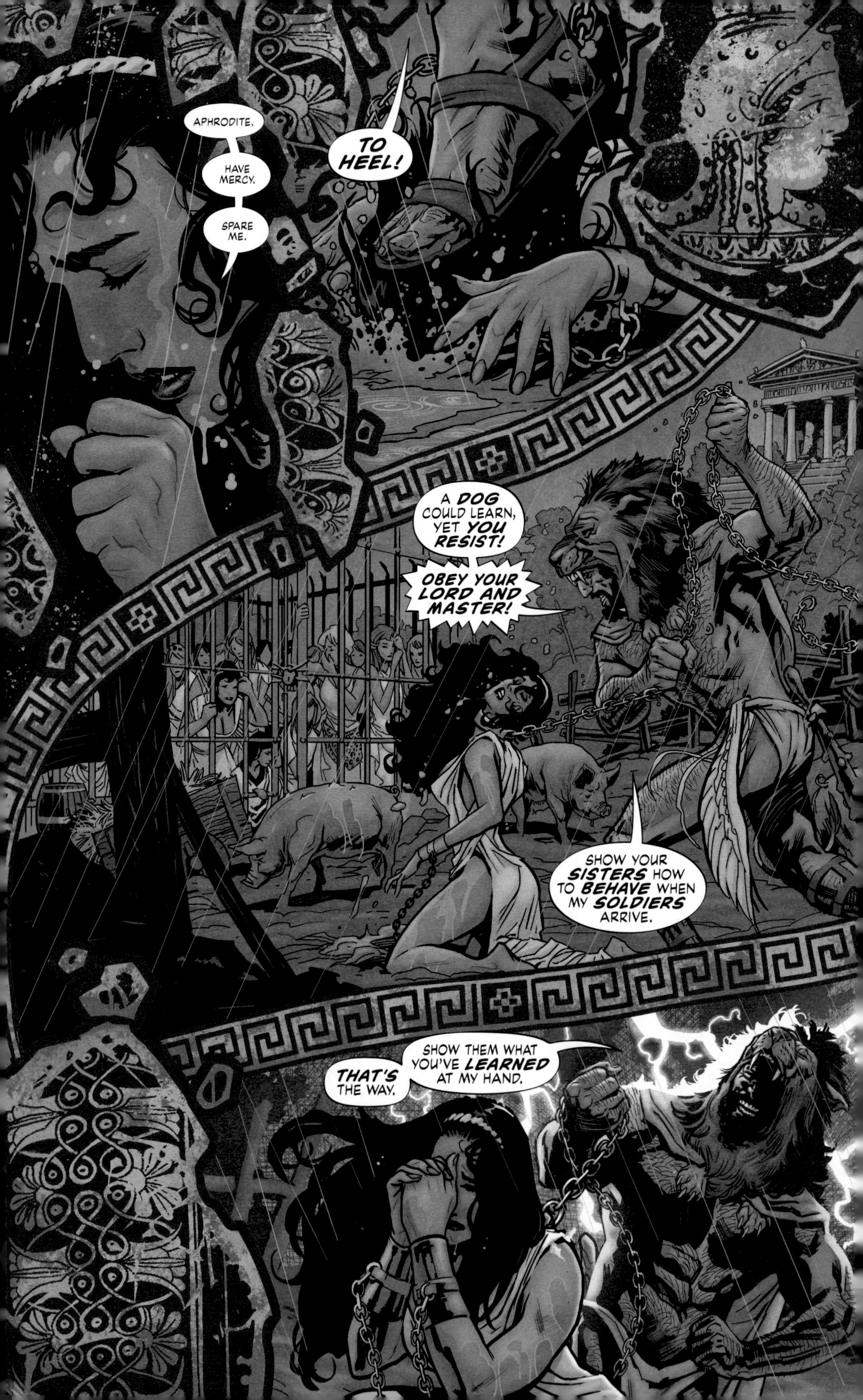
APHRODITE.
HAVE MERCY.
SPARE ME.
TO HEEL!
A DOG COULD LEARN, YET YOU RESIST!
OBEY YOUR LORD AND MASTER!
SHOW YOUR SISTERS HOW TO BEHAVE WHEN MY SOLDIERS ARRIVE.
SHOW THEM WHAT YOU'VE LEARNED AT MY HAND.
THAT'S THE WAY.

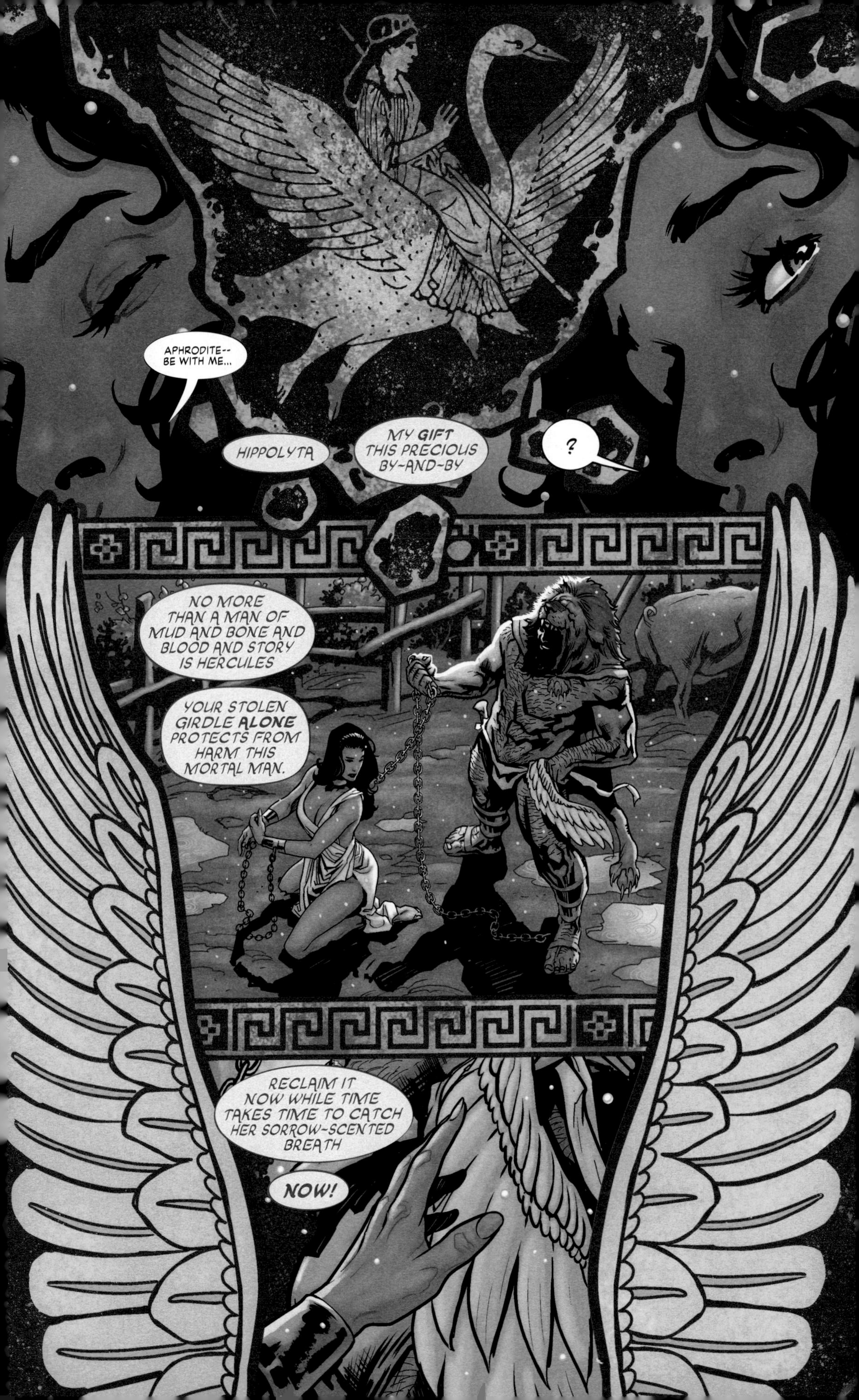
APHRODITE--
BE WITH ME...
HIPPOLYTA
MY GIFT THIS PRECIOUS BY-AND-BY
?
NO MORE THAN A MAN OF MUD AND BONE AND BLOOD AND STORY IS HERCULES
YOUR STOLEN GIRDLE ALONE PROTECTS FROM HARM THIS MORTAL MAN.
RECLAIM IT NOW WHILE TIME TAKES TIME TO CATCH HER SORROW-SCENTED BREATH
NOW!

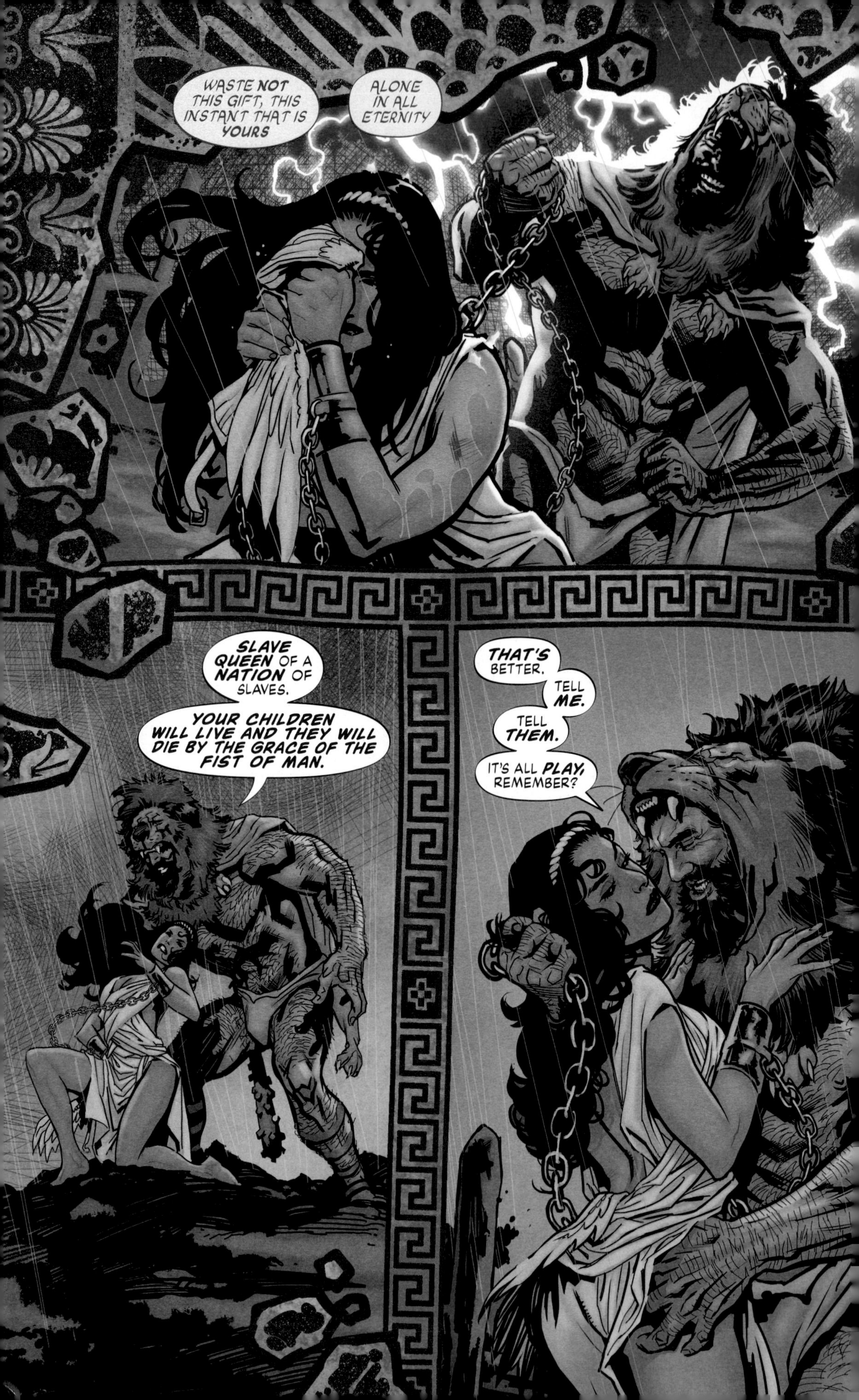
WASTE NOT THIS GIFT, THIS INSTANT THAT IS YOURS
ALONE IN ALL ETERNITY
SLAVE QUEEN OF A NATION OF SLAVES.
YOUR CHILDREN WILL LIVE AND THEY WILL DIE BY THE GRACE OF THE FIST OF MAN.
THAT'S BETTER.
TELL ME.
TELL THEM.
IT'S ALL PLAY, REMEMBER?

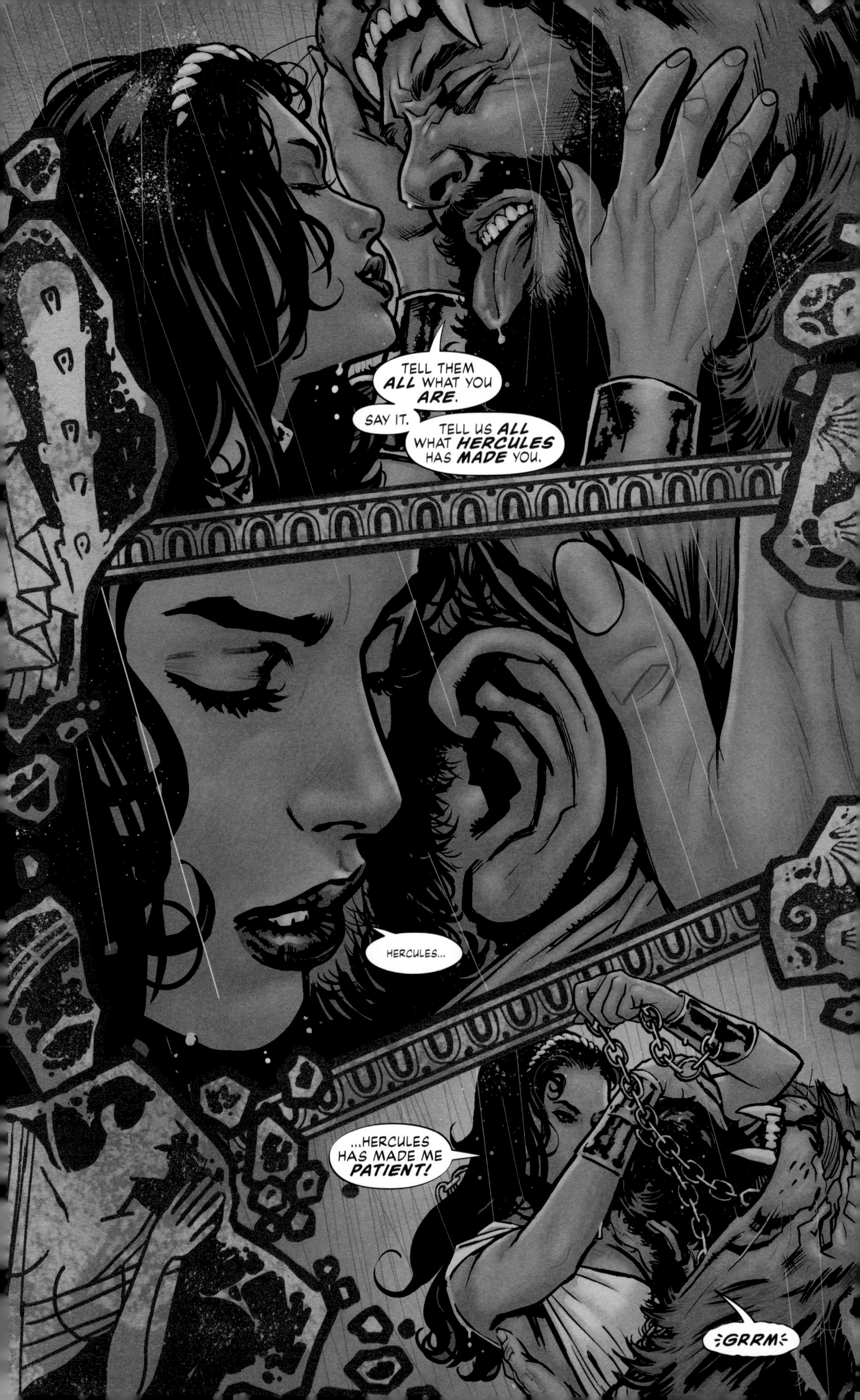
TELL THEM ALL WHAT YOU ARE.
SAY IT.
TELL US ALL WHAT HERCULES HAS MADE YOU.
HERCULES...
...HERCULES HAS MADE ME PATIENT!
GRRM

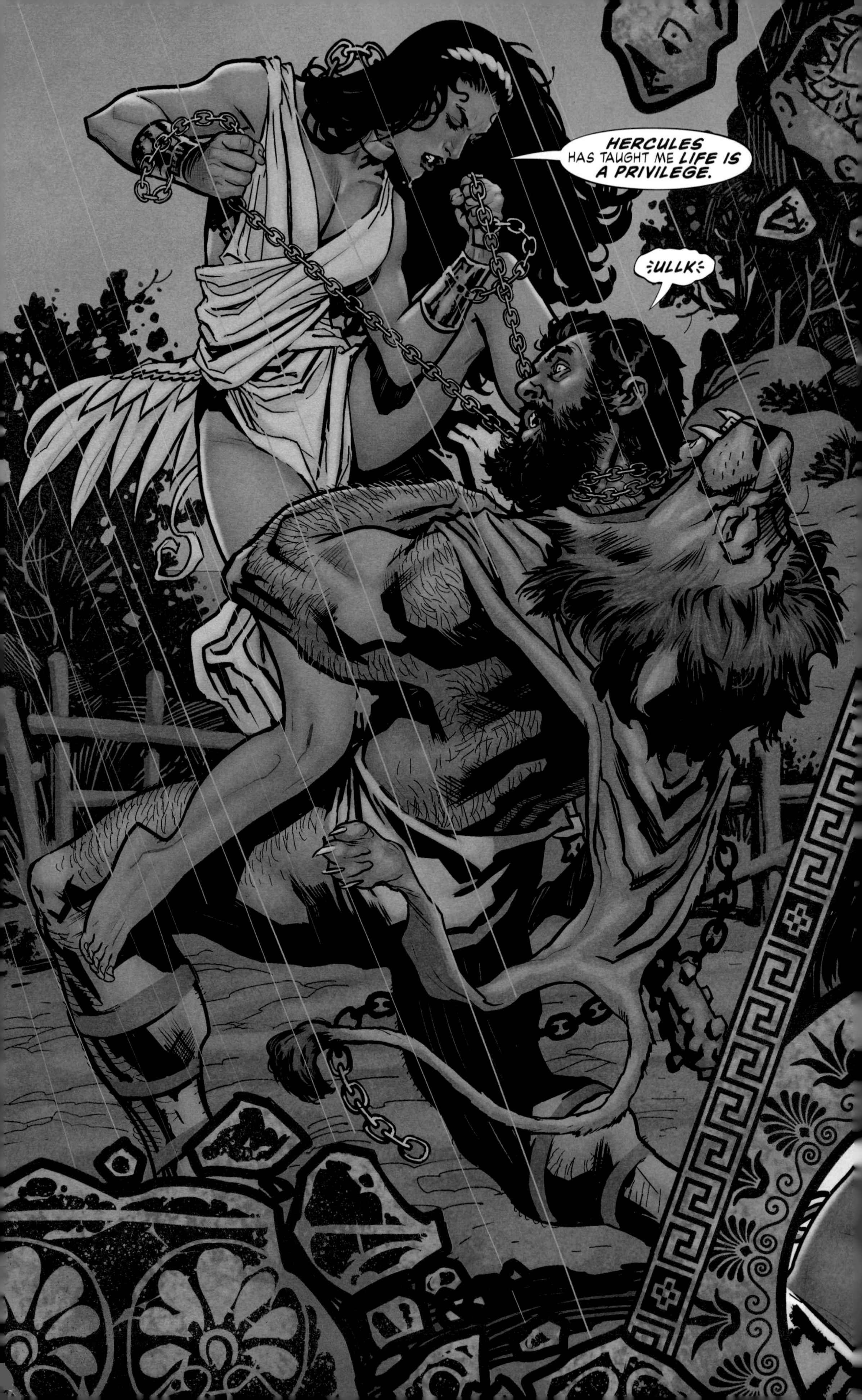
HERCULES HAS TAUGHT ME LIFE IS A PRIVILEGE.
ULLK

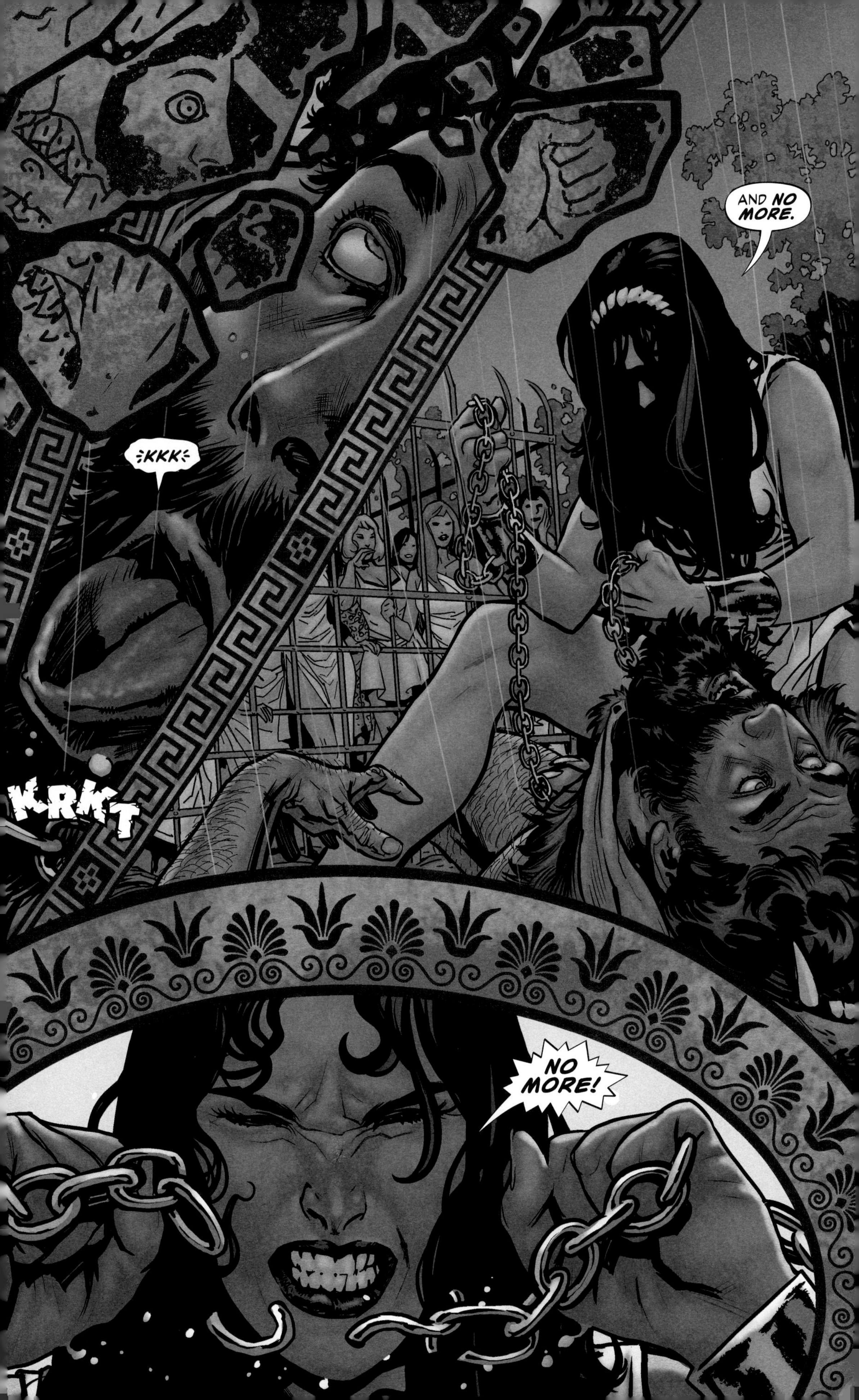
AND NO MORE.
KKK
KRKT
NO MORE!

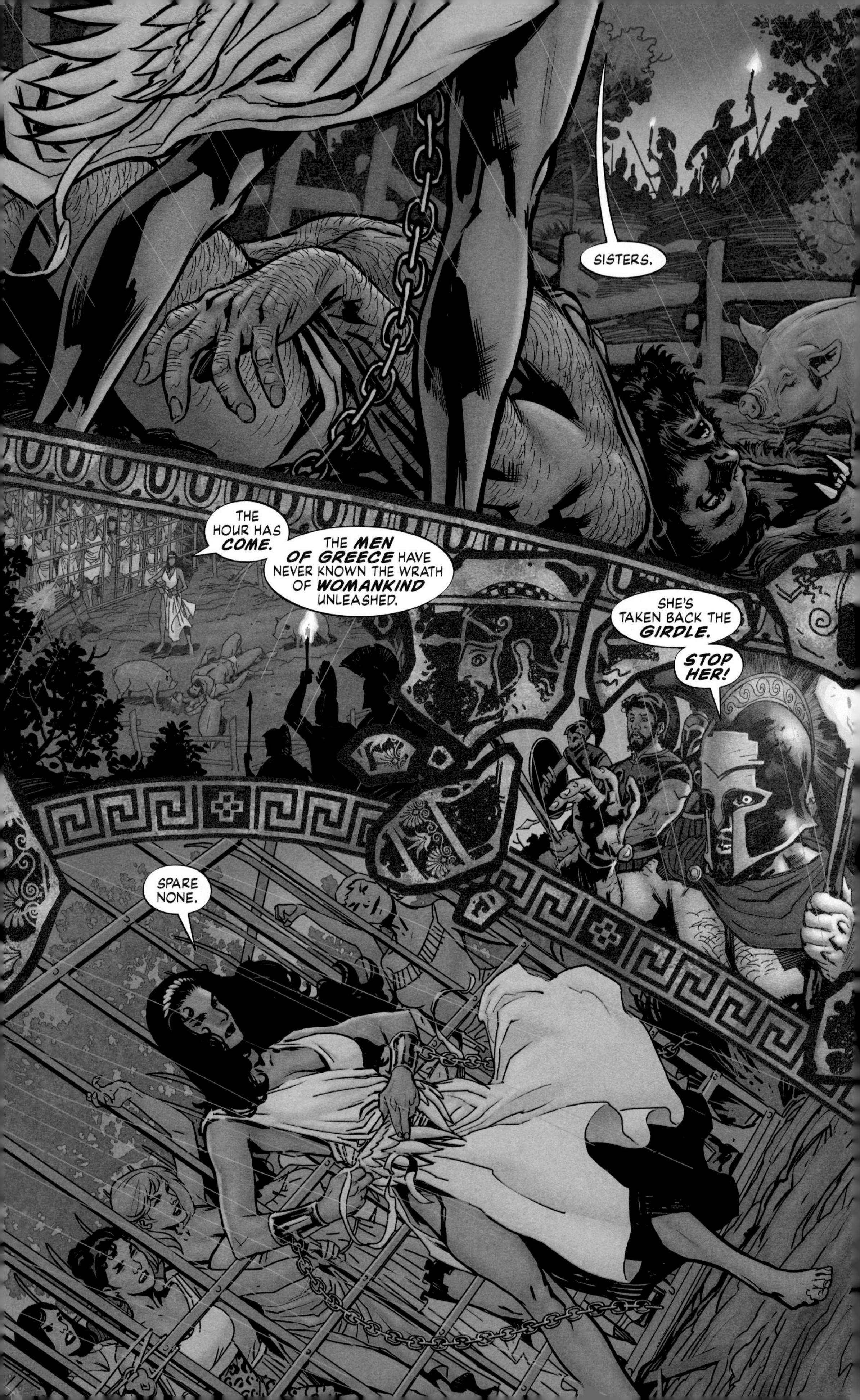
SISTERS.
THE HOUR HAS **COME.**
THE **MEN OF GREECE** HAVE NEVER KNOWN THE WRATH OF **WOMANKIND** UNLEASHED.
SHE'S TAKEN BACK THE **GIRDLE.**
STOP HER!
SPARE NONE.

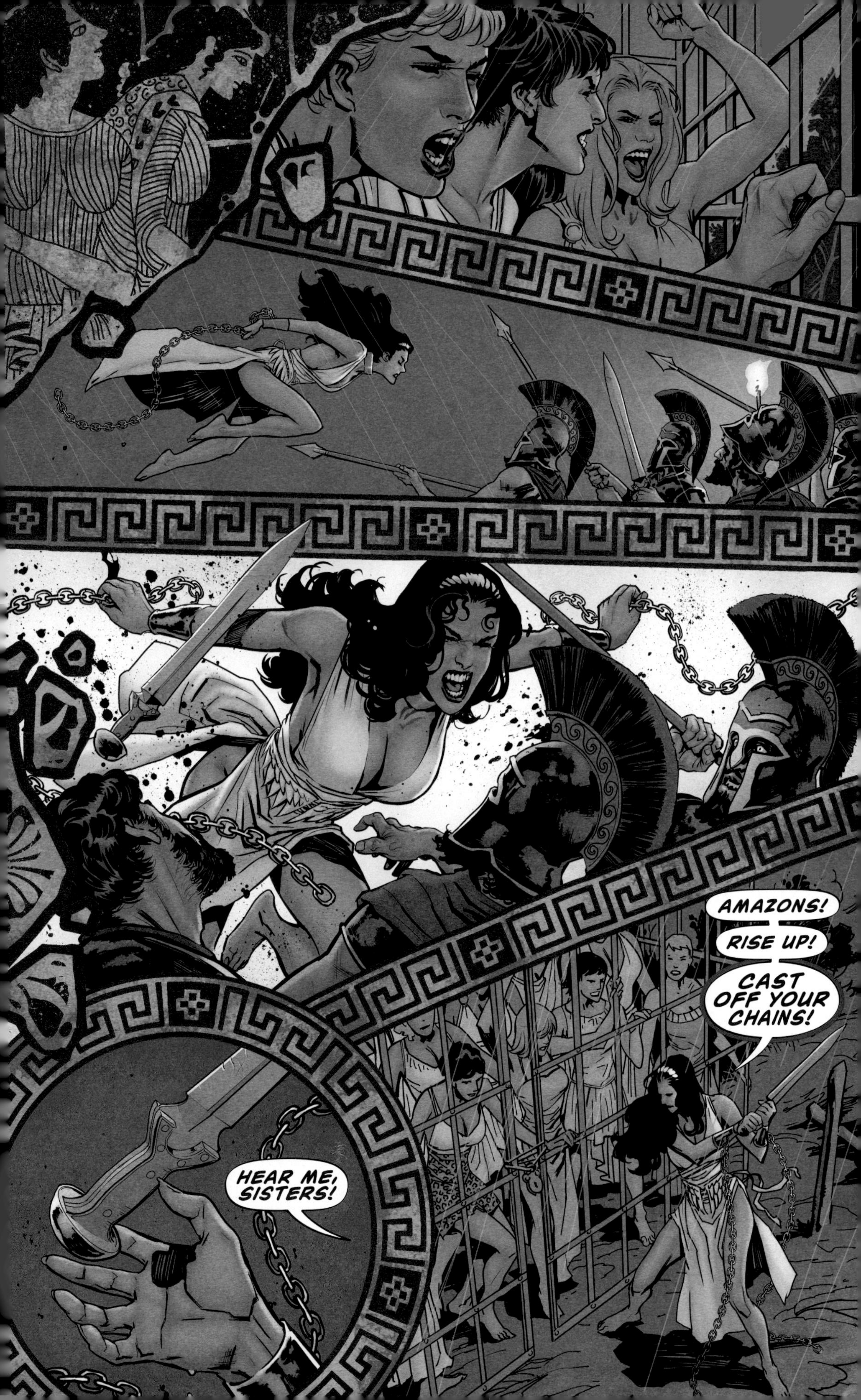
HEAR ME, SISTERS!
AMAZONS!
RISE UP!
CAST OFF YOUR CHAINS!

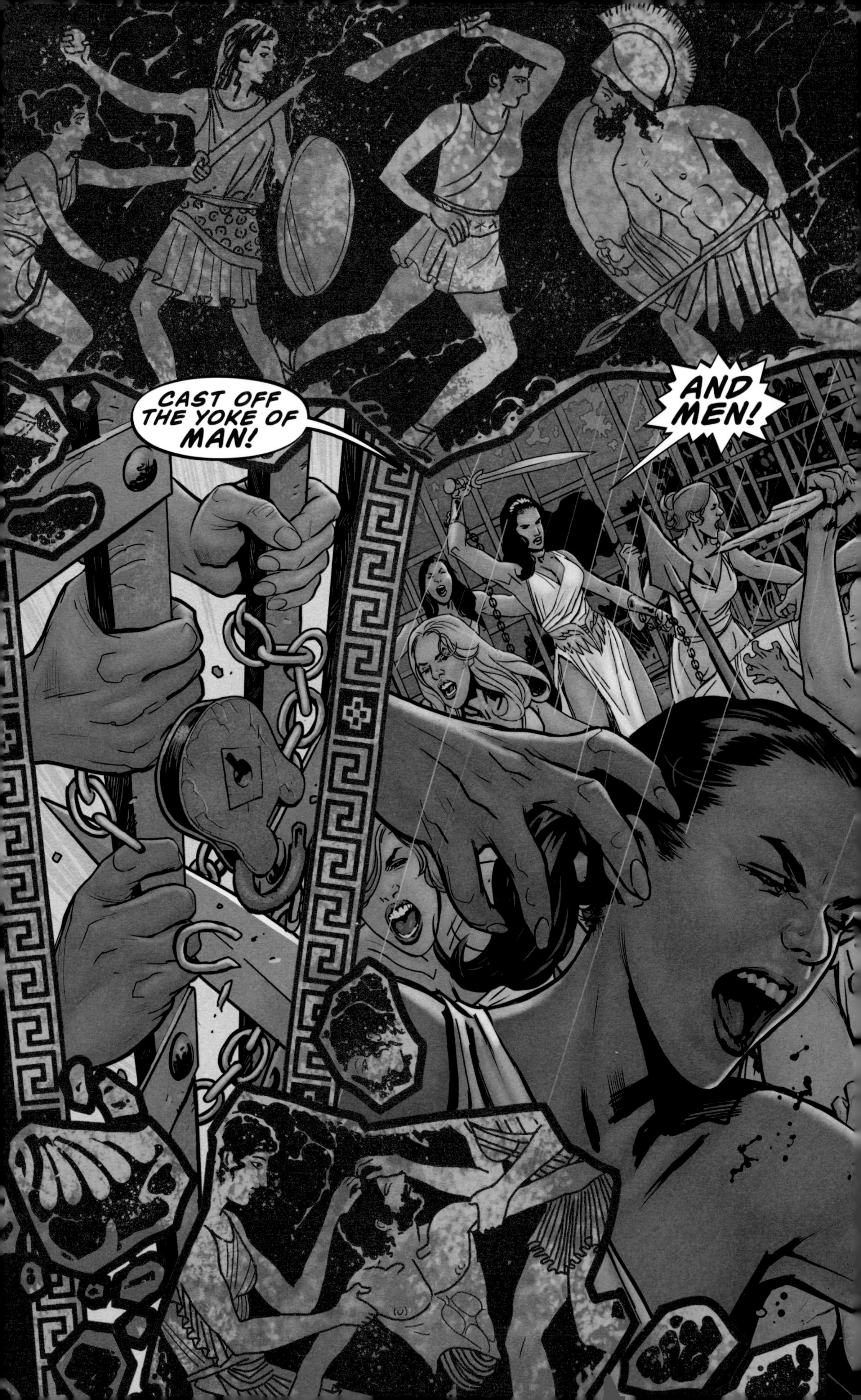
CAST OFF THE YOKE OF MAN!
AND MEN!

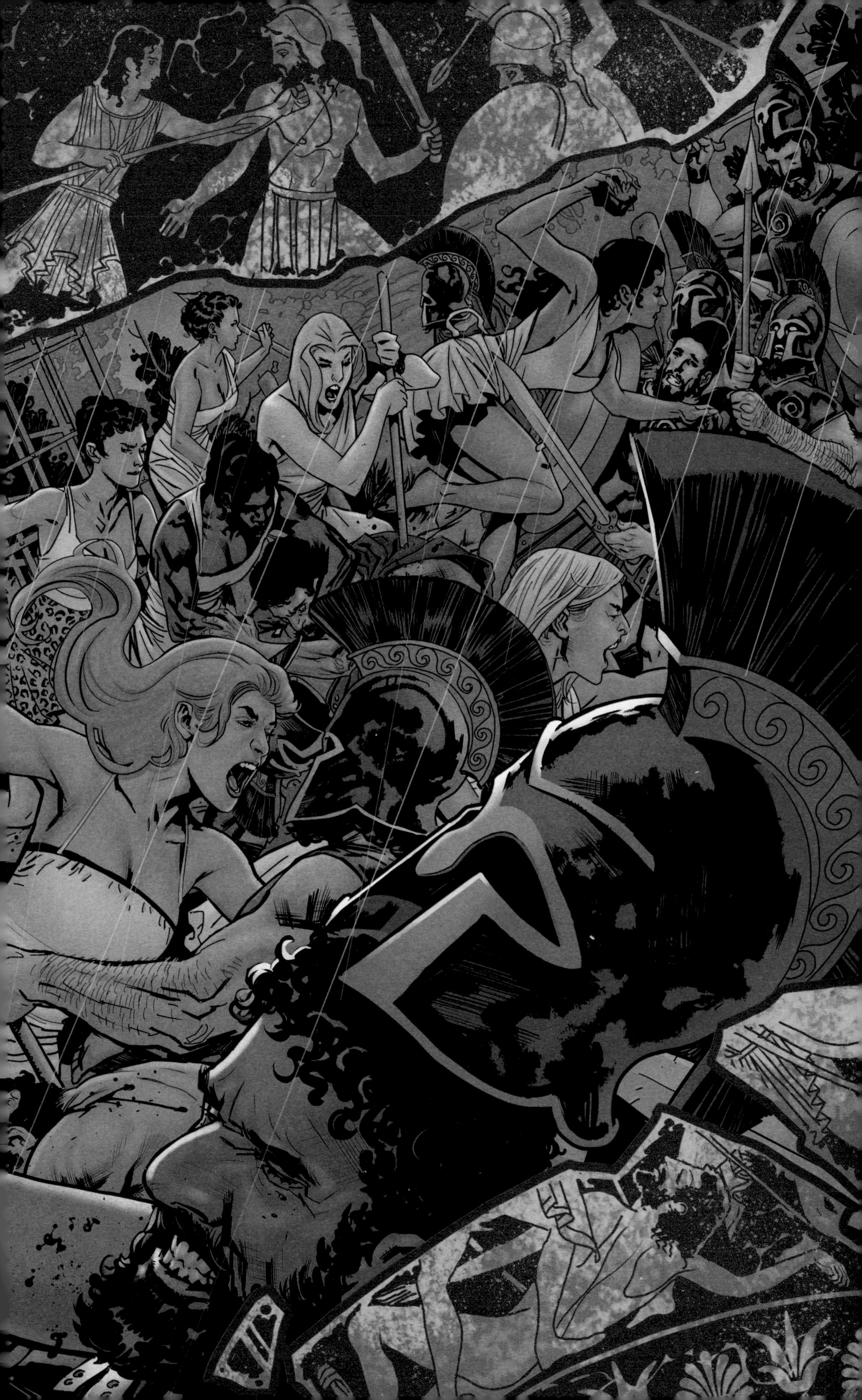

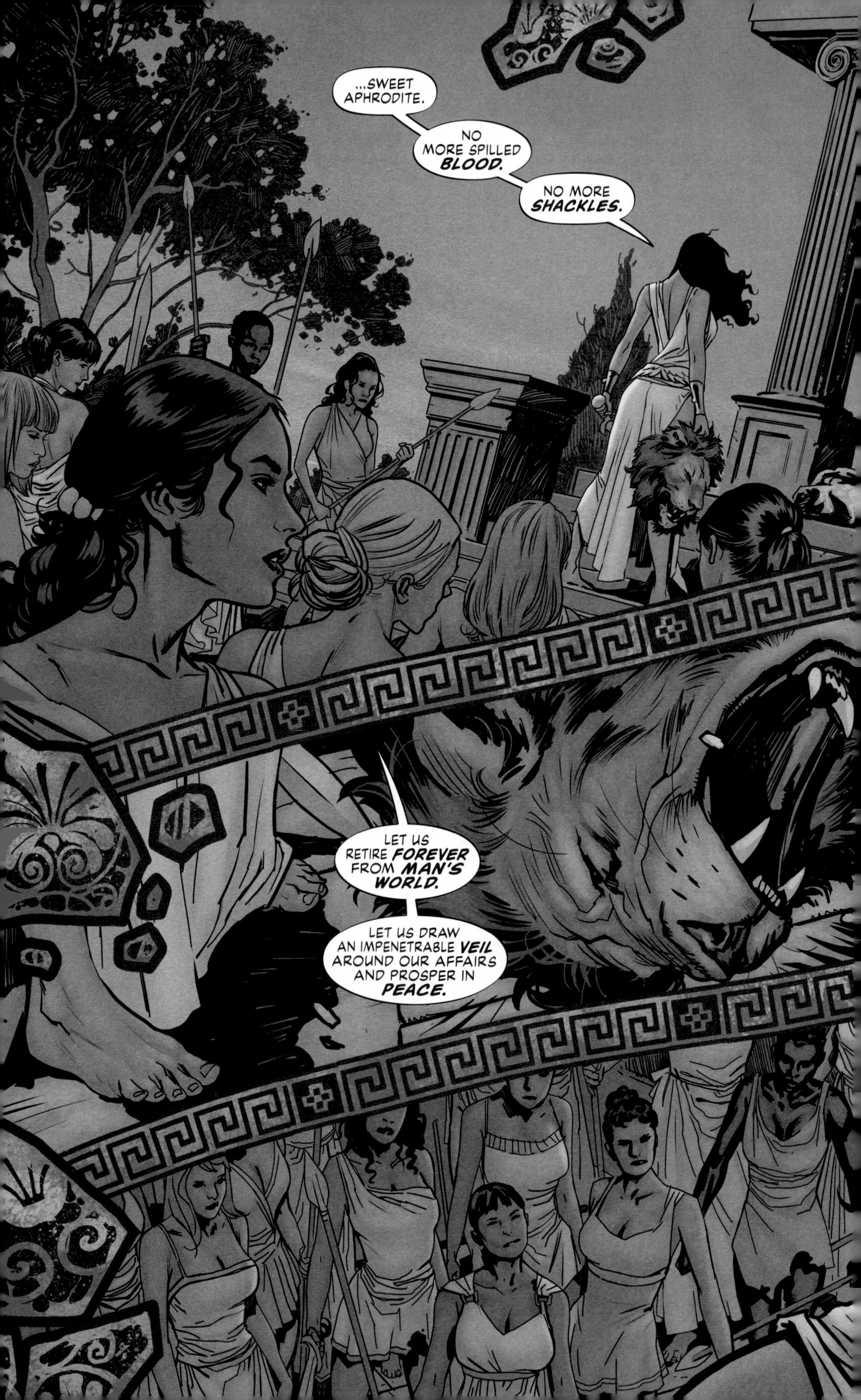
...SWEET APHRODITE.
NO MORE SPILLED BLOOD.
NO MORE SHACKLES.
LET US RETIRE FOREVER FROM MAN'S WORLD.
LET US DRAW AN IMPENETRABLE VEIL AROUND OUR AFFAIRS AND PROSPER IN PEACE.

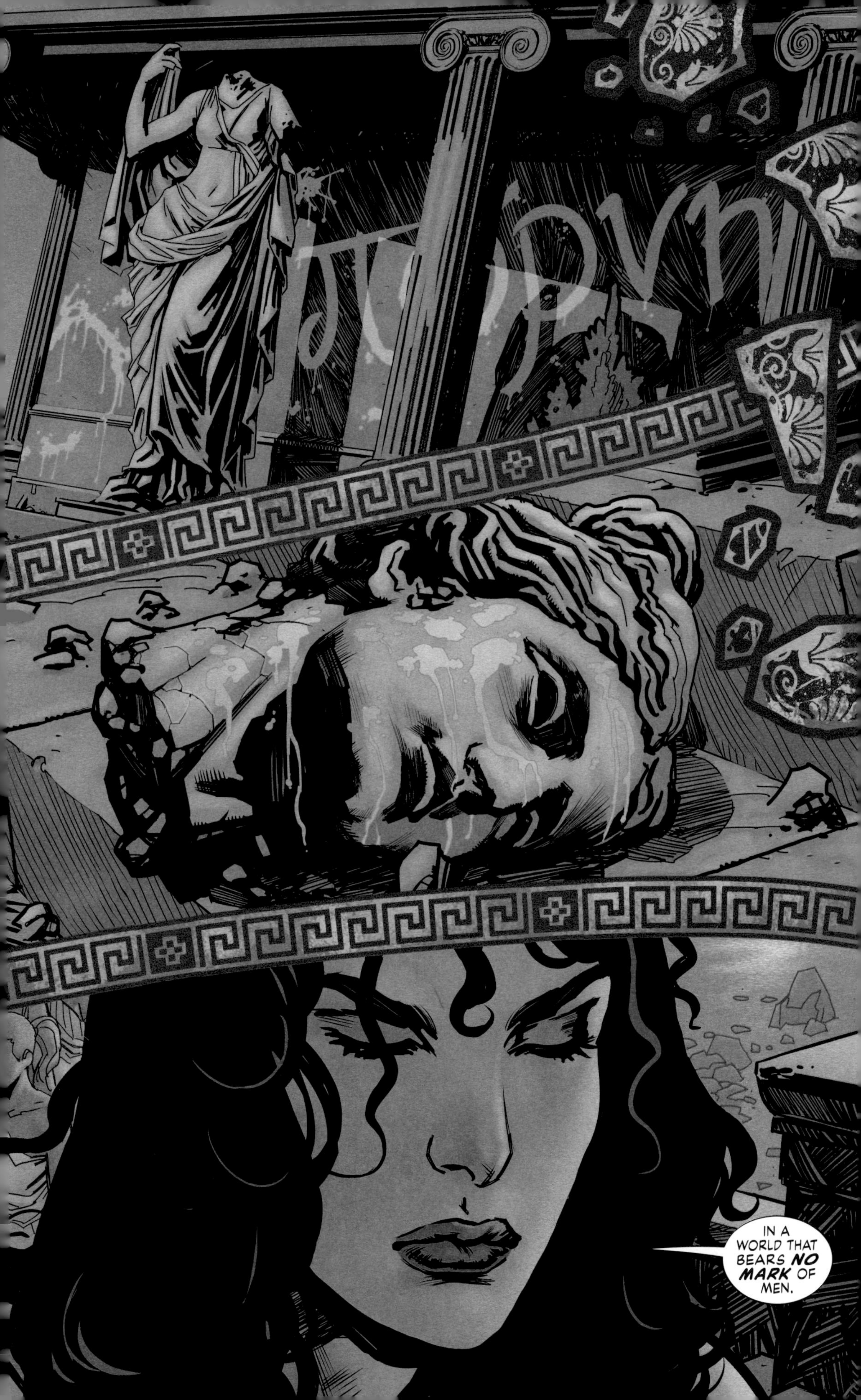
IN A WORLD THAT BEARS NO MARK OF MEN.

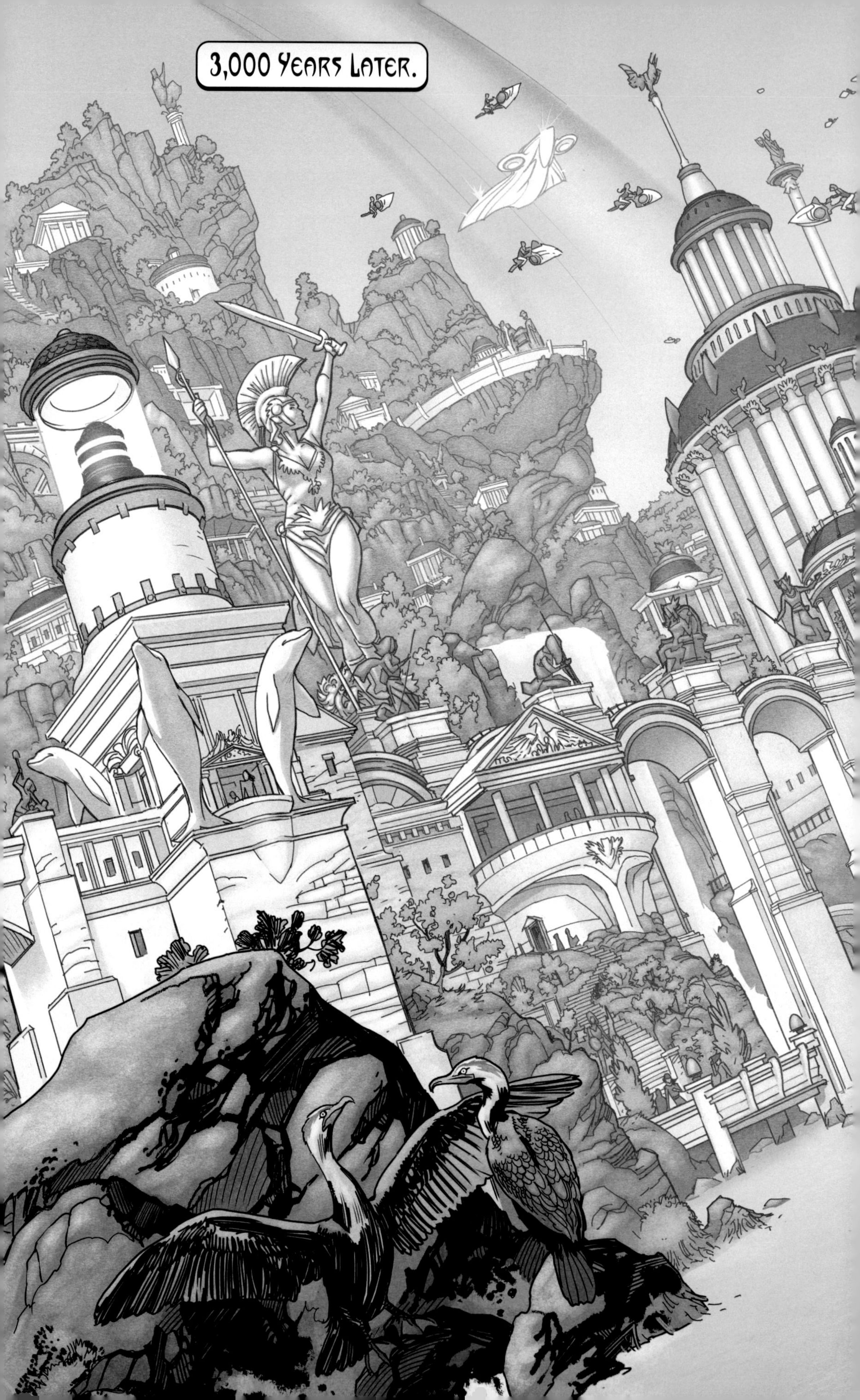
3,000 YEARS LATER.

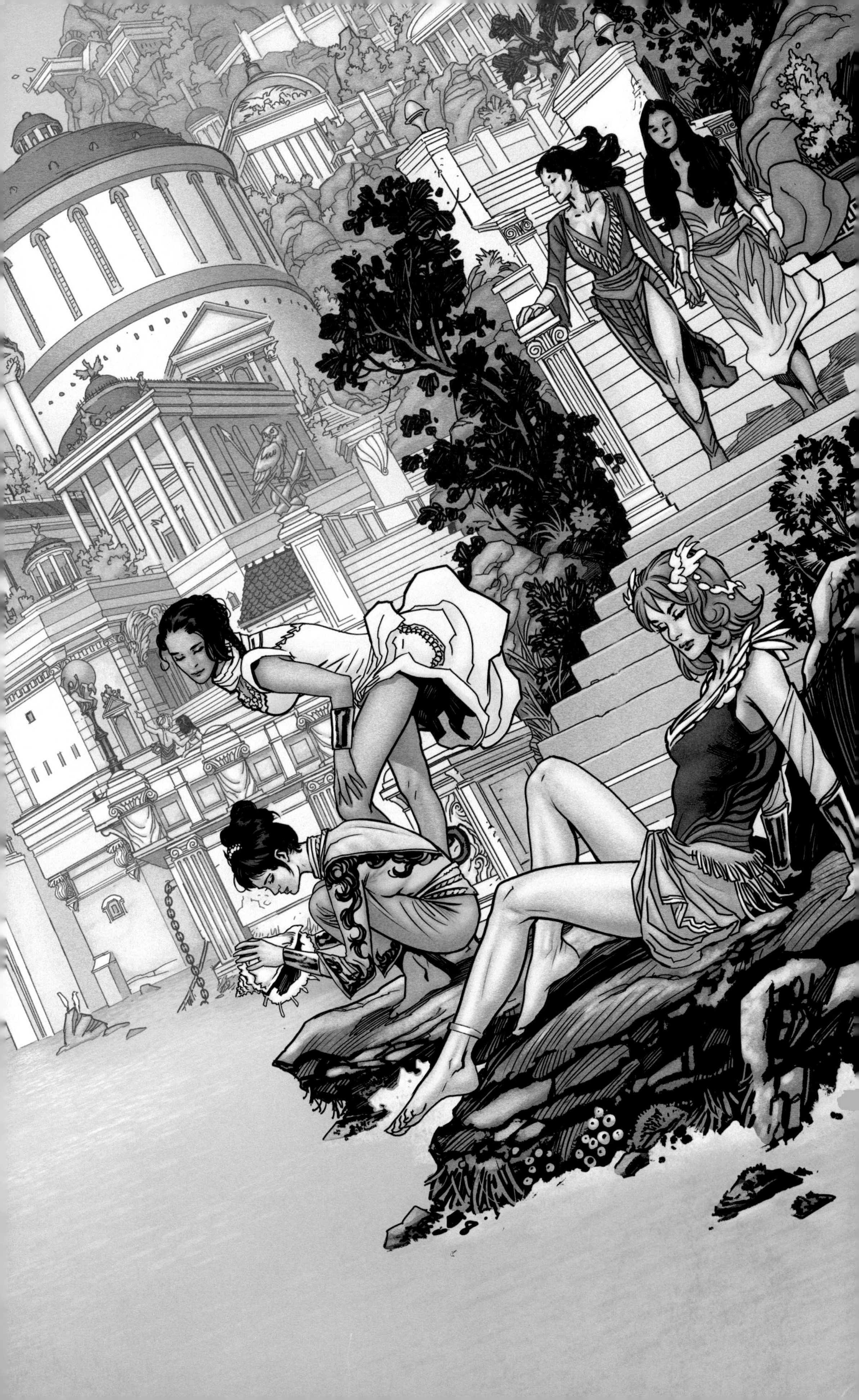

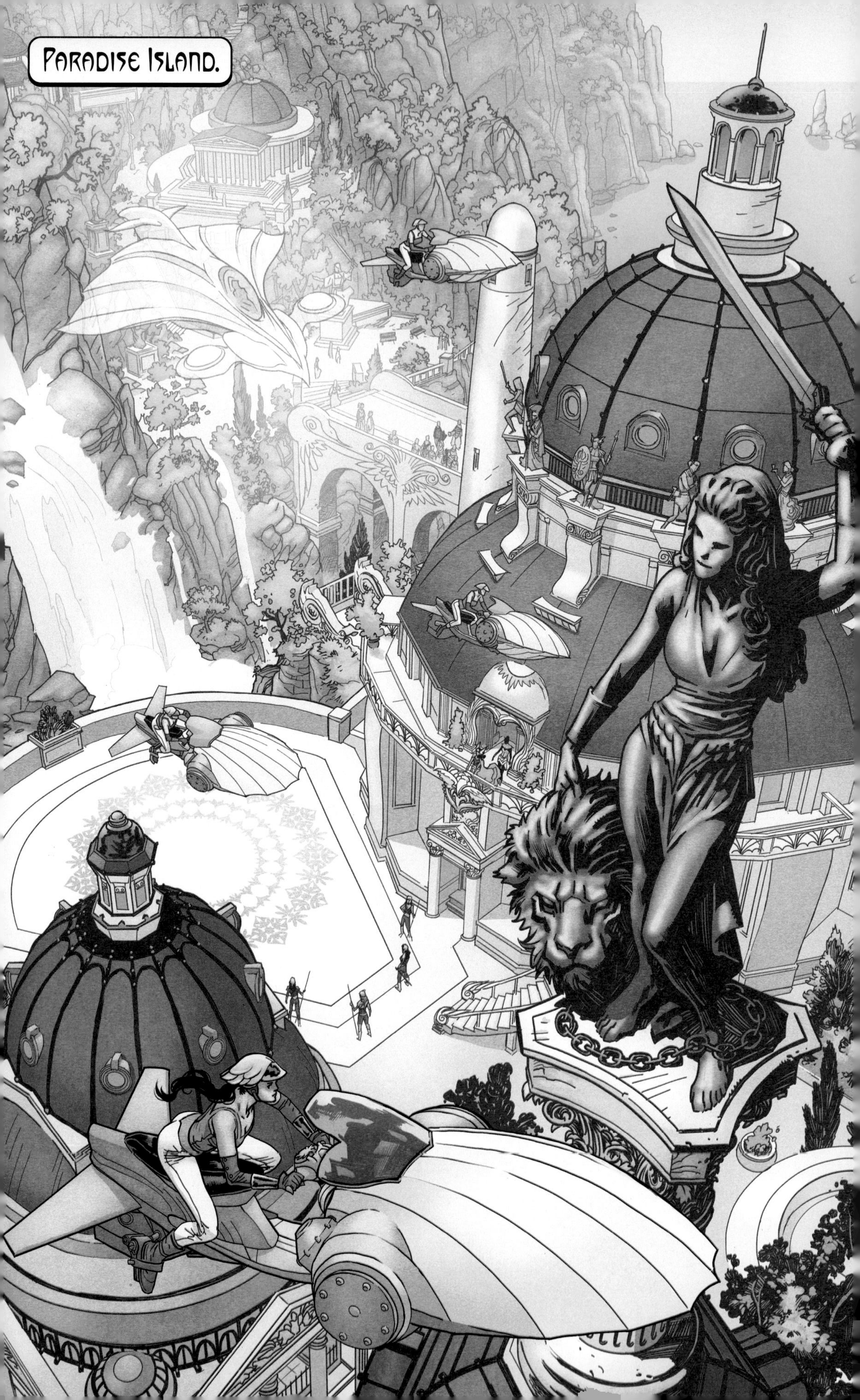
PARADISE ISLAND.

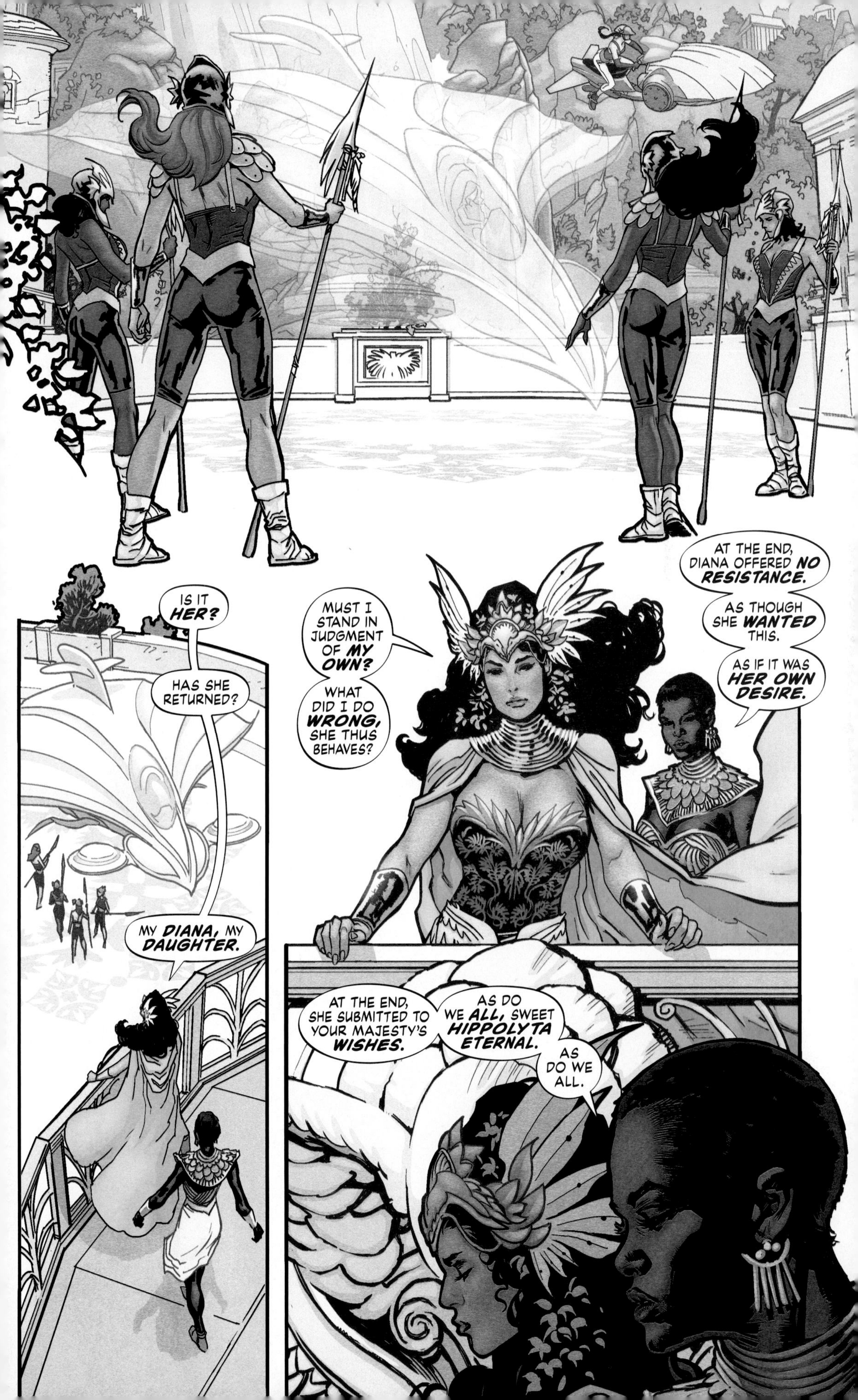
IS IT HER?
HAS SHE RETURNED?
MY DIANA, MY DAUGHTER.
MUST I STAND IN JUDGMENT OF MY OWN?
WHAT DID I DO WRONG, SHE THUS BEHAVES?
AT THE END, DIANA OFFERED NO RESISTANCE.
AS THOUGH SHE WANTED THIS.
AS IF IT WAS HER OWN DESIRE.
AT THE END, SHE SUBMITTED TO YOUR MAJESTY'S WISHES.
AS DO WE ALL, SWEET HIPPOLYTA ETERNAL.
AS DO WE ALL.

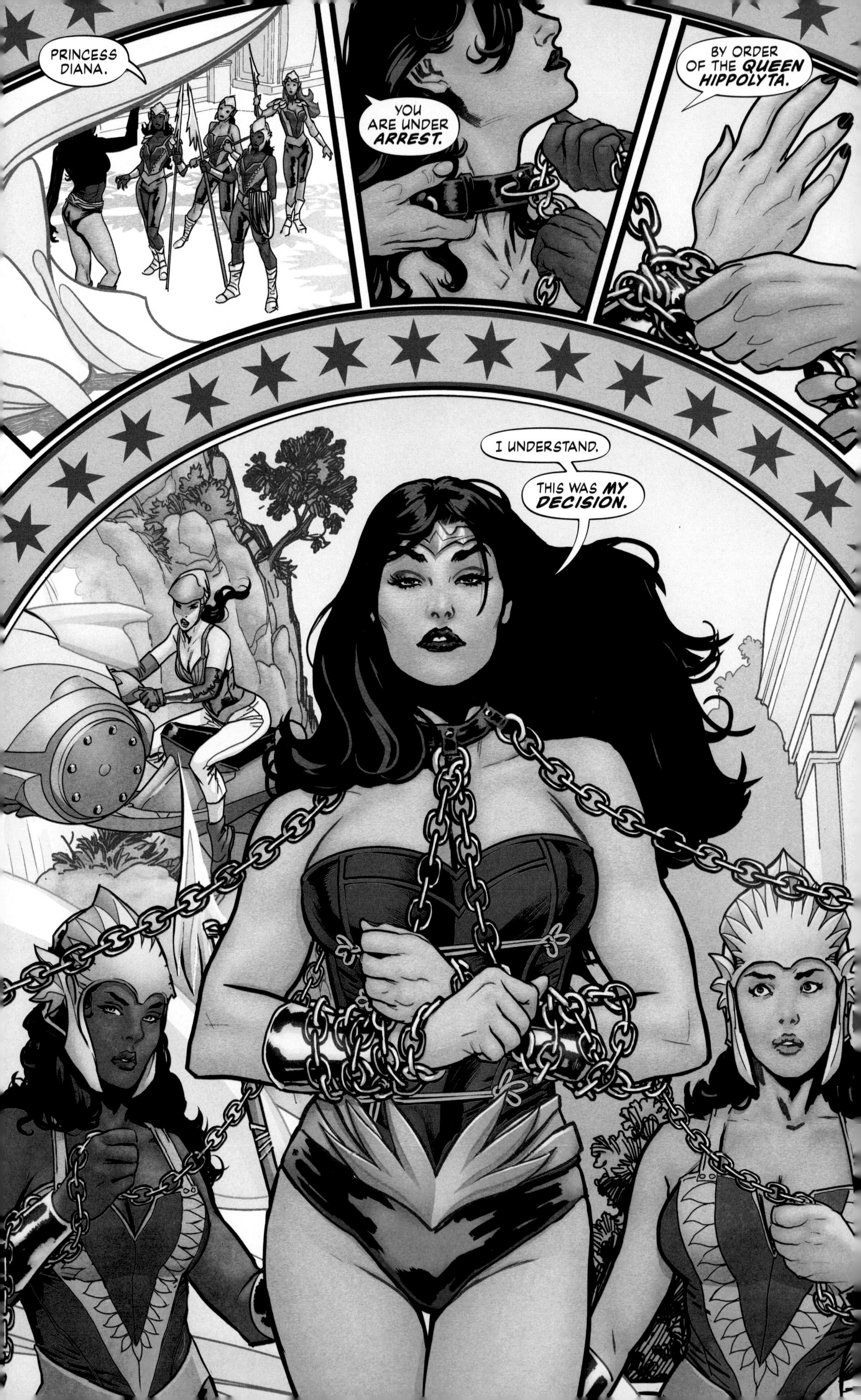
PRINCESS DIANA.
YOU ARE UNDER ARREST.
BY ORDER OF THE QUEEN HIPPOLYTA.
I UNDERSTAND.
THIS WAS MY DECISION.

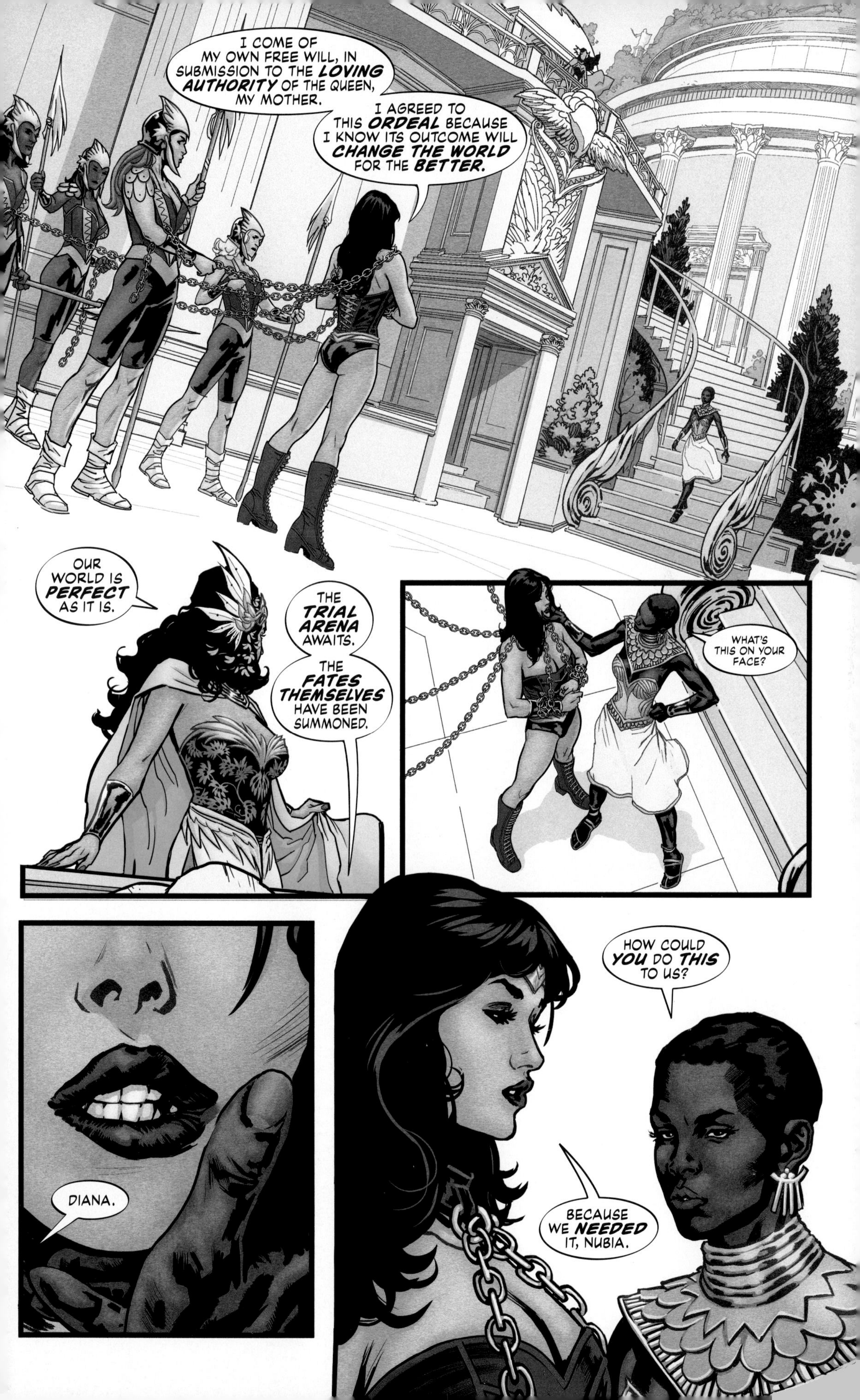
I COME OF MY OWN FREE WILL, IN SUBMISSION TO THE LOVING AUTHORITY OF THE QUEEN, MY MOTHER.
I AGREED TO THIS ORDEAL BECAUSE I KNOW ITS OUTCOME WILL CHANGE THE WORLD FOR THE BETTER.
OUR WORLD IS PERFECT AS IT IS.
THE TRIAL ARENA AWAITS.
THE FATES THEMSELVES HAVE BEEN SUMMONED.
WHAT'S THIS ON YOUR FACE?
DIANA.
HOW COULD YOU DO THIS TO US?
BECAUSE WE NEEDED IT, NUBIA.

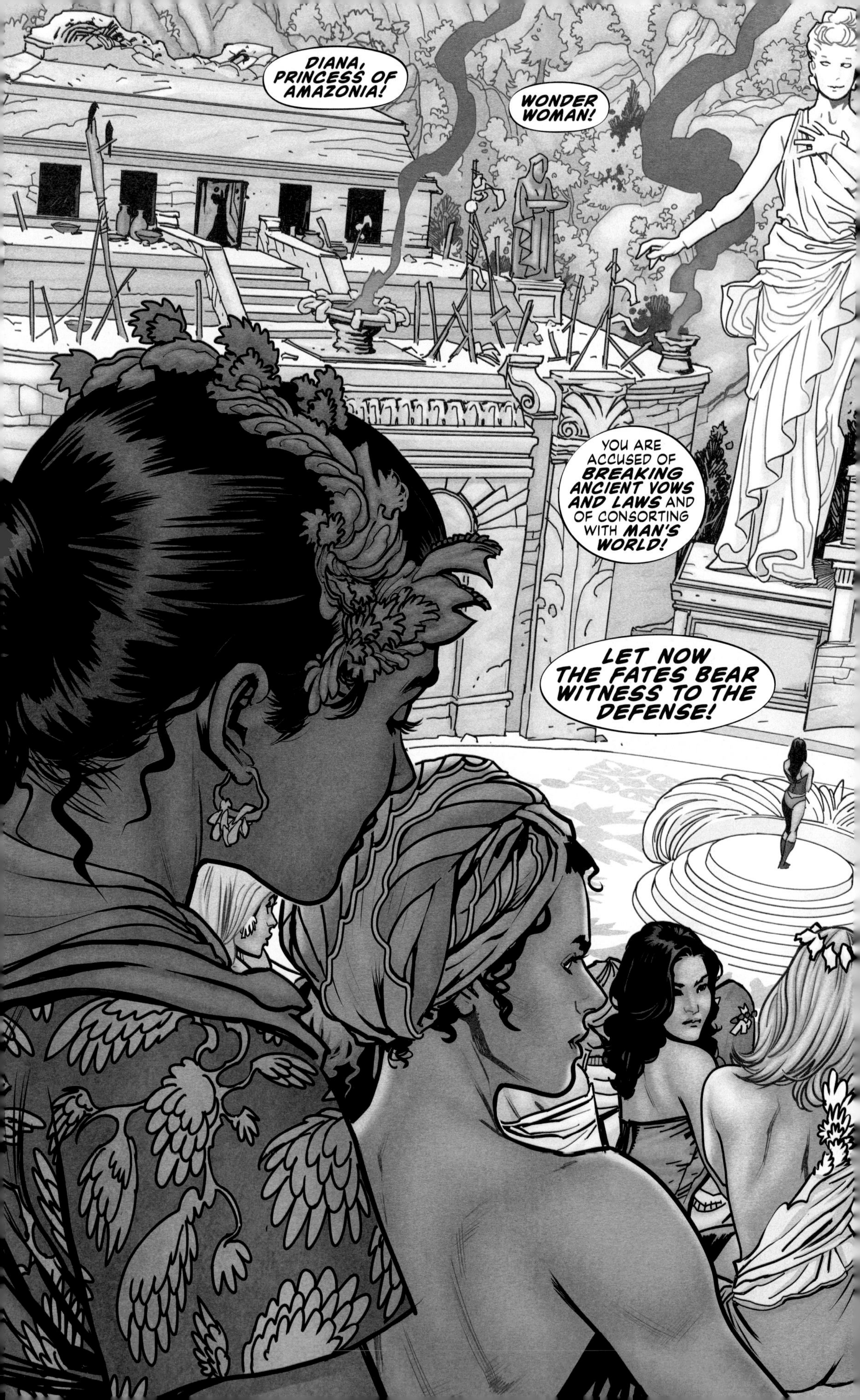
DIANA, PRINCESS OF AMAZONIA!
WONDER WOMAN!
YOU ARE ACCUSED OF BREAKING ANCIENT VOWS AND LAWS AND OF CONSORTING WITH MAN'S WORLD!
LET NOW THE FATES BEAR WITNESS TO THE DEFENSE!

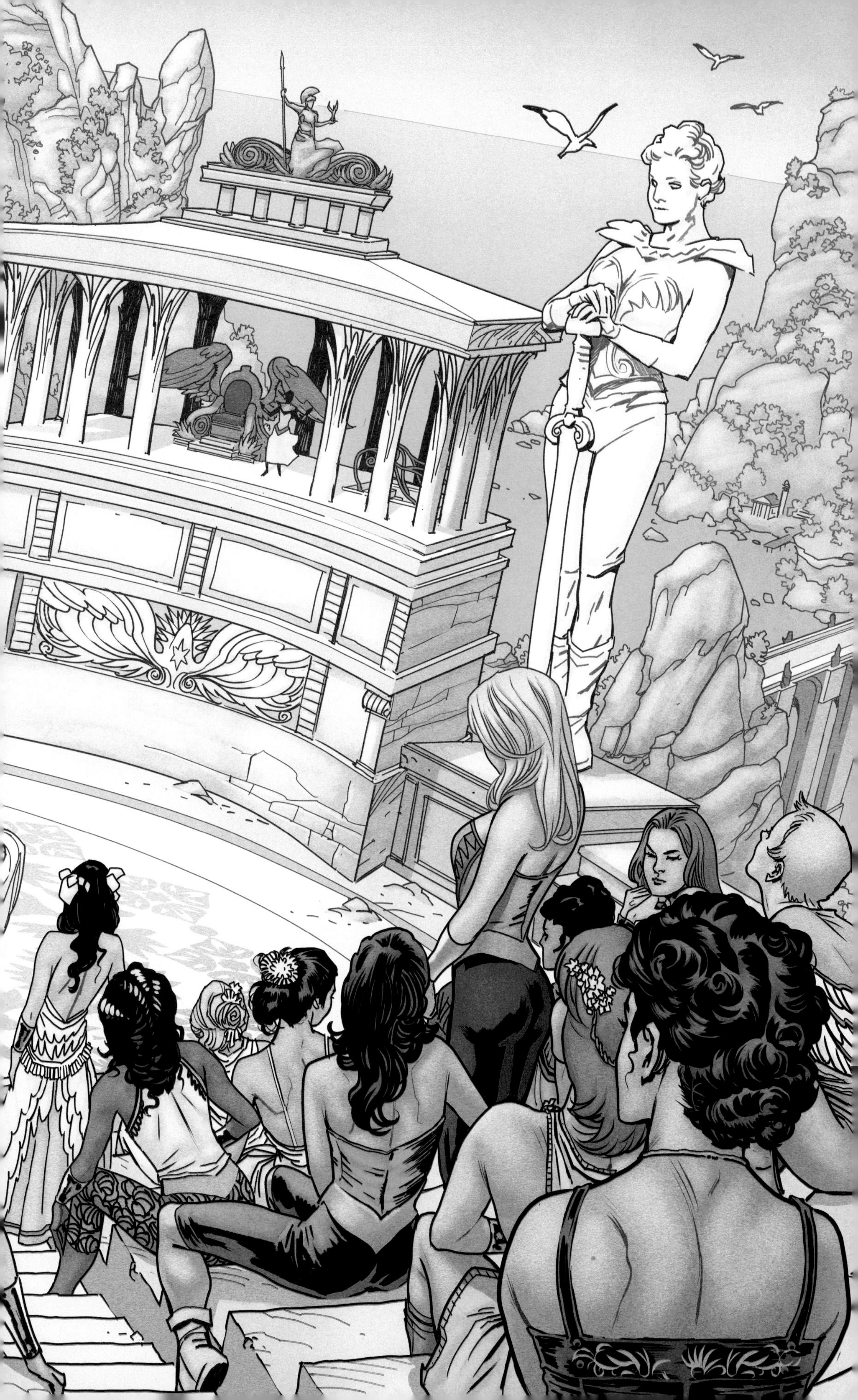

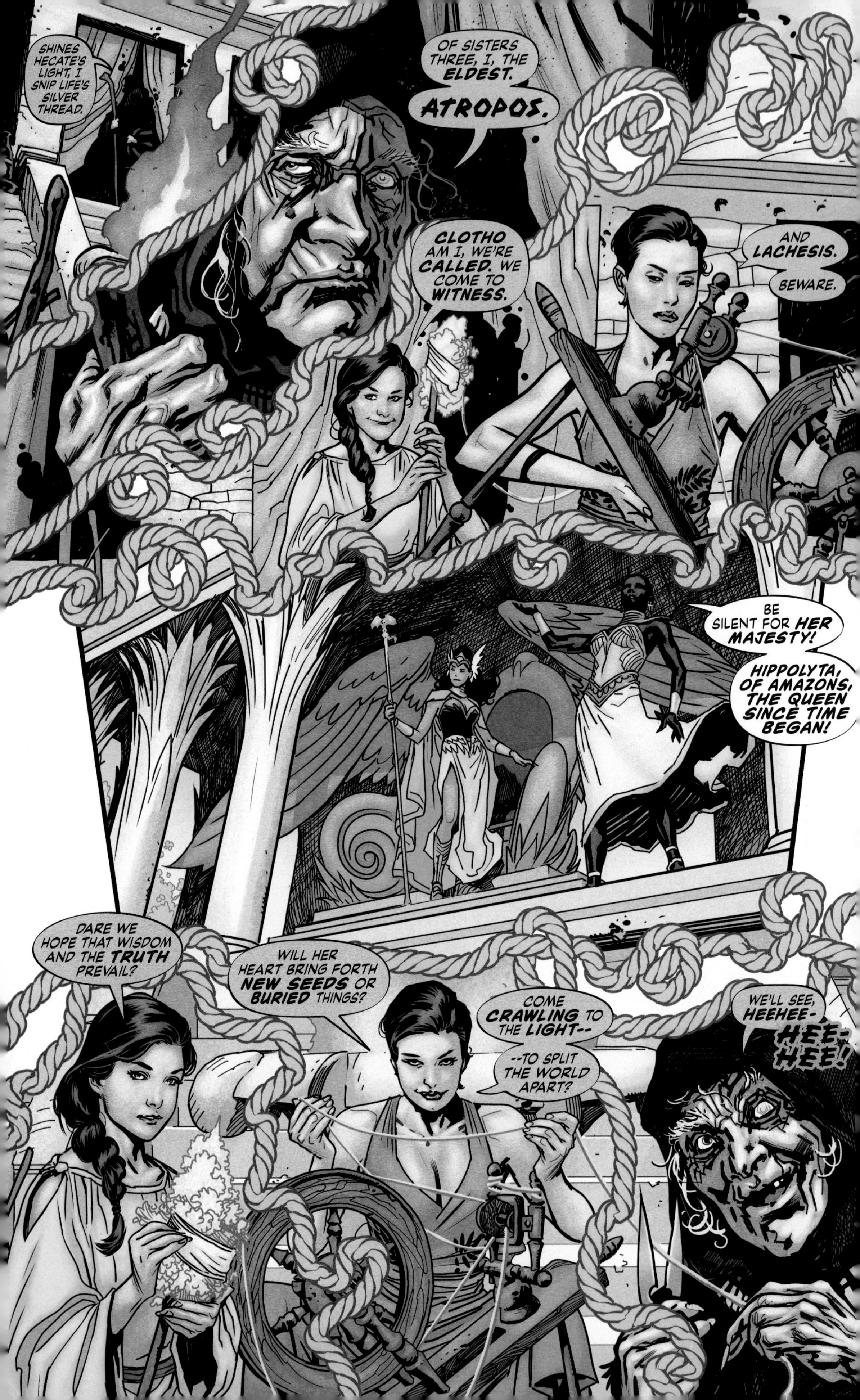
SHINES HECATE'S LIGHT, I SNIP LIFE'S SILVER THREAD.
OF SISTERS THREE, I, THE ELDEST.
ATROPOS.
CLOTHO AM I, WE'RE CALLED. WE COME TO WITNESS.
AND LACHESIS.
BEWARE.
BE SILENT FOR HER MAJESTY!
HIPPOLYTA, OF AMAZONS, THE QUEEN SINCE TIME BEGAN!
DARE WE HOPE THAT WISDOM AND THE TRUTH PREVAIL?
WILL HER HEART BRING FORTH NEW SEEDS OR BURIED THINGS?
COME CRAWLING TO THE LIGHT--
--TO SPLIT THE WORLD APART?
WE'LL SEE, HEEHEE-
HEE-HEE!

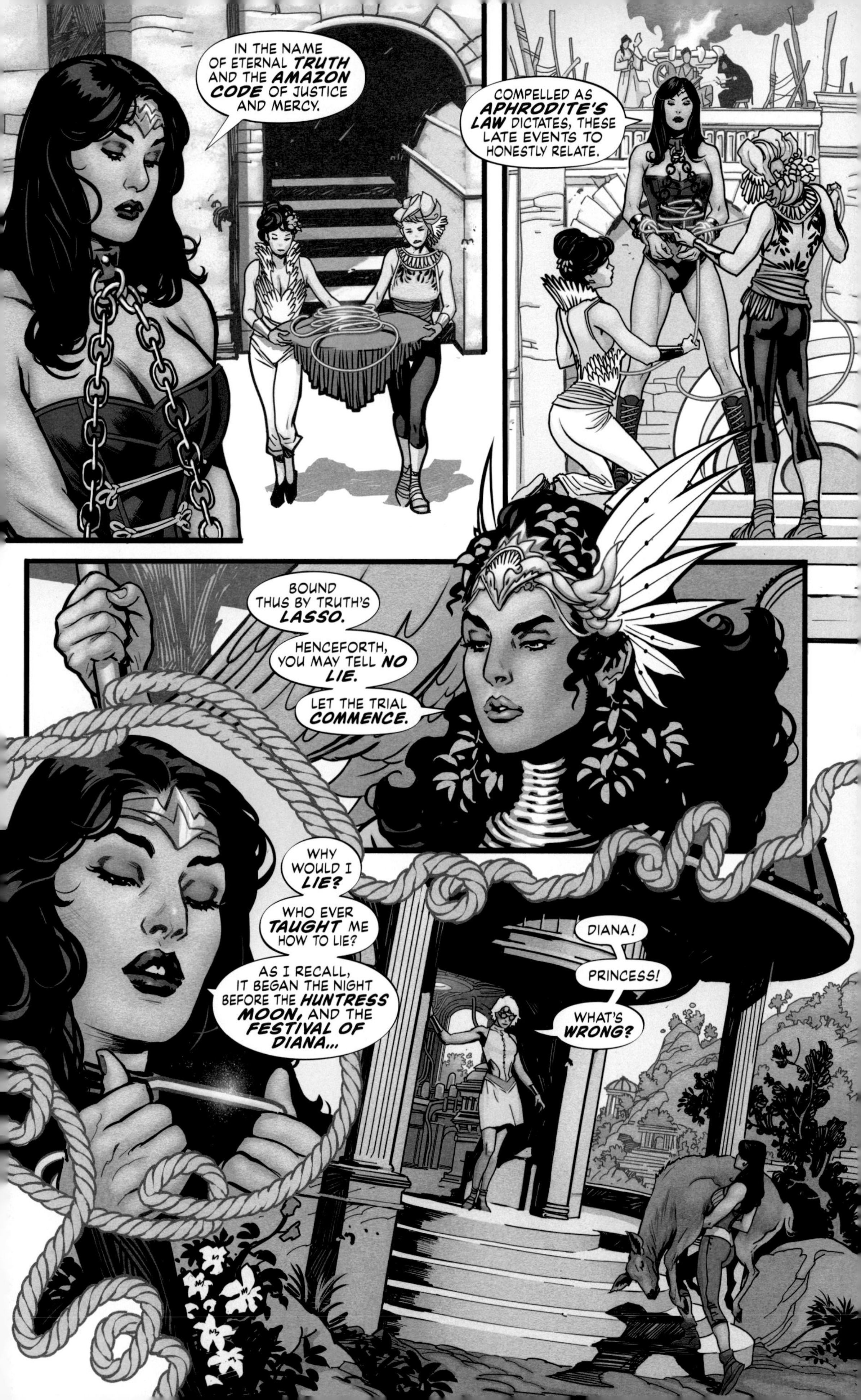
IN THE NAME OF ETERNAL TRUTH AND THE AMAZON CODE OF JUSTICE AND MERCY.
COMPELLED AS APHRODITE'S LAW DICTATES, THESE LATE EVENTS TO HONESTLY RELATE.
BOUND THUS BY TRUTH'S LASSO.
HENCEFORTH, YOU MAY TELL NO LIE.
LET THE TRIAL COMMENCE.
WHY WOULD I LIE?
WHO EVER TAUGHT ME HOW TO LIE?
AS I RECALL, IT BEGAN THE NIGHT BEFORE THE HUNTRESS MOON, AND THE FESTIVAL OF DIANA...
DIANA!
PRINCESS!
WHAT'S WRONG?

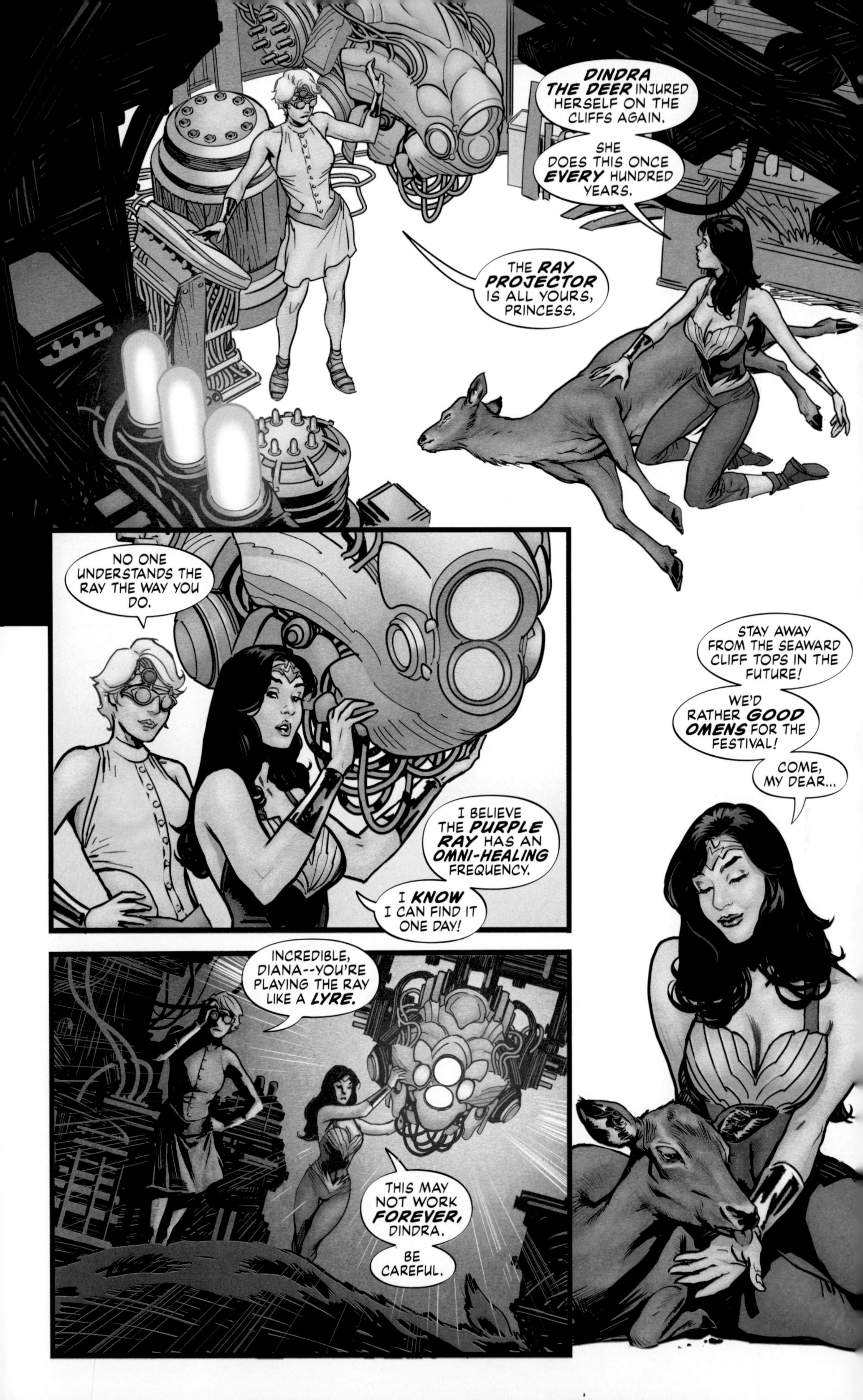
DINDRA THE DEER INJURED HERSELF ON THE CLIFFS AGAIN.
SHE DOES THIS ONCE EVERY HUNDRED YEARS.
THE RAY PROJECTOR IS ALL YOURS, PRINCESS.
NO ONE UNDERSTANDS THE RAY THE WAY YOU DO.
I BELIEVE THE PURPLE RAY HAS AN OMNI-HEALING FREQUENCY.
I KNOW I CAN FIND IT ONE DAY!
INCREDIBLE, DIANA--YOU'RE PLAYING THE RAY LIKE A LYRE.
THIS MAY NOT WORK FOREVER, DINDRA.
BE CAREFUL.
STAY AWAY FROM THE SEAWARD CLIFF TOPS IN THE FUTURE!
WE'D RATHER GOOD OMENS FOR THE FESTIVAL!
COME, MY DEAR...

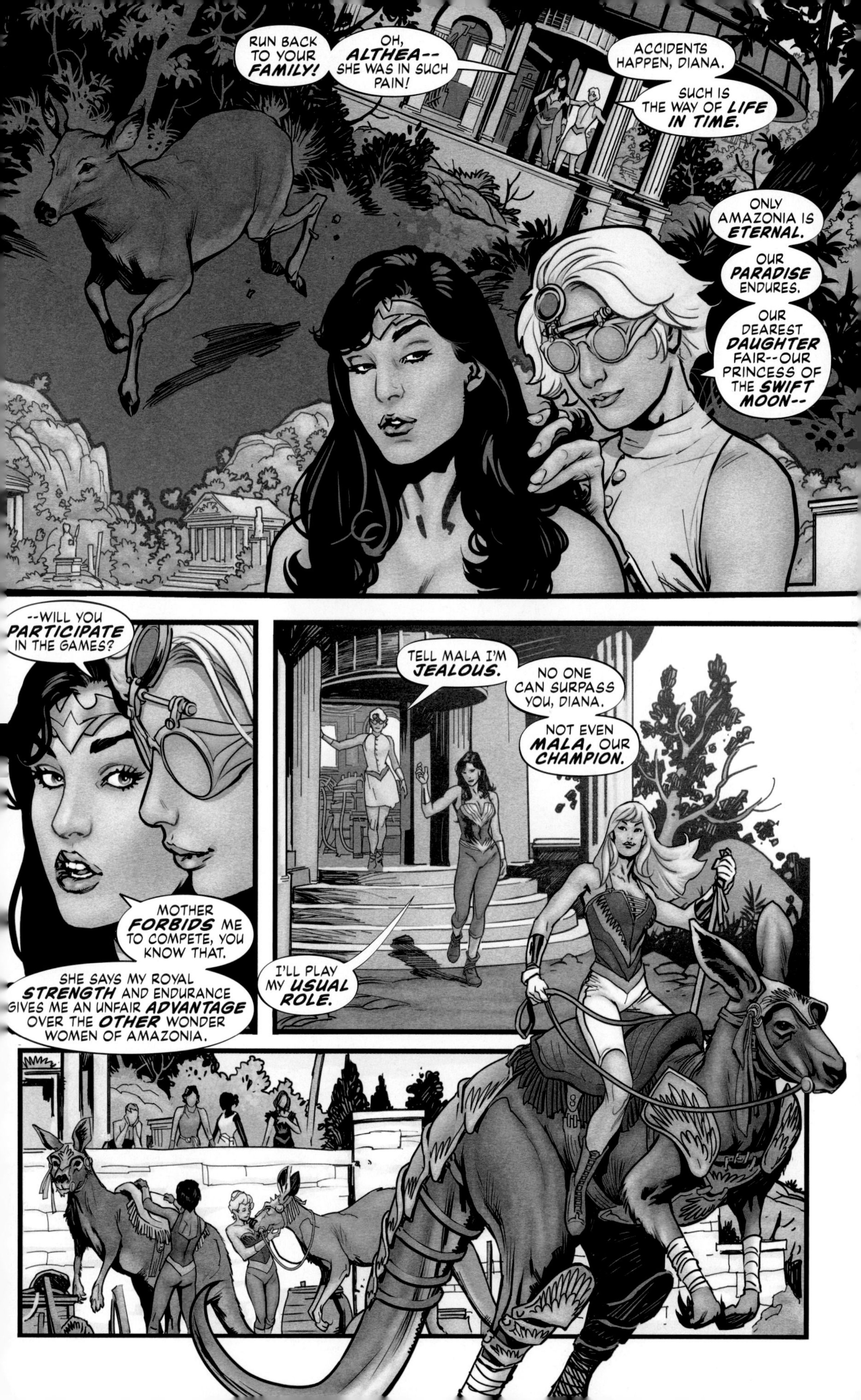
RUN BACK TO YOUR FAMILY!
OH, ALTHEA-- SHE WAS IN SUCH PAIN!
ACCIDENTS HAPPEN, DIANA.
SUCH IS THE WAY OF LIFE IN TIME.
ONLY AMAZONIA IS ETERNAL.
OUR PARADISE ENDURES.
OUR DEAREST DAUGHTER FAIR--OUR PRINCESS OF THE SWIFT MOON--
--WILL YOU PARTICIPATE IN THE GAMES?
MOTHER FORBIDS ME TO COMPETE, YOU KNOW THAT.
SHE SAYS MY ROYAL STRENGTH AND ENDURANCE GIVES ME AN UNFAIR ADVANTAGE OVER THE OTHER WONDER WOMEN OF AMAZONIA.
TELL MALA I'M JEALOUS.
NO ONE CAN SURPASS YOU, DIANA.
NOT EVEN MALA, OUR CHAMPION.
I'LL PLAY MY USUAL ROLE.

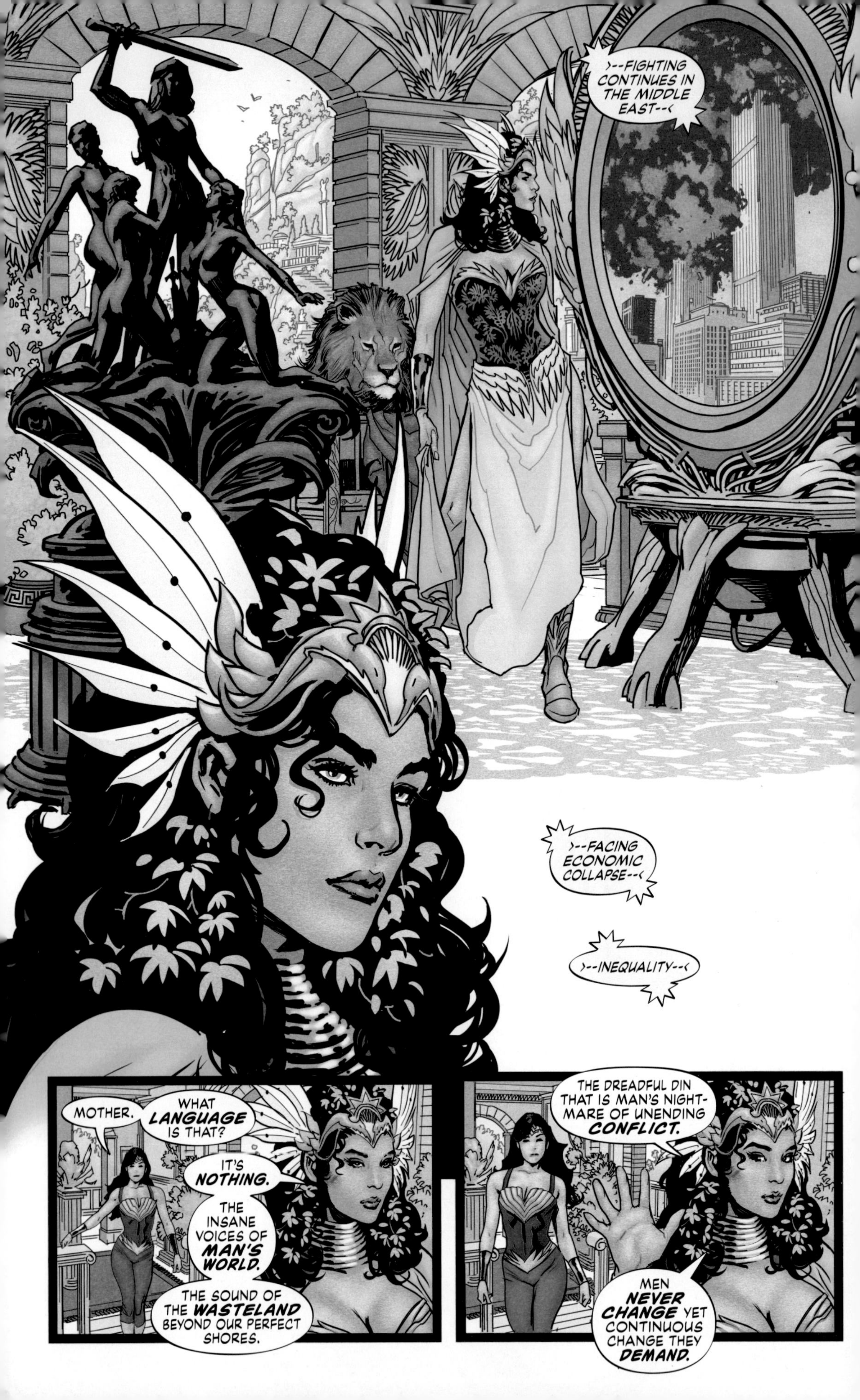
›--FIGHTING CONTINUES IN THE MIDDLE EAST--‹
›--FACING ECONOMIC COLLAPSE--‹
›--INEQUALITY--‹
MOTHER.
WHAT LANGUAGE IS THAT?
IT'S NOTHING.
THE INSANE VOICES OF MAN'S WORLD.
THE SOUND OF THE WASTELAND BEYOND OUR PERFECT SHORES.
THE DREADFUL DIN THAT IS MAN'S NIGHT-MARE OF UNENDING CONFLICT.
MEN NEVER CHANGE YET CONTINUOUS CHANGE THEY DEMAND.

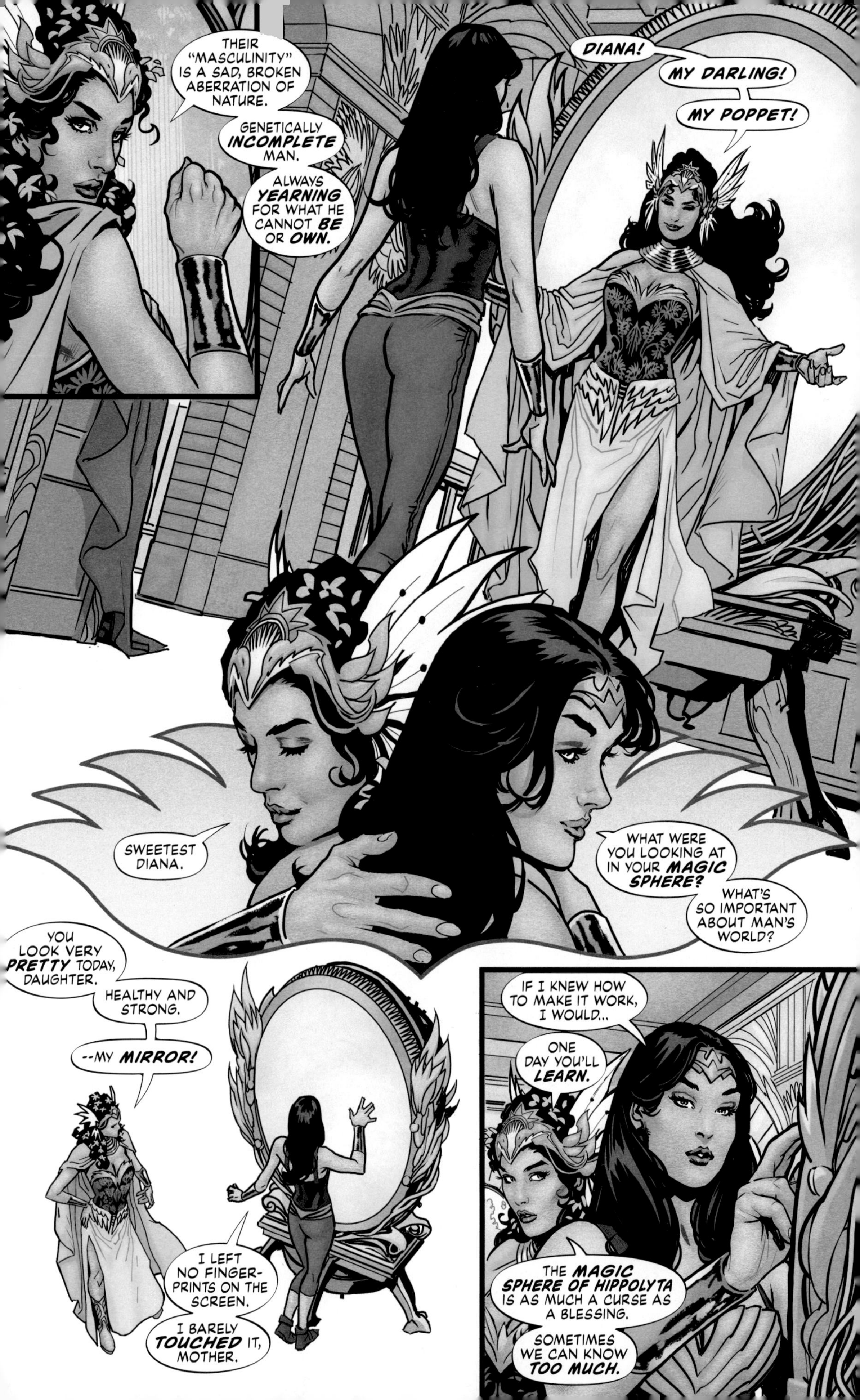
THEIR "MASCULINITY" IS A SAD, BROKEN ABERRATION OF NATURE.
GENETICALLY INCOMPLETE MAN.
ALWAYS YEARNING FOR WHAT HE CANNOT BE OR OWN.
DIANA!
MY DARLING!
MY POPPET!
SWEETEST DIANA.
WHAT WERE YOU LOOKING AT IN YOUR MAGIC SPHERE?
WHAT'S SO IMPORTANT ABOUT MAN'S WORLD?
YOU LOOK VERY PRETTY TODAY, DAUGHTER.
HEALTHY AND STRONG.
--MY MIRROR!
I LEFT NO FINGER-PRINTS ON THE SCREEN.
I BARELY TOUCHED IT, MOTHER.
IF I KNEW HOW TO MAKE IT WORK, I WOULD...
ONE DAY YOU'LL LEARN.
THE MAGIC SPHERE OF HIPPOLYTA IS AS MUCH A CURSE AS A BLESSING.
SOMETIMES WE CAN KNOW TOO MUCH.

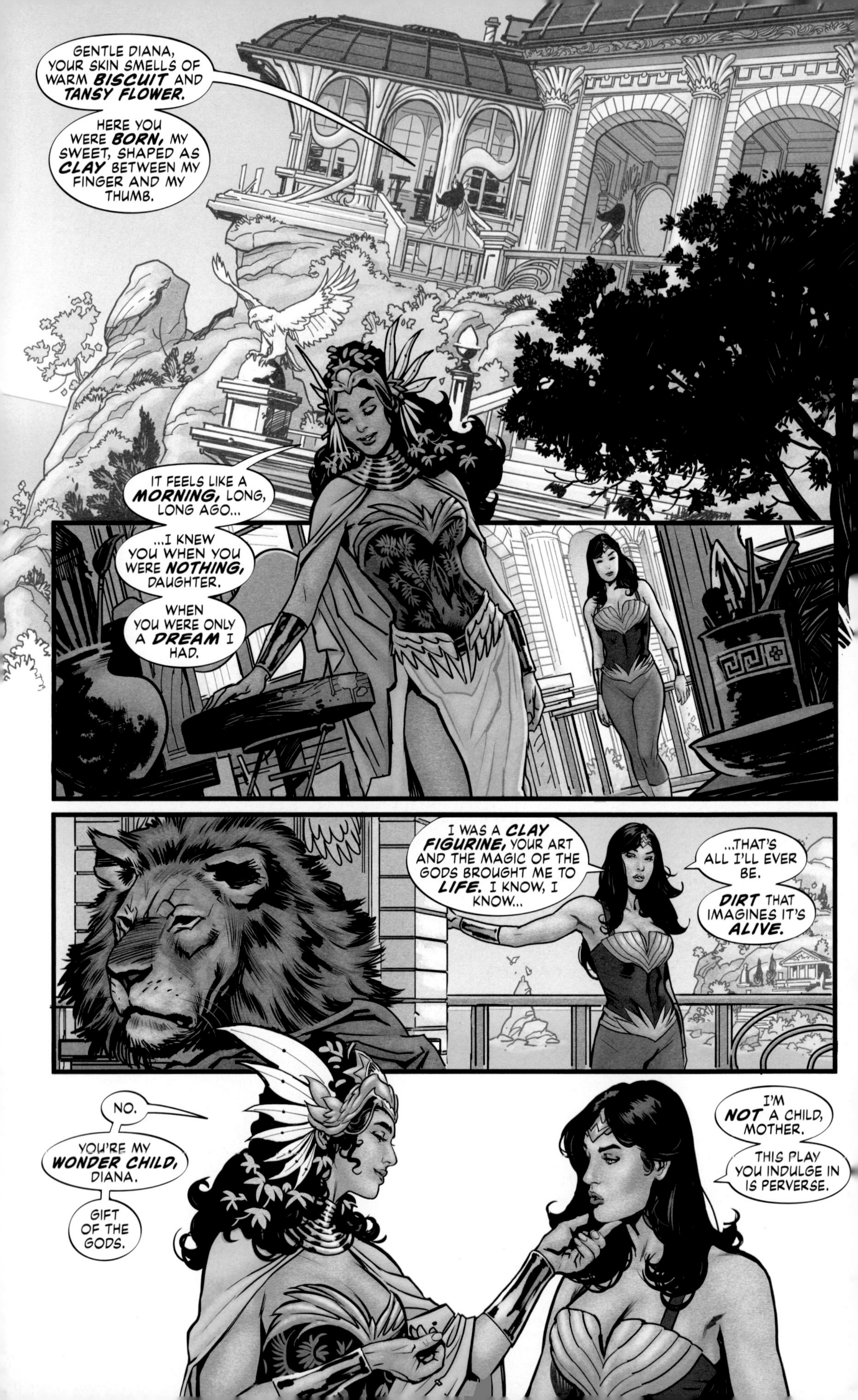
GENTLE DIANA, YOUR SKIN SMELLS OF WARM BISCUIT AND TANSY FLOWER.
HERE YOU WERE BORN, MY SWEET, SHAPED AS CLAY BETWEEN MY FINGER AND MY THUMB.
IT FEELS LIKE A MORNING, LONG, LONG AGO...
...I KNEW YOU WHEN YOU WERE NOTHING, DAUGHTER.
WHEN YOU WERE ONLY A DREAM I HAD.
I WAS A CLAY FIGURINE, YOUR ART AND THE MAGIC OF THE GODS BROUGHT ME TO LIFE. I KNOW, I KNOW...
...THAT'S ALL I'LL EVER BE.
DIRT THAT IMAGINES IT'S ALIVE.
NO.
YOU'RE MY WONDER CHILD, DIANA.
GIFT OF THE GODS.
I'M NOT A CHILD, MOTHER.
THIS PLAY YOU INDULGE IN IS PERVERSE.

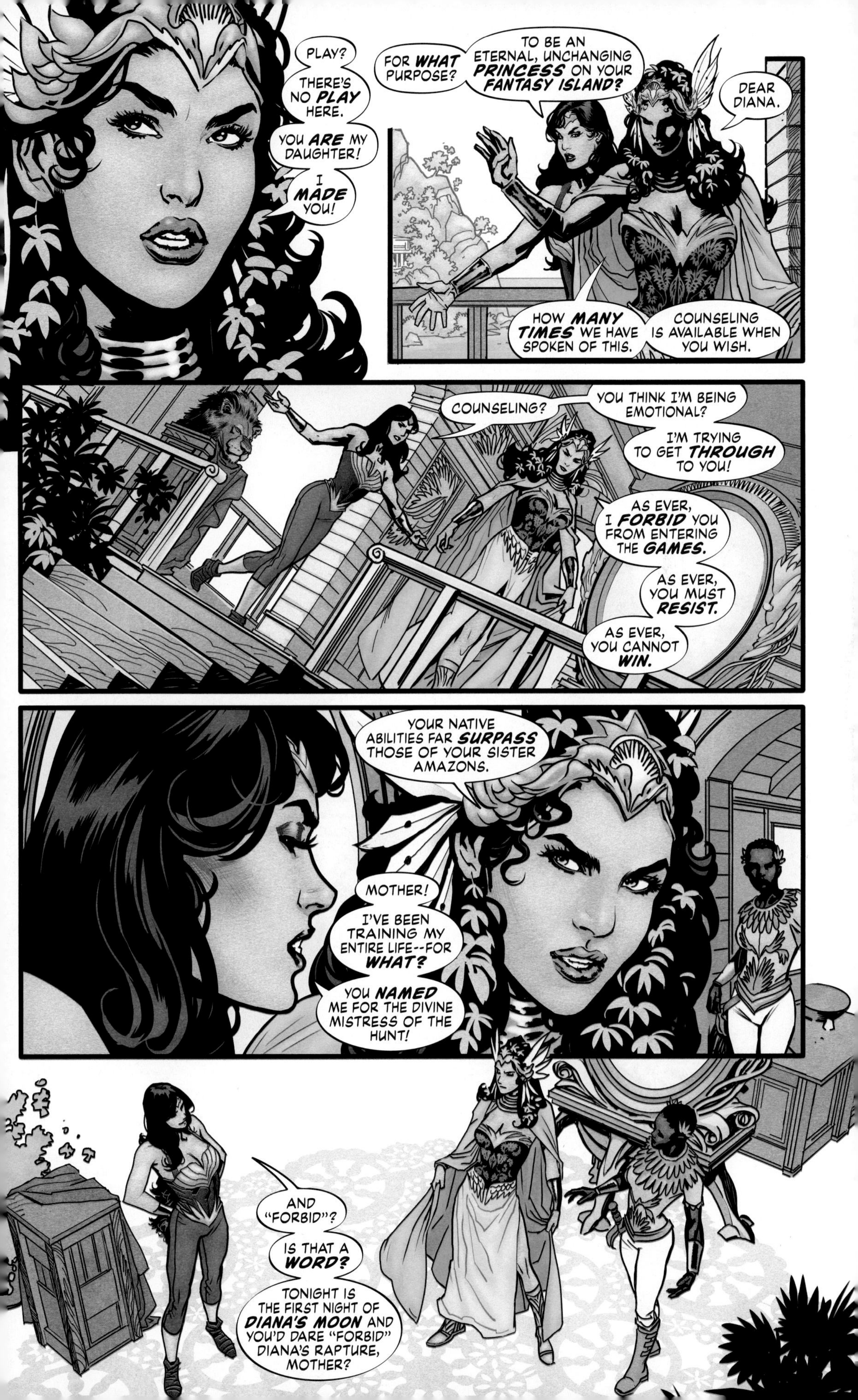
PLAY?
THERE'S NO PLAY HERE.
YOU ARE MY DAUGHTER!
I MADE YOU!
FOR WHAT PURPOSE?
TO BE AN ETERNAL, UNCHANGING PRINCESS ON YOUR FANTASY ISLAND?
DEAR DIANA.
HOW MANY TIMES WE HAVE SPOKEN OF THIS.
COUNSELING IS AVAILABLE WHEN YOU WISH.
COUNSELING?
YOU THINK I'M BEING EMOTIONAL?
I'M TRYING TO GET THROUGH TO YOU!
AS EVER, I FORBID YOU FROM ENTERING THE GAMES.
AS EVER, YOU MUST RESIST.
AS EVER, YOU CANNOT WIN.
YOUR NATIVE ABILITIES FAR SURPASS THOSE OF YOUR SISTER AMAZONS.
MOTHER!
I'VE BEEN TRAINING MY ENTIRE LIFE--FOR WHAT?
YOU NAMED ME FOR THE DIVINE MISTRESS OF THE HUNT!
AND "FORBID"?
IS THAT A WORD?
TONIGHT IS THE FIRST NIGHT OF DIANA'S MOON AND YOU'D DARE "FORBID" DIANA'S RAPTURE, MOTHER?

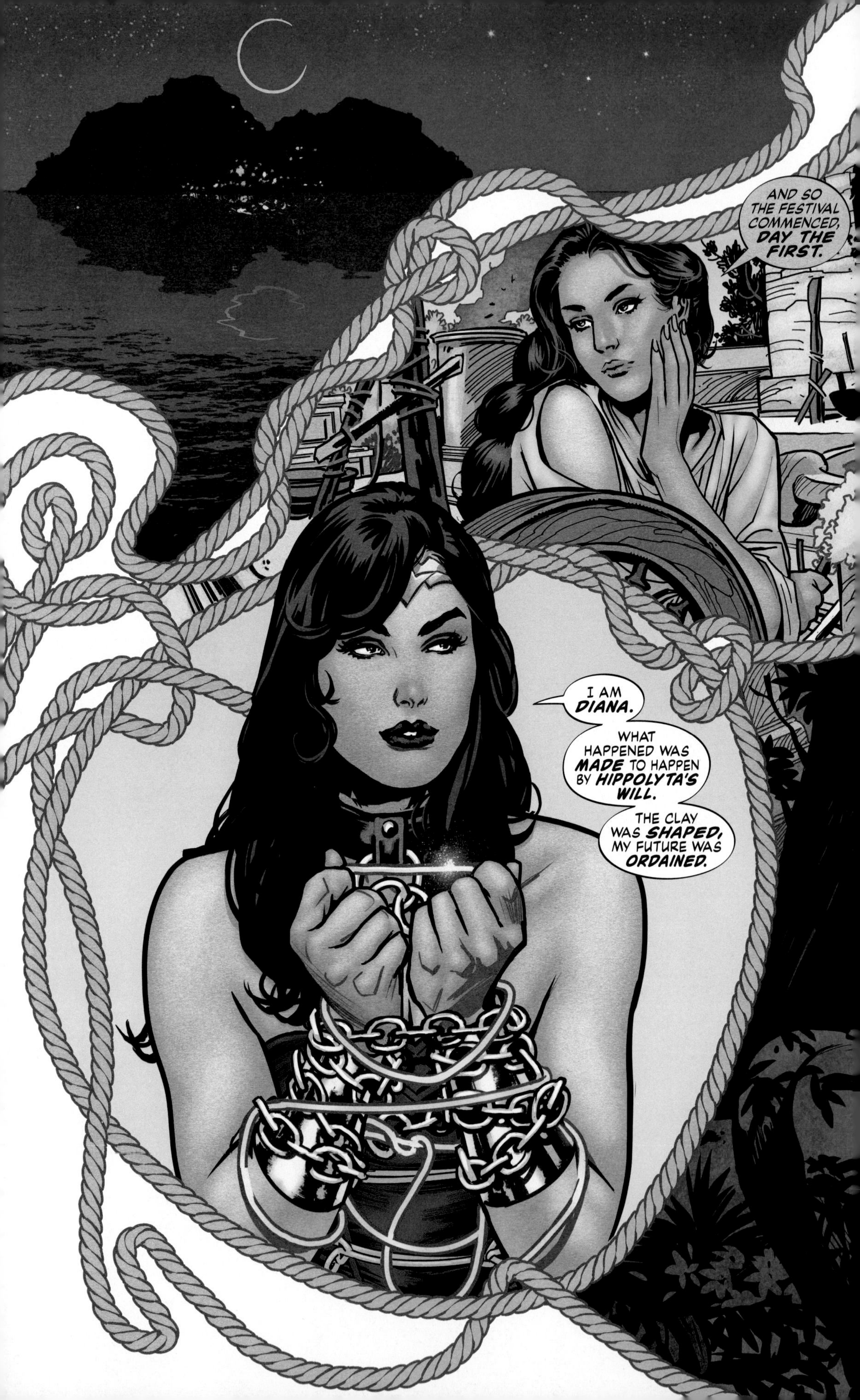
AND SO THE FESTIVAL COMMENCED, DAY THE FIRST.
I AM DIANA.
WHAT HAPPENED WAS MADE TO HAPPEN BY HIPPOLYTA'S WILL.
THE CLAY WAS SHAPED, MY FUTURE WAS ORDAINED.

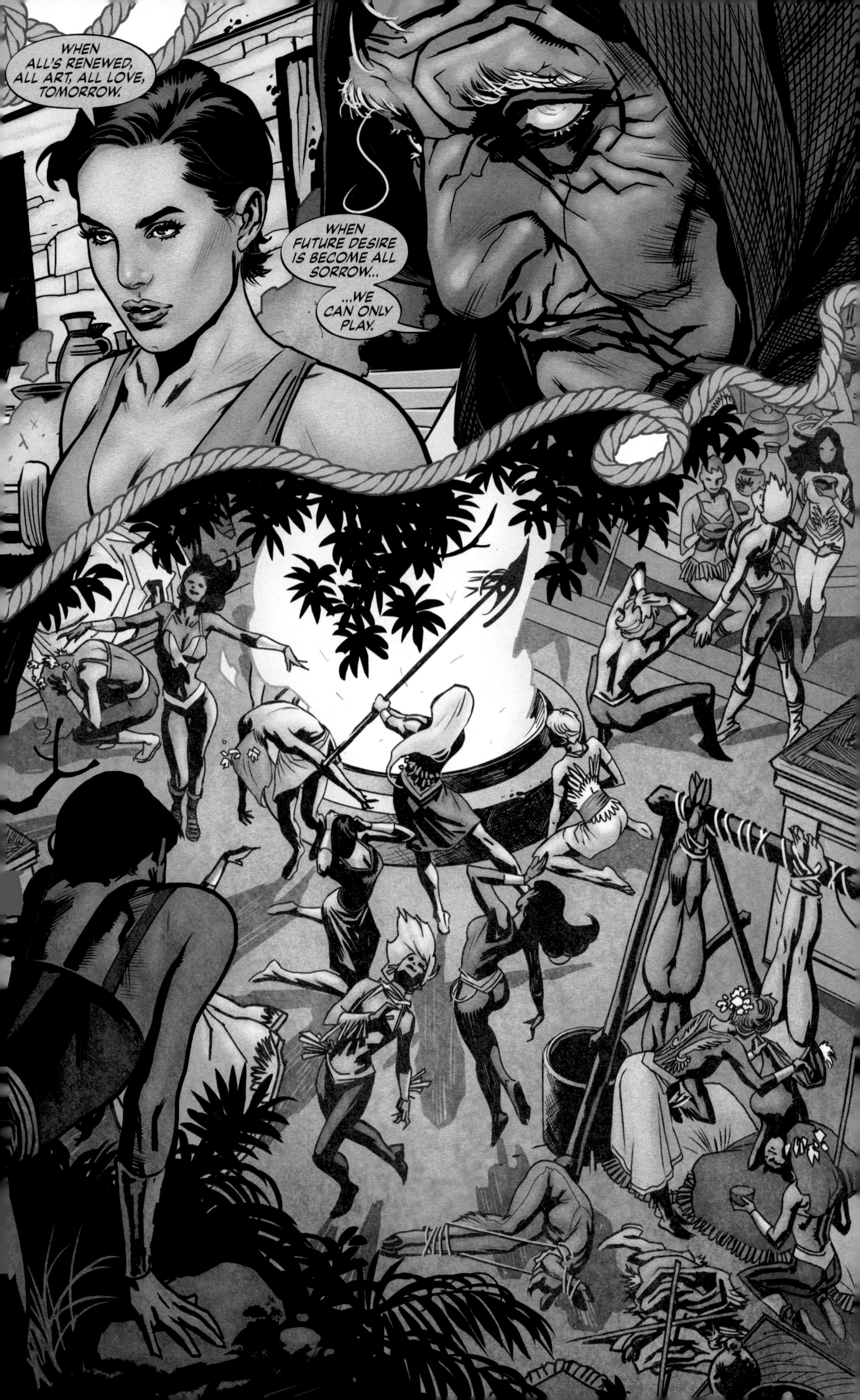
WHEN ALL'S RENEWED, ALL ART, ALL LOVE, TOMORROW.
WHEN FUTURE DESIRE IS BECOME ALL SORROW...
...WE CAN ONLY PLAY.

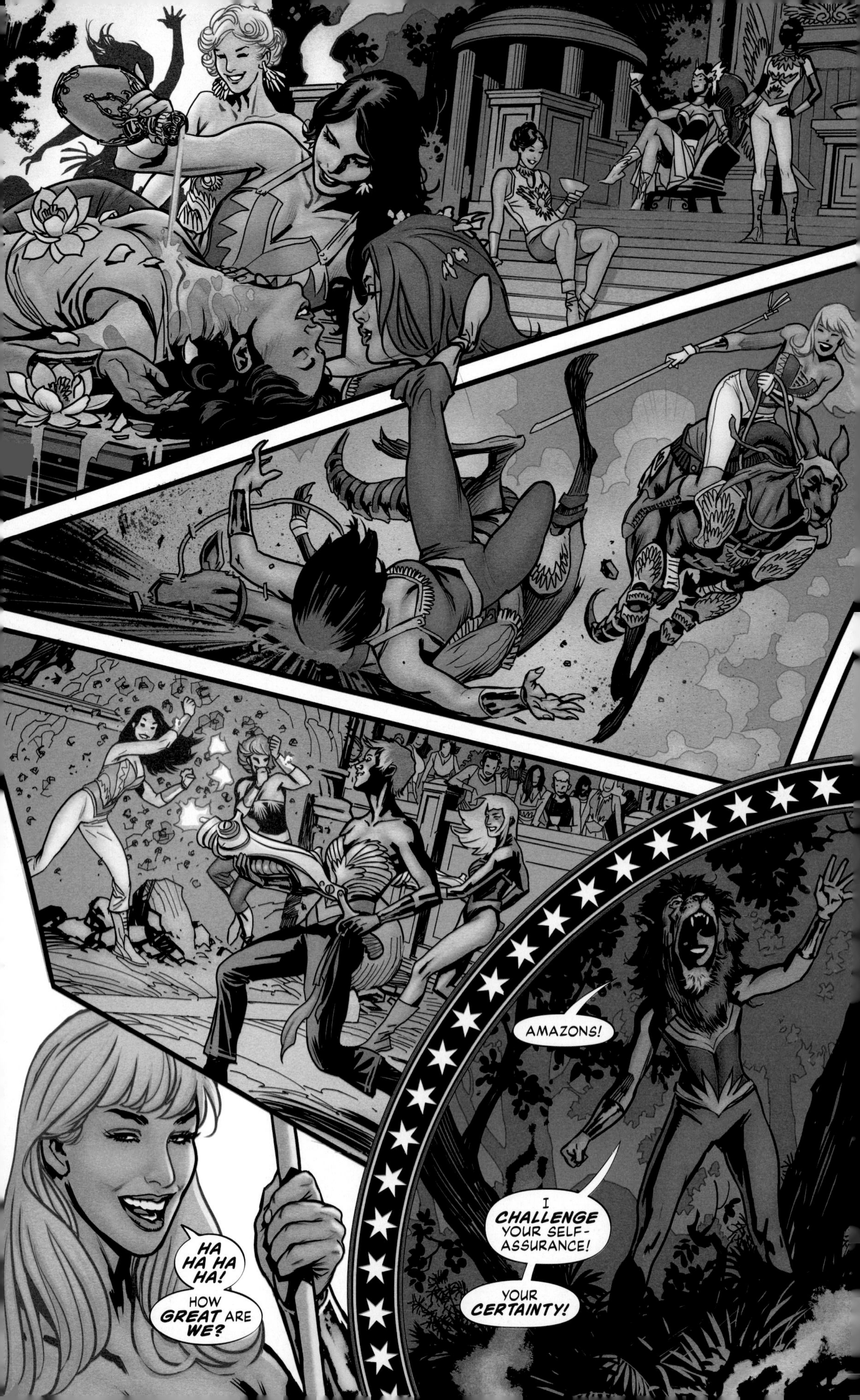
HA HA HA HA! HOW GREAT ARE WE?
AMAZONS!
I CHALLENGE YOUR SELF-ASSURANCE!
YOUR CERTAINTY!

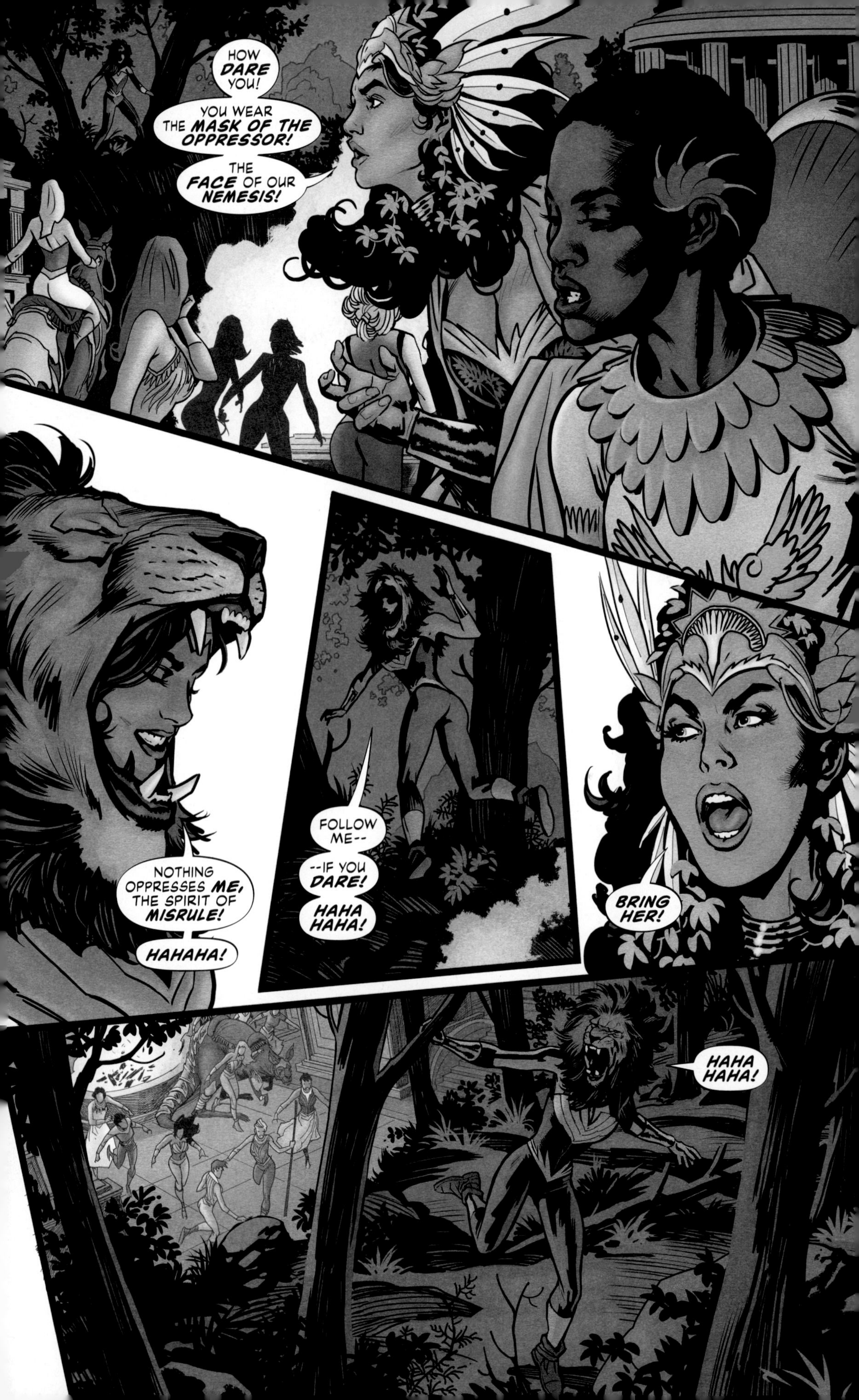
HOW DARE YOU!
YOU WEAR THE MASK OF THE OPPRESSOR!
THE FACE OF OUR NEMESIS!
NOTHING OPPRESSES ME, THE SPIRIT OF MISRULE!
HAHAHA!
FOLLOW ME--
--IF YOU DARE!
HAHA HAHA!
BRING HER!
HAHA HAHA!

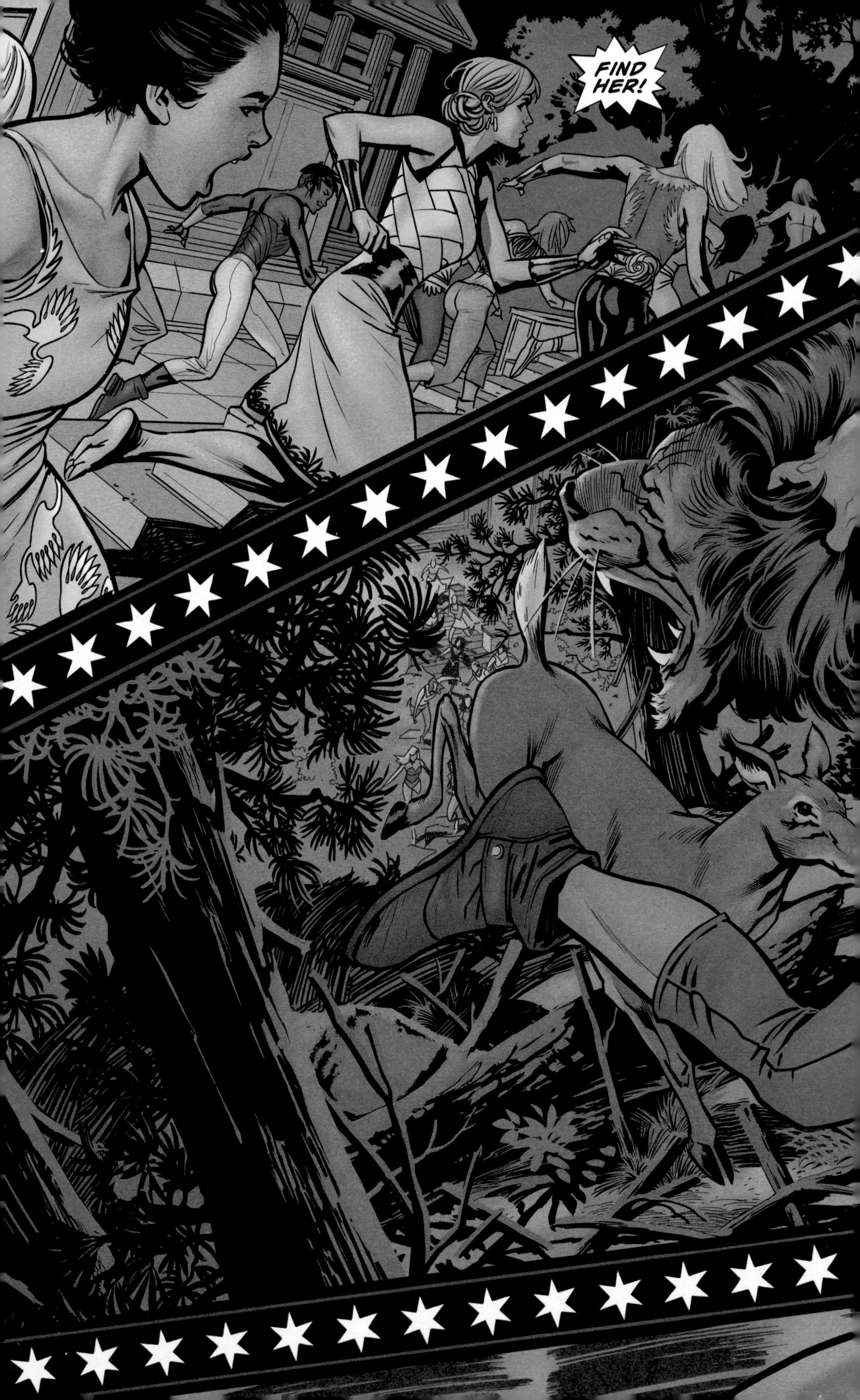
FIND HER!

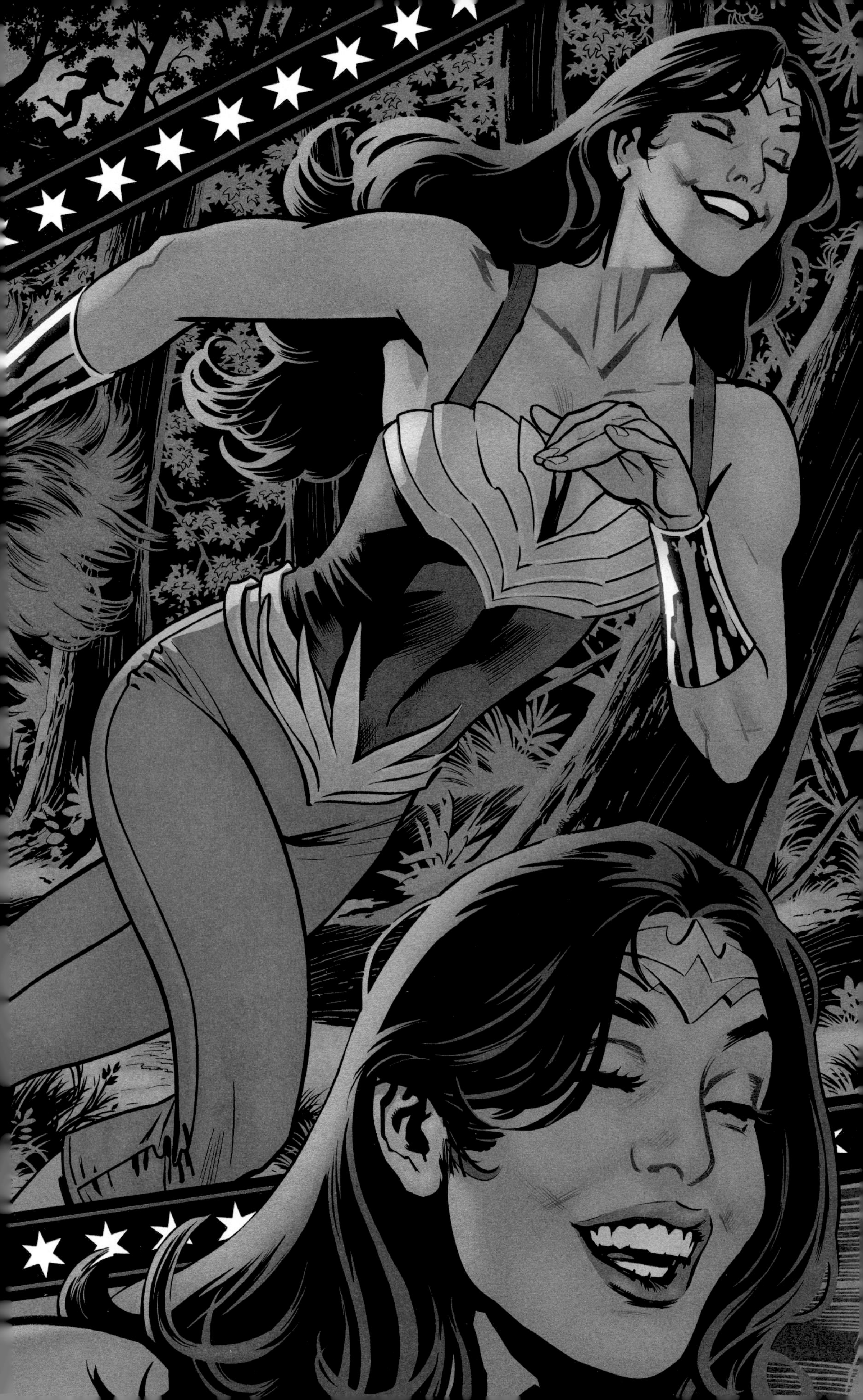

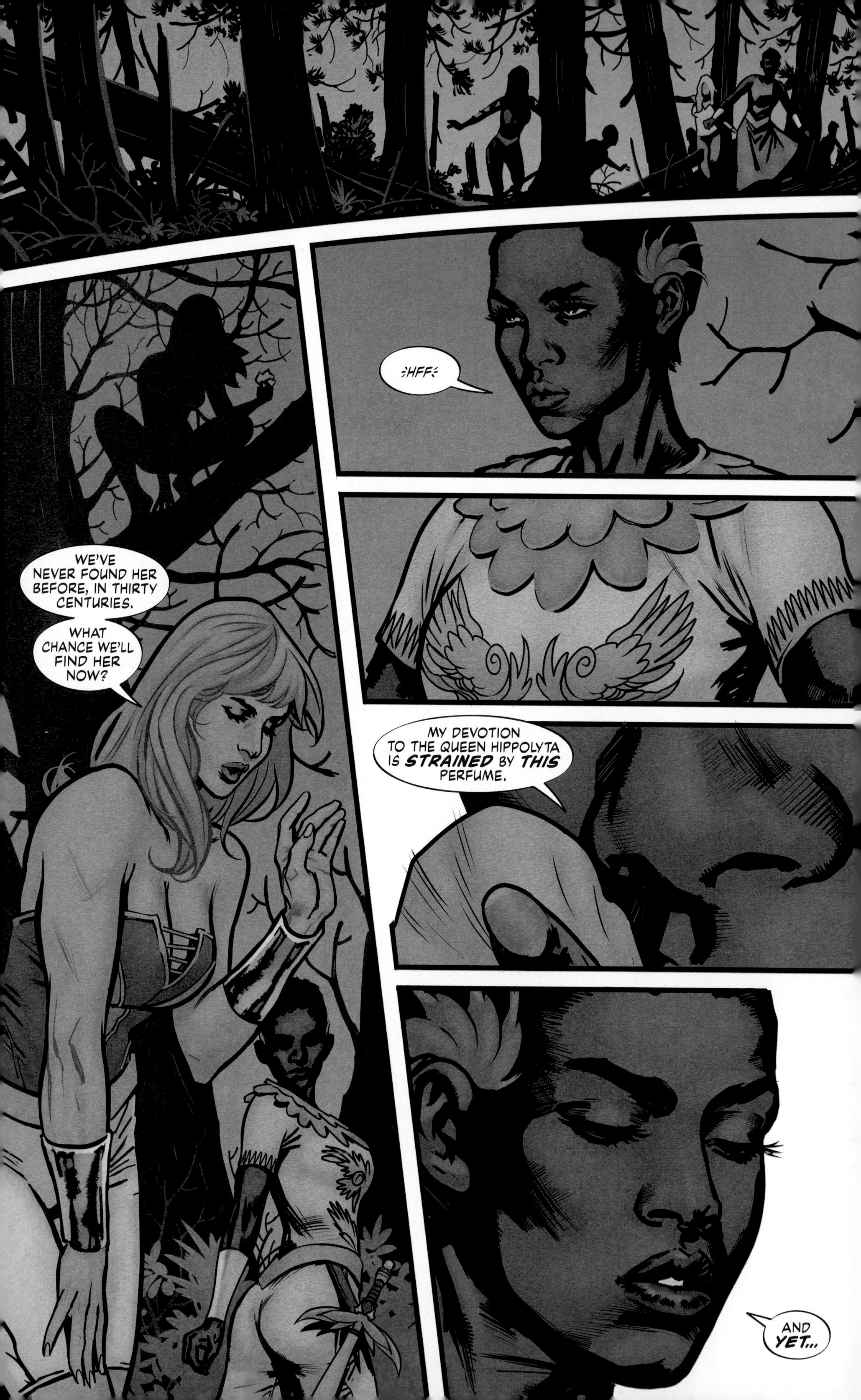
WE'VE NEVER FOUND HER BEFORE, IN THIRTY CENTURIES.
WHAT CHANCE WE'LL FIND HER NOW?
HFF
MY DEVOTION TO THE QUEEN HIPPOLYTA IS STRAINED BY THIS PERFUME.
AND YET...

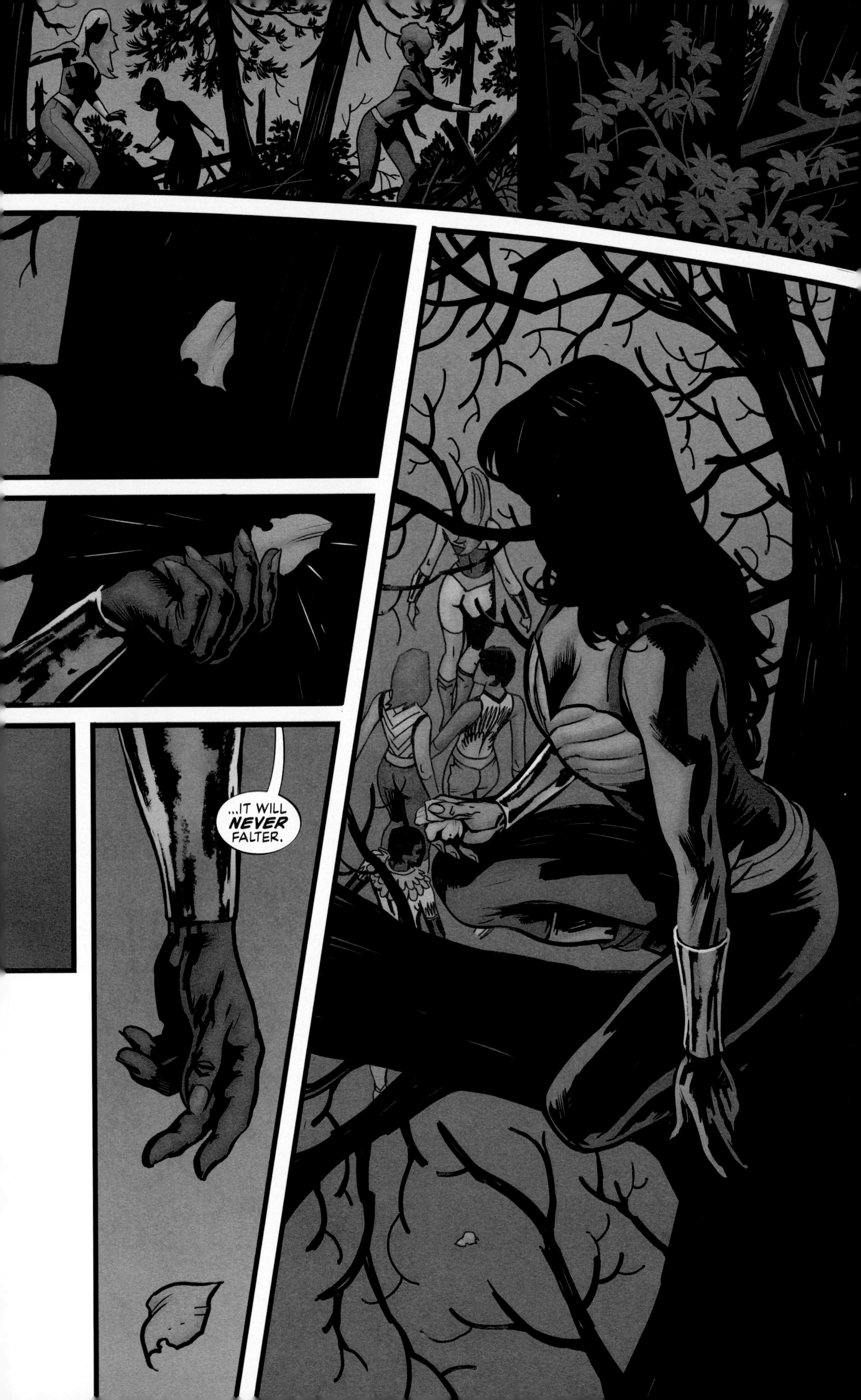
...IT WILL NEVER FALTER.

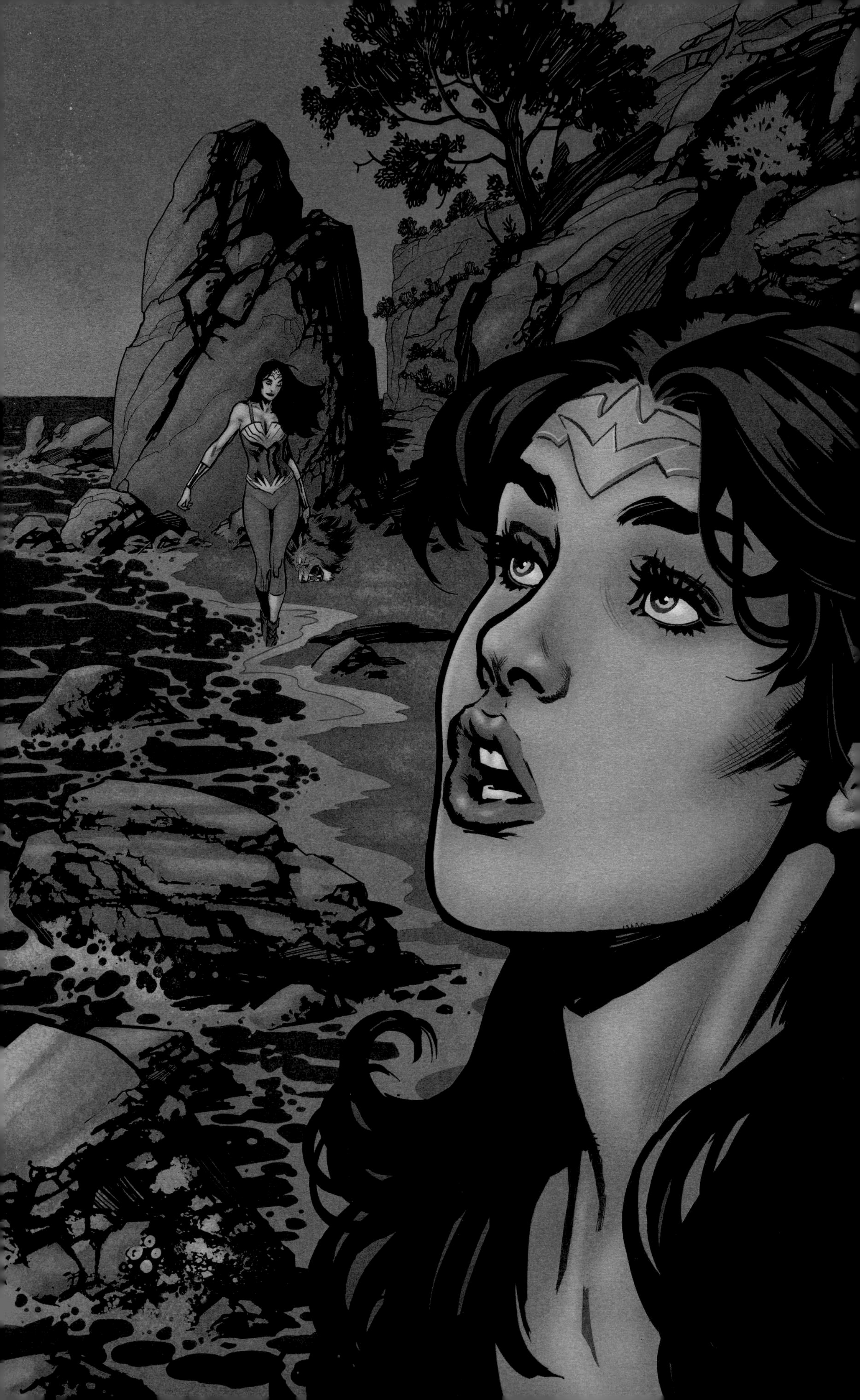

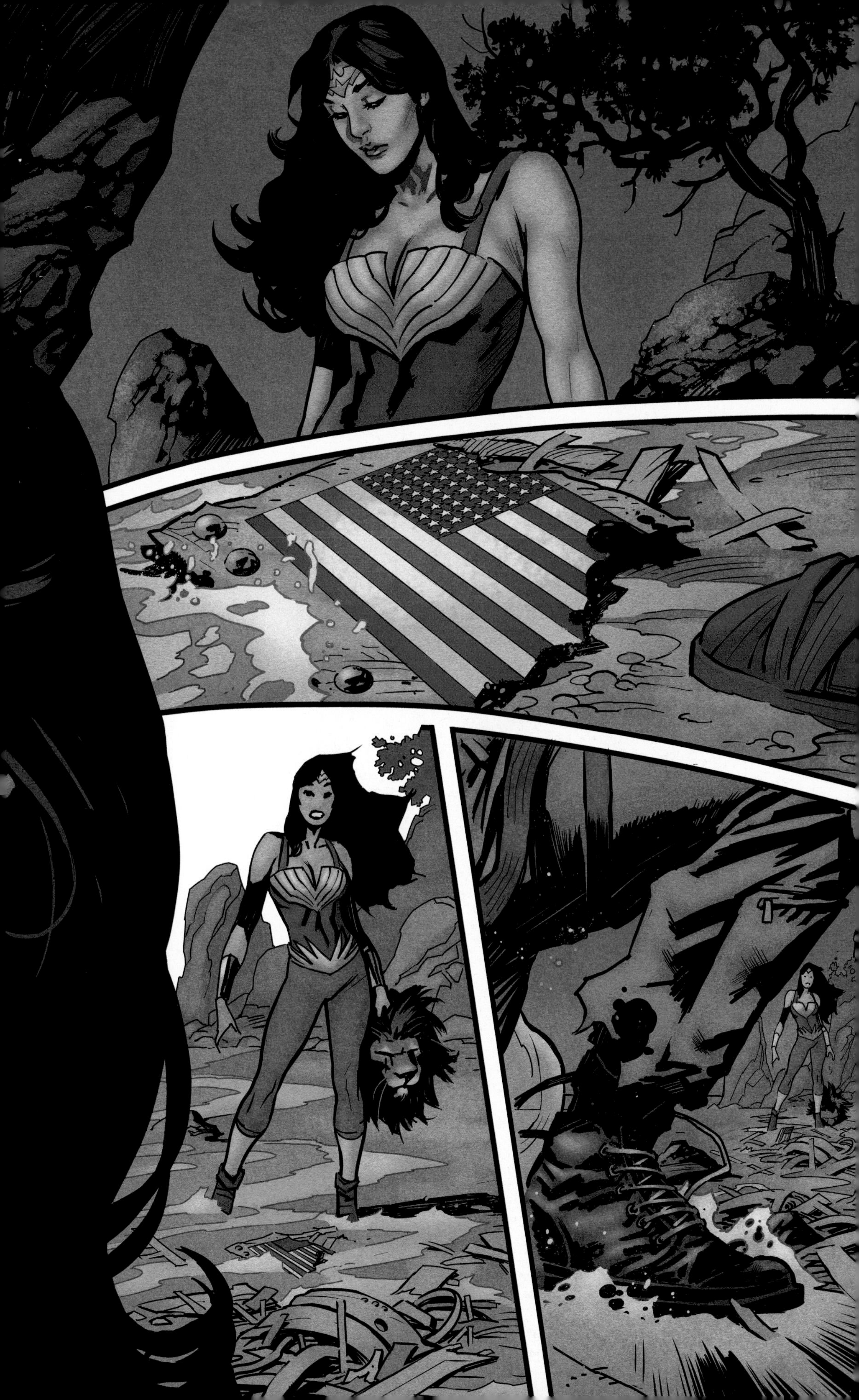

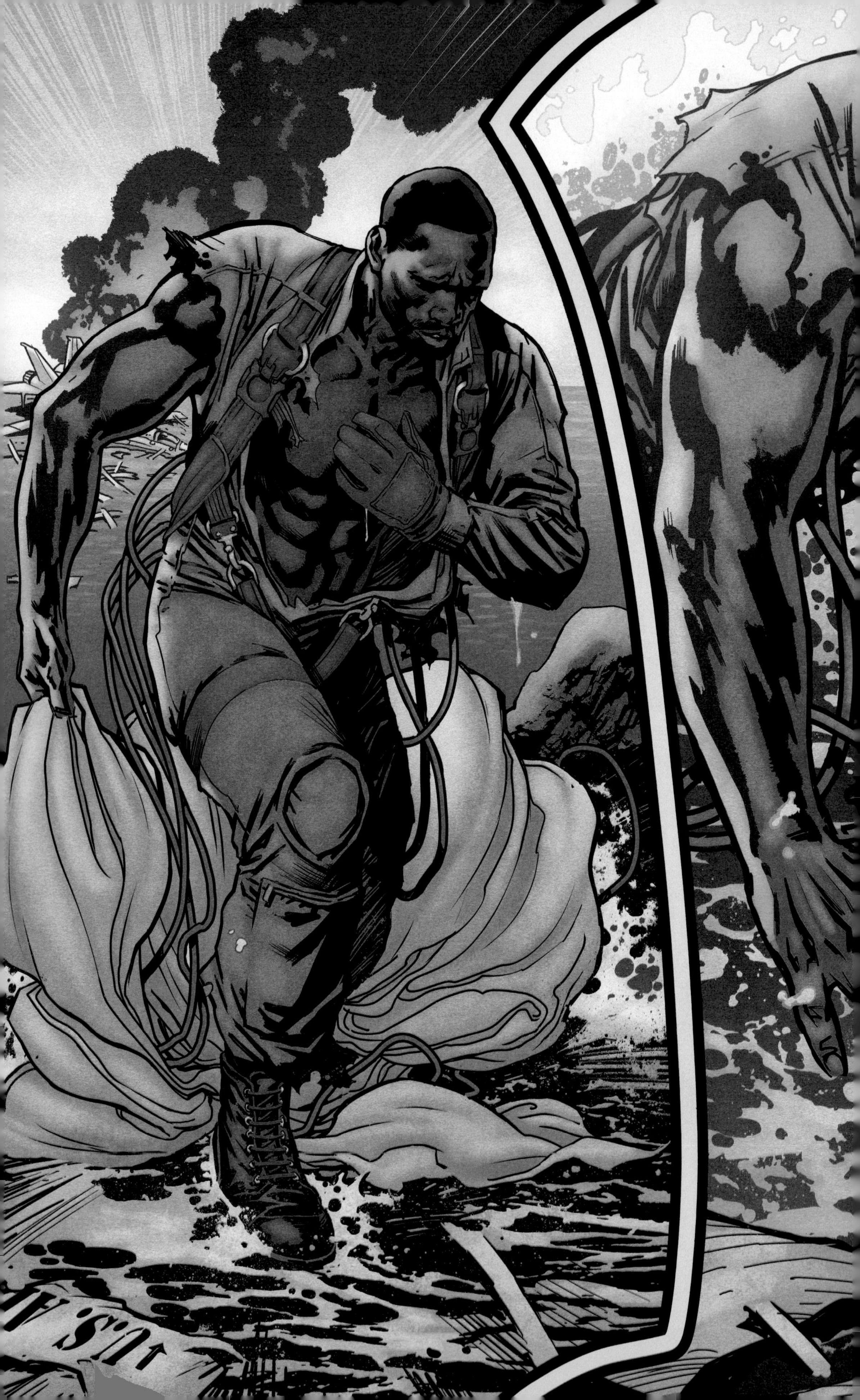

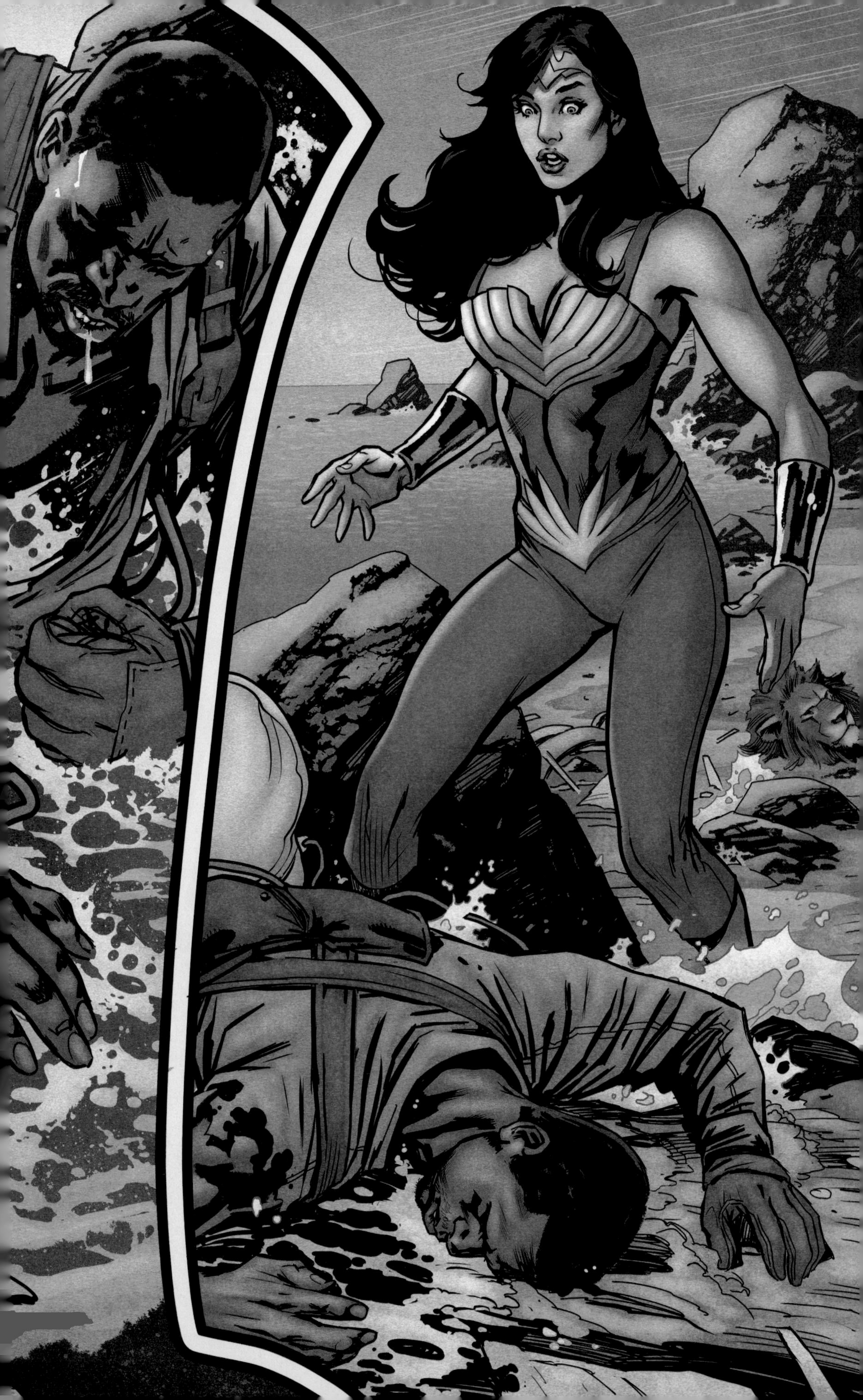

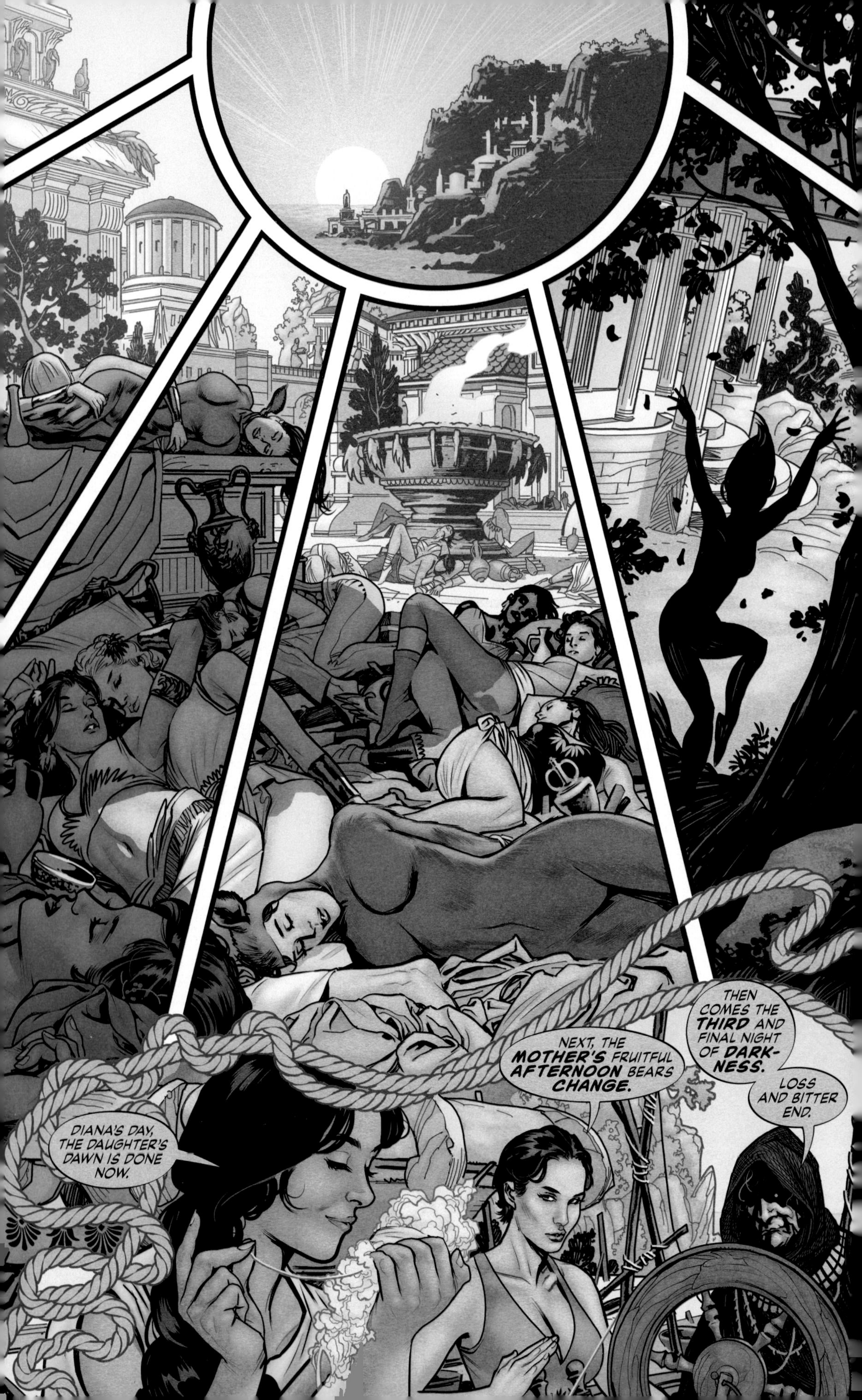
DIANA'S DAY, THE DAUGHTER'S DAWN IS DONE NOW.
NEXT, THE MOTHER'S FRUITFUL AFTERNOON BEARS CHANGE.
THEN COMES THE THIRD AND FINAL NIGHT OF DARK-NESS.
LOSS AND BITTER END.

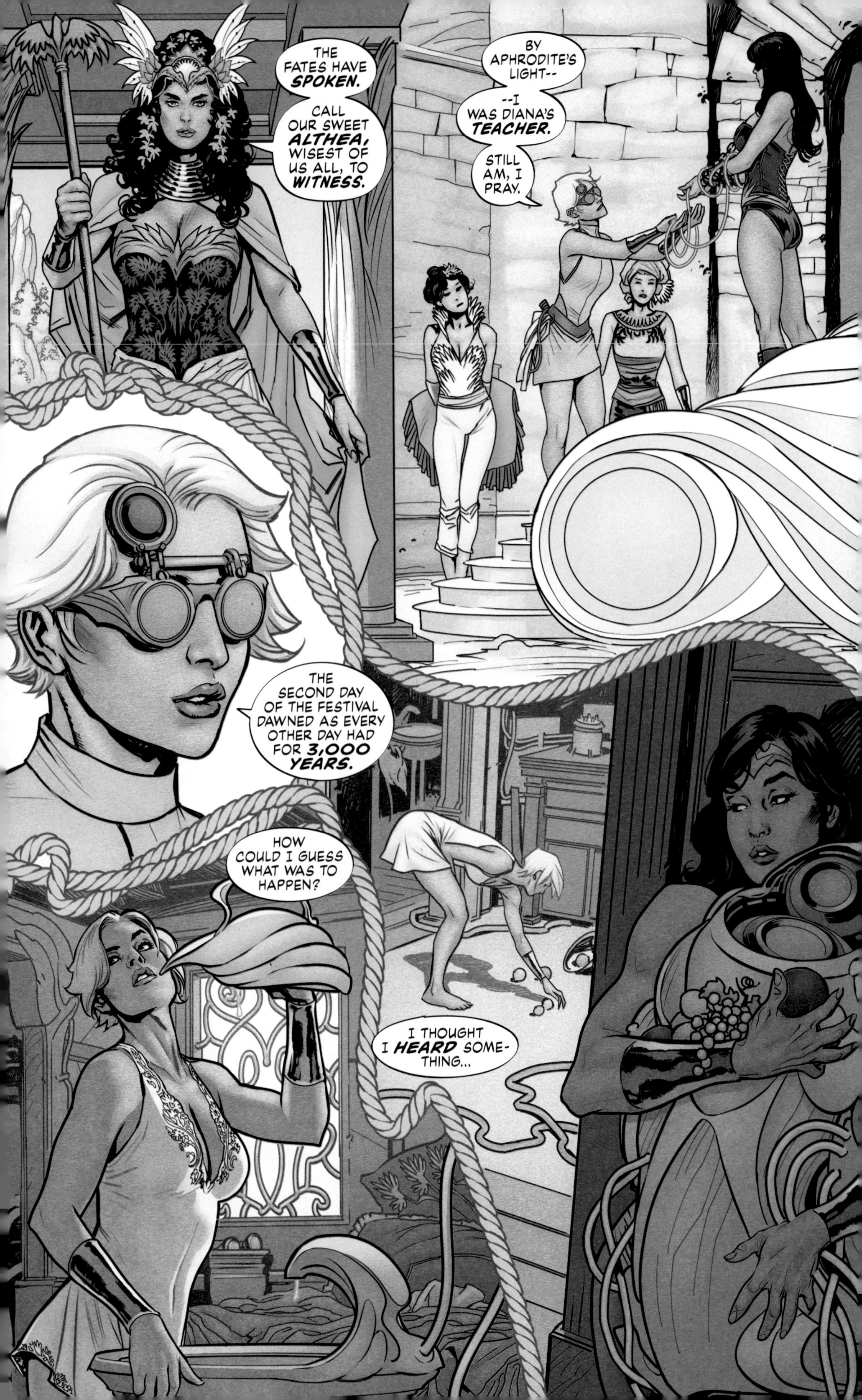
THE FATES HAVE SPOKEN.
CALL OUR SWEET ALTHEA, WISEST OF US ALL, TO WITNESS.
BY APHRODITE'S LIGHT--
--I WAS DIANA'S TEACHER.
STILL AM, I PRAY.
THE SECOND DAY OF THE FESTIVAL DAWNED AS EVERY OTHER DAY HAD FOR 3,000 YEARS.
HOW COULD I GUESS WHAT WAS TO HAPPEN?
I THOUGHT I HEARD SOME-THING...

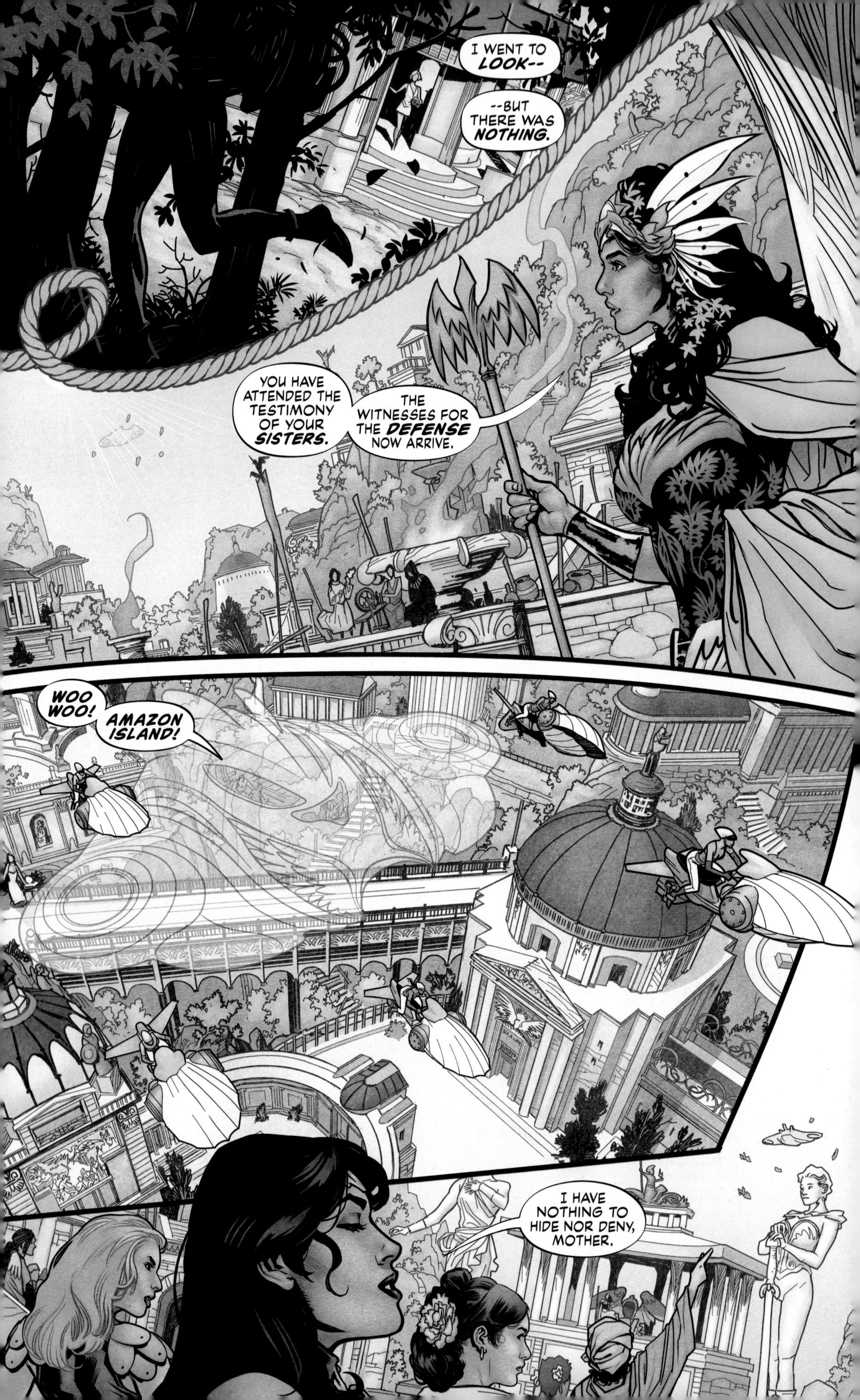
I WENT TO LOOK--
--BUT THERE WAS NOTHING.
YOU HAVE ATTENDED THE TESTIMONY OF YOUR SISTERS.
THE WITNESSES FOR THE DEFENSE NOW ARRIVE.
WOO WOO!
AMAZON ISLAND!
I HAVE NOTHING TO HIDE NOR DENY, MOTHER.

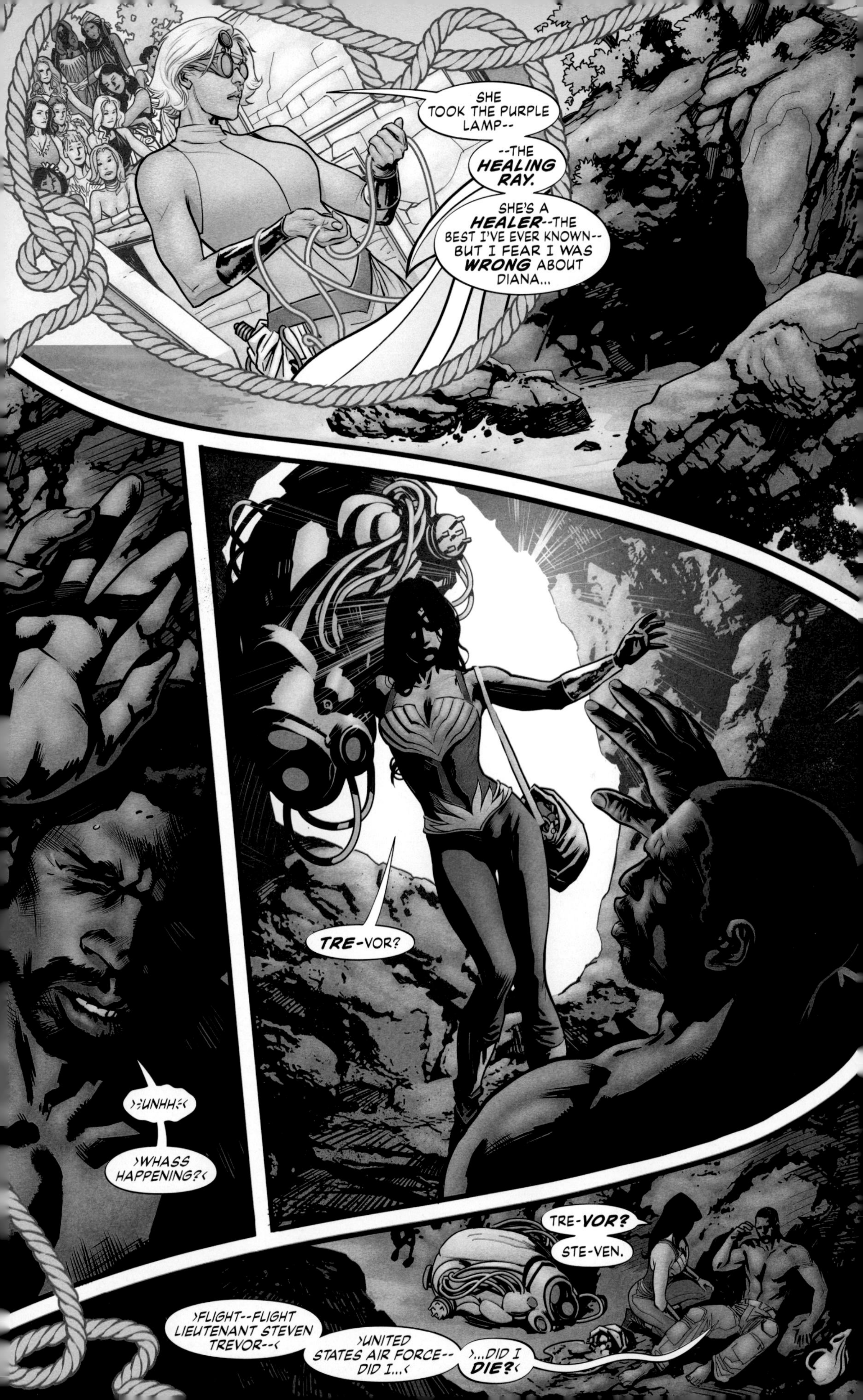
SHE TOOK THE PURPLE LAMP--
--THE HEALING RAY.
SHE'S A HEALER--THE BEST I'VE EVER KNOWN--BUT I FEAR I WAS WRONG ABOUT DIANA...
TRE-VOR?
›UNHH‹
›WHASS HAPPENING?‹
TRE-VOR?
STE-VEN.
›FLIGHT--FLIGHT LIEUTENANT STEVEN TREVOR--‹
›UNITED STATES AIR FORCE--DID I...‹
›...DID I DIE?‹

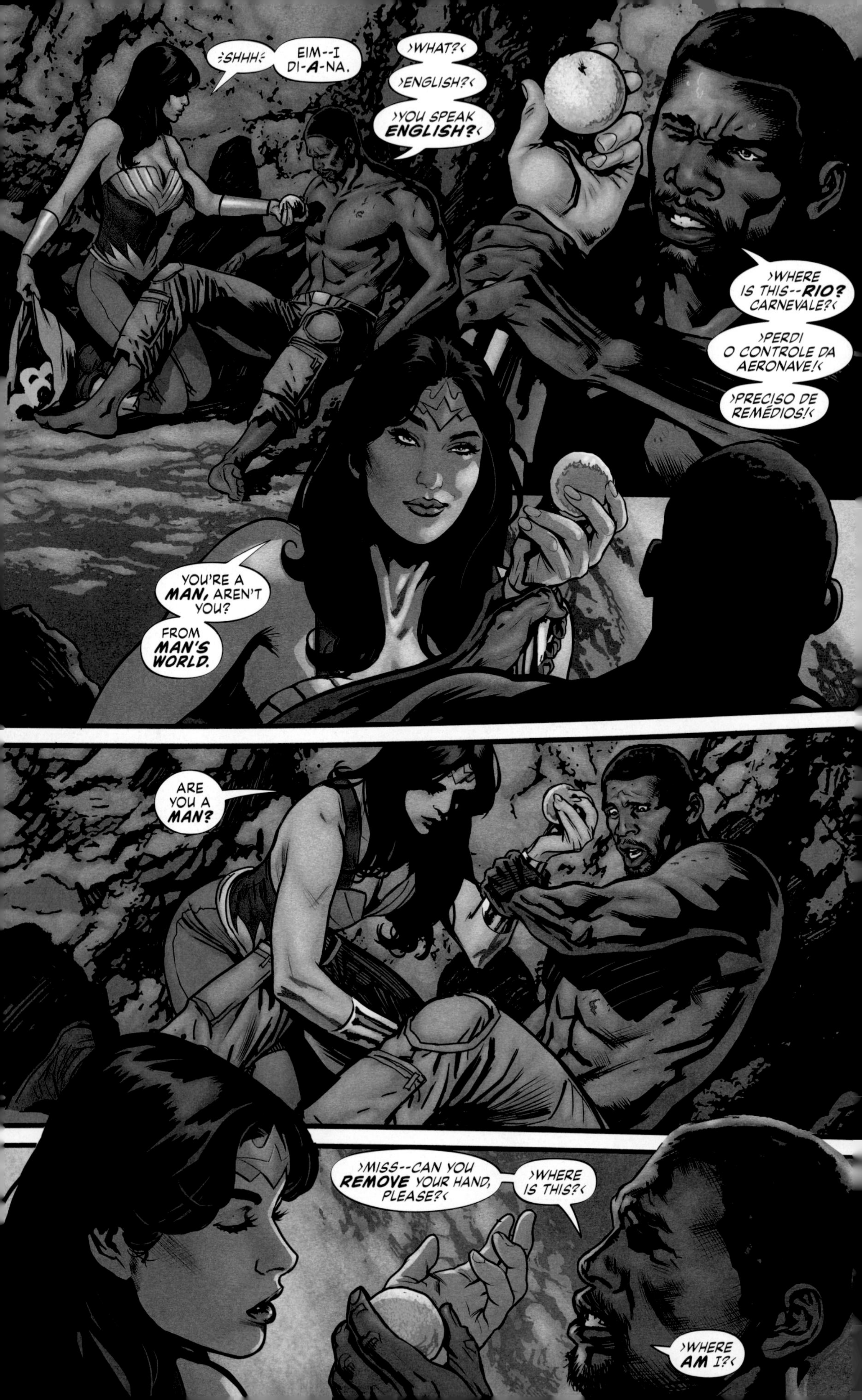
›SHHH‹
EIM--I DI-A-NA.
›WHAT?‹
›ENGLISH?‹
›YOU SPEAK ENGLISH?‹
›WHERE IS THIS--RIO? CARNEVALE?‹
›PERDI O CONTROLE DA AERONAVE!‹
›PRECISO DE REMÉDIOS!‹
YOU'RE A MAN, AREN'T YOU?
FROM MAN'S WORLD.
ARE YOU A MAN?
›MISS--CAN YOU REMOVE YOUR HAND, PLEASE?‹
›WHERE IS THIS?‹
›WHERE AM I?‹

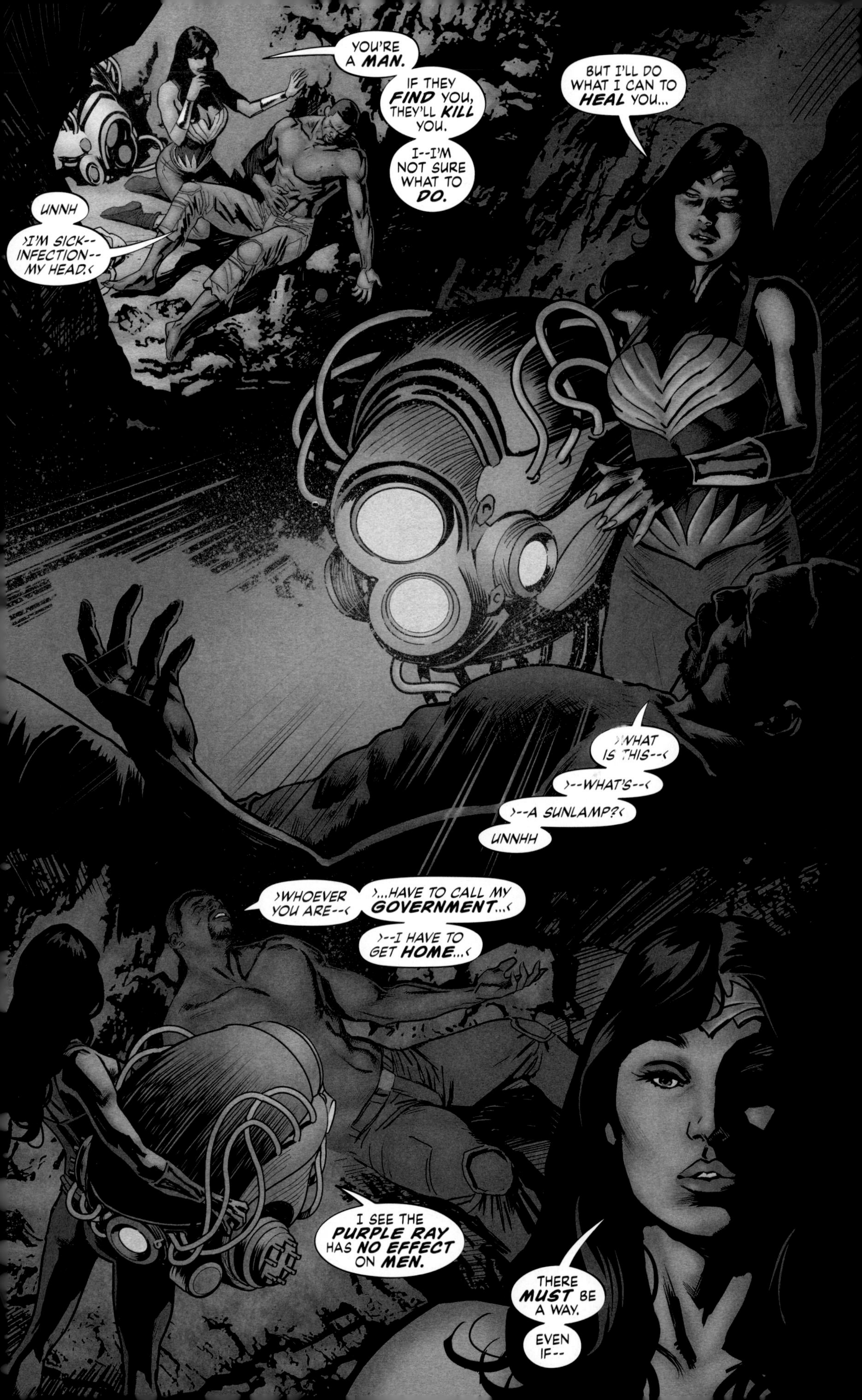
YOU'RE A MAN.
IF THEY FIND YOU, THEY'LL KILL YOU.
I--I'M NOT SURE WHAT TO DO.
UNNH
›I'M SICK-- INFECTION-- MY HEAD.‹
BUT I'LL DO WHAT I CAN TO HEAL YOU...
›WHAT IS THIS--‹
›--WHAT'S--‹
›--A SUNLAMP?‹
UNNHH
›WHOEVER YOU ARE--‹
›...HAVE TO CALL MY GOVERNMENT...‹
›--I HAVE TO GET HOME...‹
I SEE THE PURPLE RAY HAS NO EFFECT ON MEN.
THERE MUST BE A WAY.
EVEN IF--

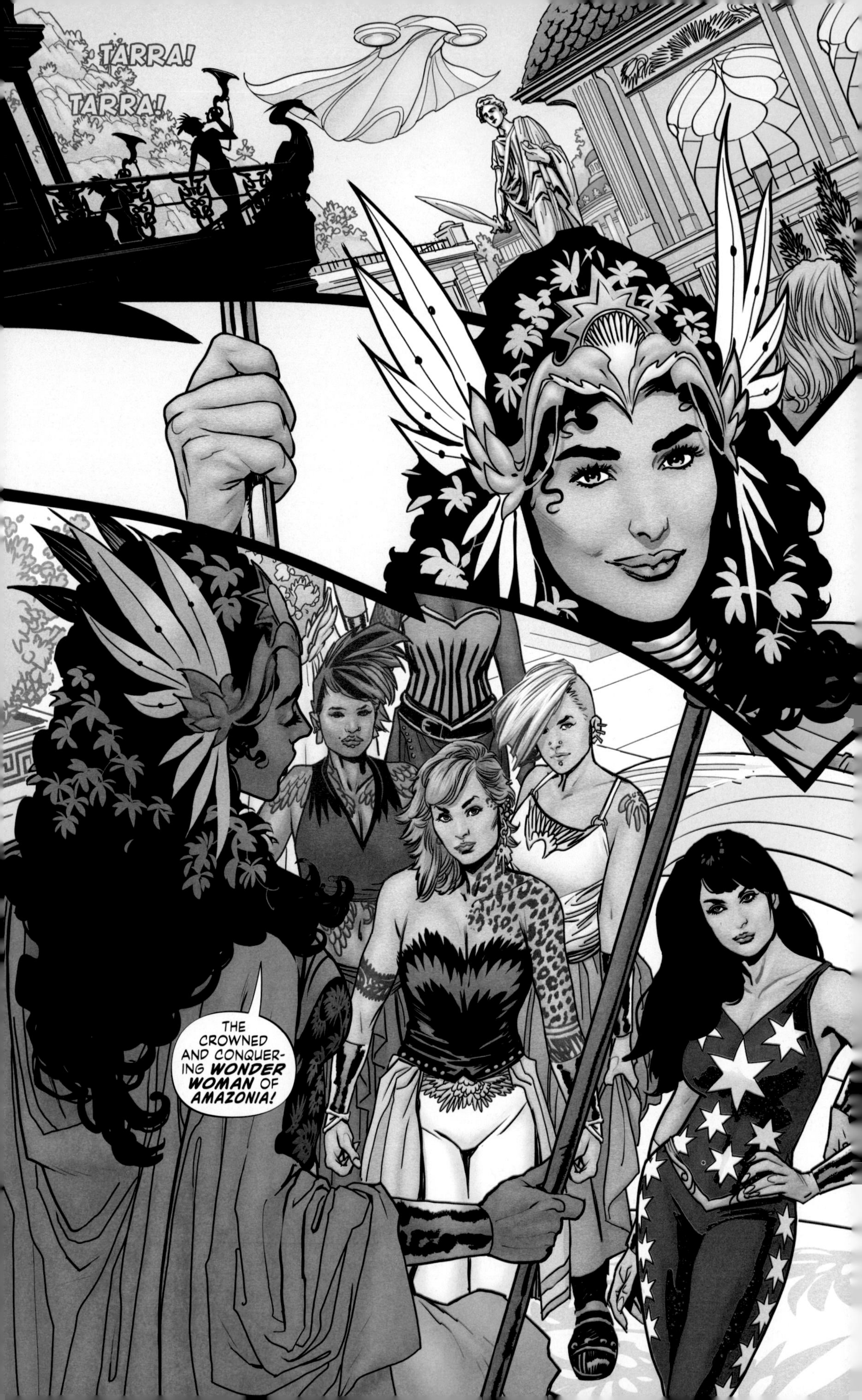
TARRA!
TARRA!
THE CROWNED AND CONQUERING **WONDER WOMAN** OF **AMAZONIA!**

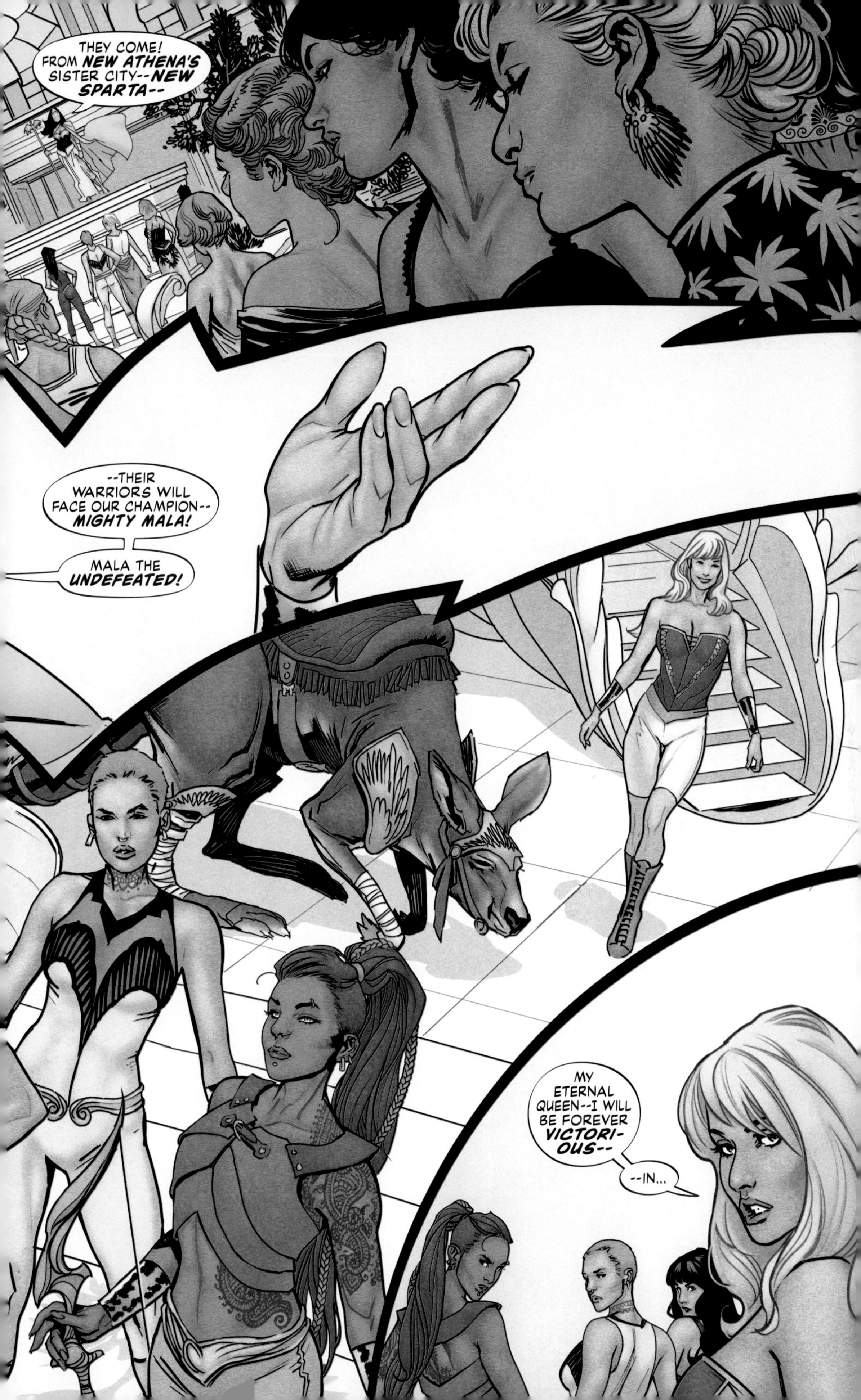
THEY COME! FROM **NEW ATHENA'S** SISTER CITY--**NEW SPARTA**--
--THEIR WARRIORS WILL FACE OUR CHAMPION--**MIGHTY MALA!**
MALA THE **UNDEFEATED!**
MY ETERNAL QUEEN--I WILL BE FOREVER **VICTORI-OUS**--
--IN...

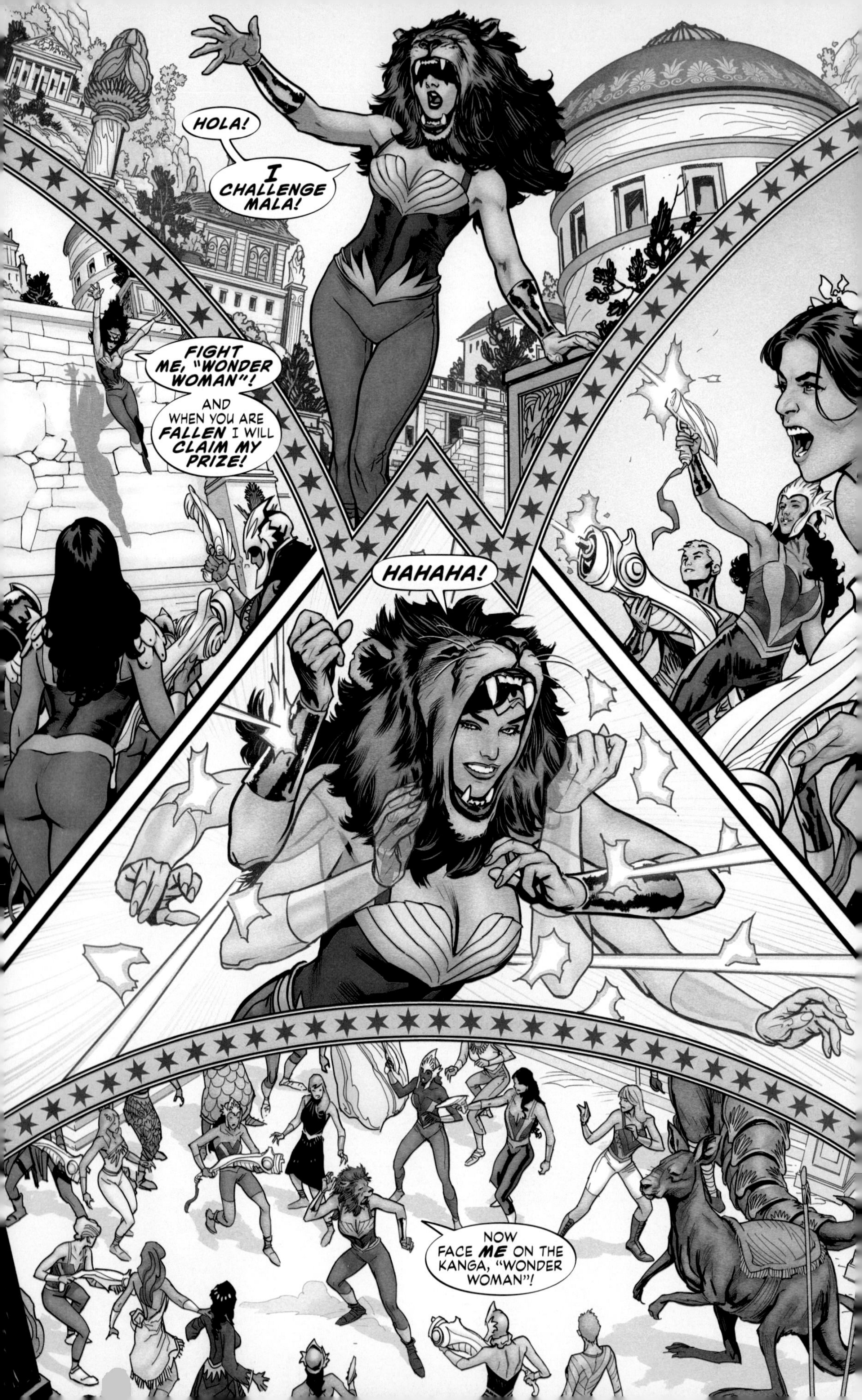
HOLA!
I CHALLENGE MALA!
FIGHT ME, "WONDER WOMAN"!
AND WHEN YOU ARE FALLEN I WILL CLAIM MY PRIZE!
HAHAHA!
NOW FACE ME ON THE KANGA, "WONDER WOMAN"!

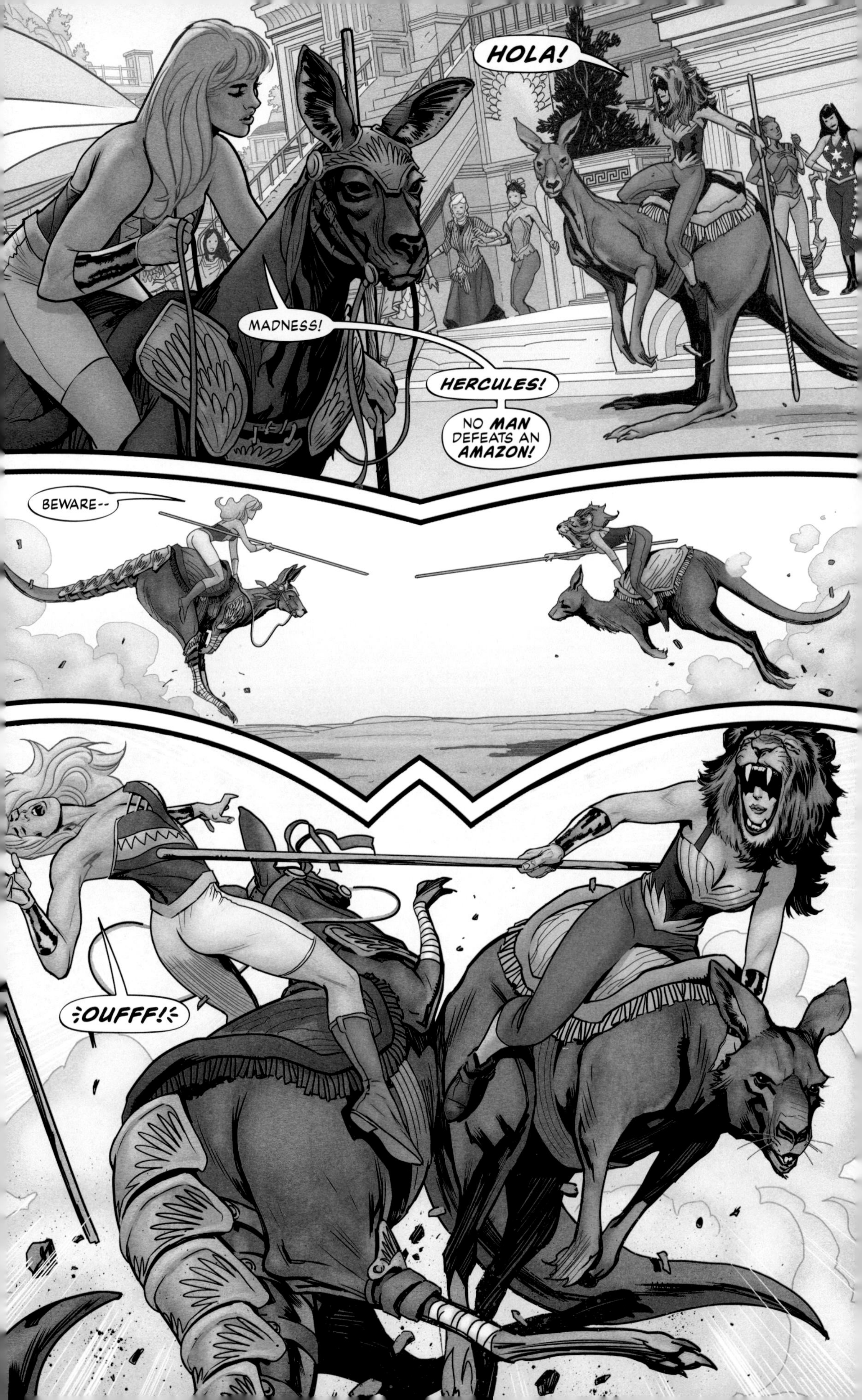
HOLA!
MADNESS!
HERCULES!
NO MAN DEFEATS AN AMAZON!
BEWARE--
OUFFF!

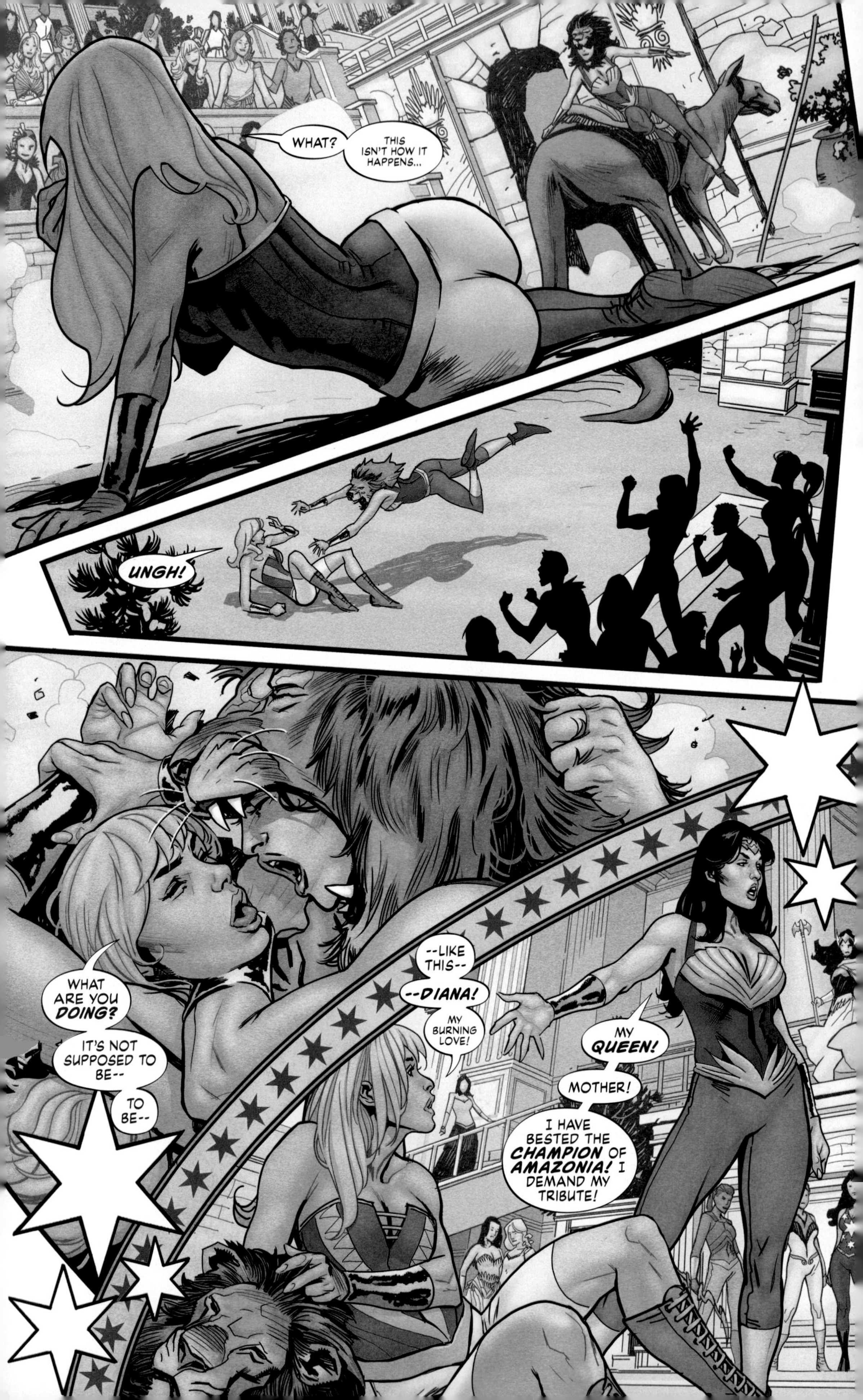
WHAT?
THIS ISN'T HOW IT HAPPENS...
UNGH!
WHAT ARE YOU DOING?
IT'S NOT SUPPOSED TO BE--
TO BE--
--LIKE THIS--
--DIANA!
MY BURNING LOVE!
MY QUEEN!
MOTHER!
I HAVE BESTED THE CHAMPION OF AMAZONIA! I DEMAND MY TRIBUTE!

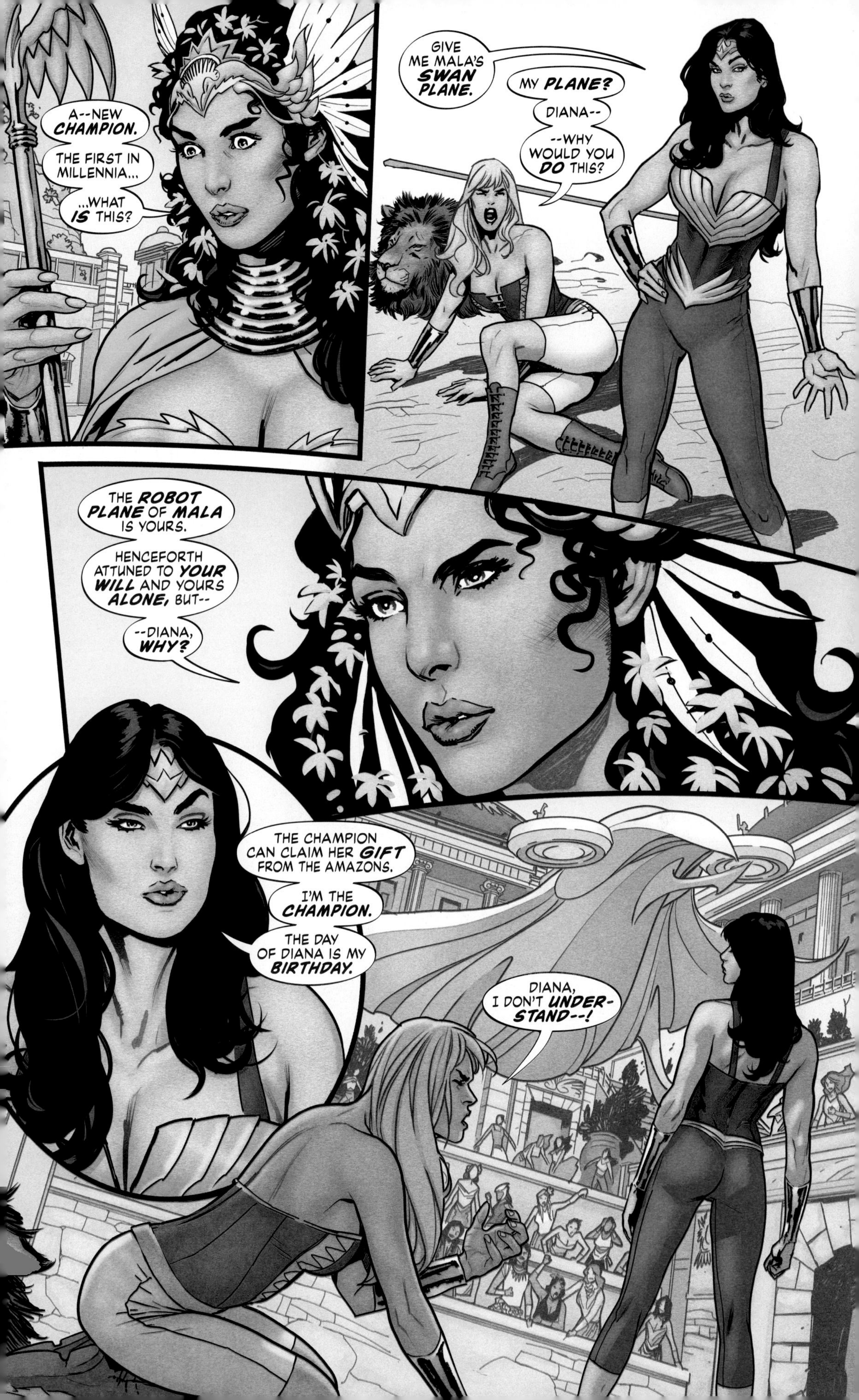
A--NEW CHAMPION.
THE FIRST IN MILLENNIA...
...WHAT IS THIS?
GIVE ME MALA'S SWAN PLANE.
MY PLANE?
DIANA--
--WHY WOULD YOU DO THIS?
THE ROBOT PLANE OF MALA IS YOURS.
HENCEFORTH ATTUNED TO YOUR WILL AND YOURS ALONE, BUT--
--DIANA, WHY?
THE CHAMPION CAN CLAIM HER GIFT FROM THE AMAZONS.
I'M THE CHAMPION.
THE DAY OF DIANA IS MY BIRTHDAY.
DIANA, I DON'T UNDER-STAND--!

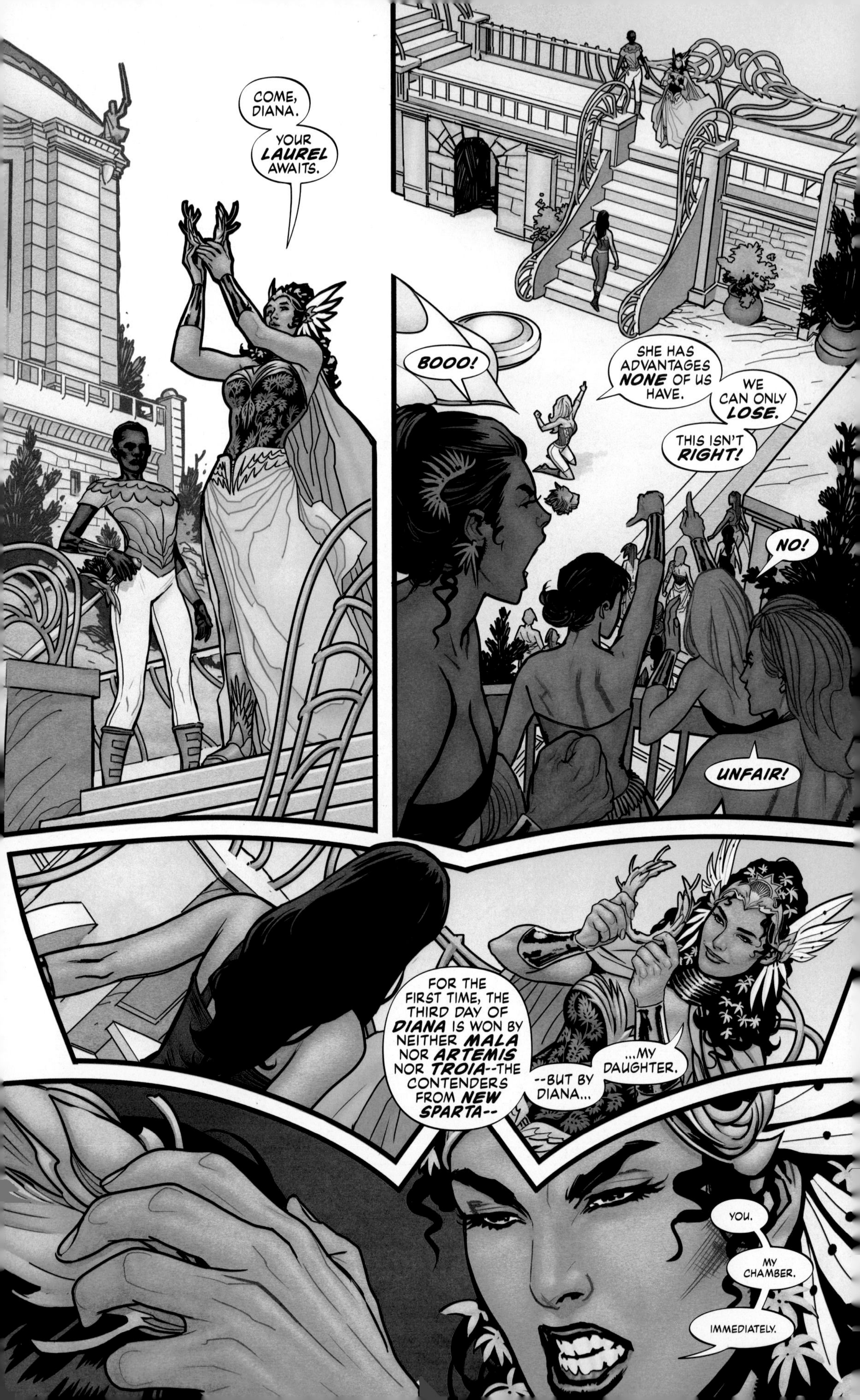

COME, DIANA.
YOUR LAUREL AWAITS.
BOOO!
SHE HAS ADVANTAGES NONE OF US HAVE.
WE CAN ONLY LOSE.
THIS ISN'T RIGHT!
NO!
UNFAIR!
FOR THE FIRST TIME, THE THIRD DAY OF DIANA IS WON BY NEITHER MALA NOR ARTEMIS NOR TROIA--THE CONTENDERS FROM NEW SPARTA--
--BUT BY DIANA...
...MY DAUGHTER.
YOU.
MY CHAMBER.
IMMEDIATELY.

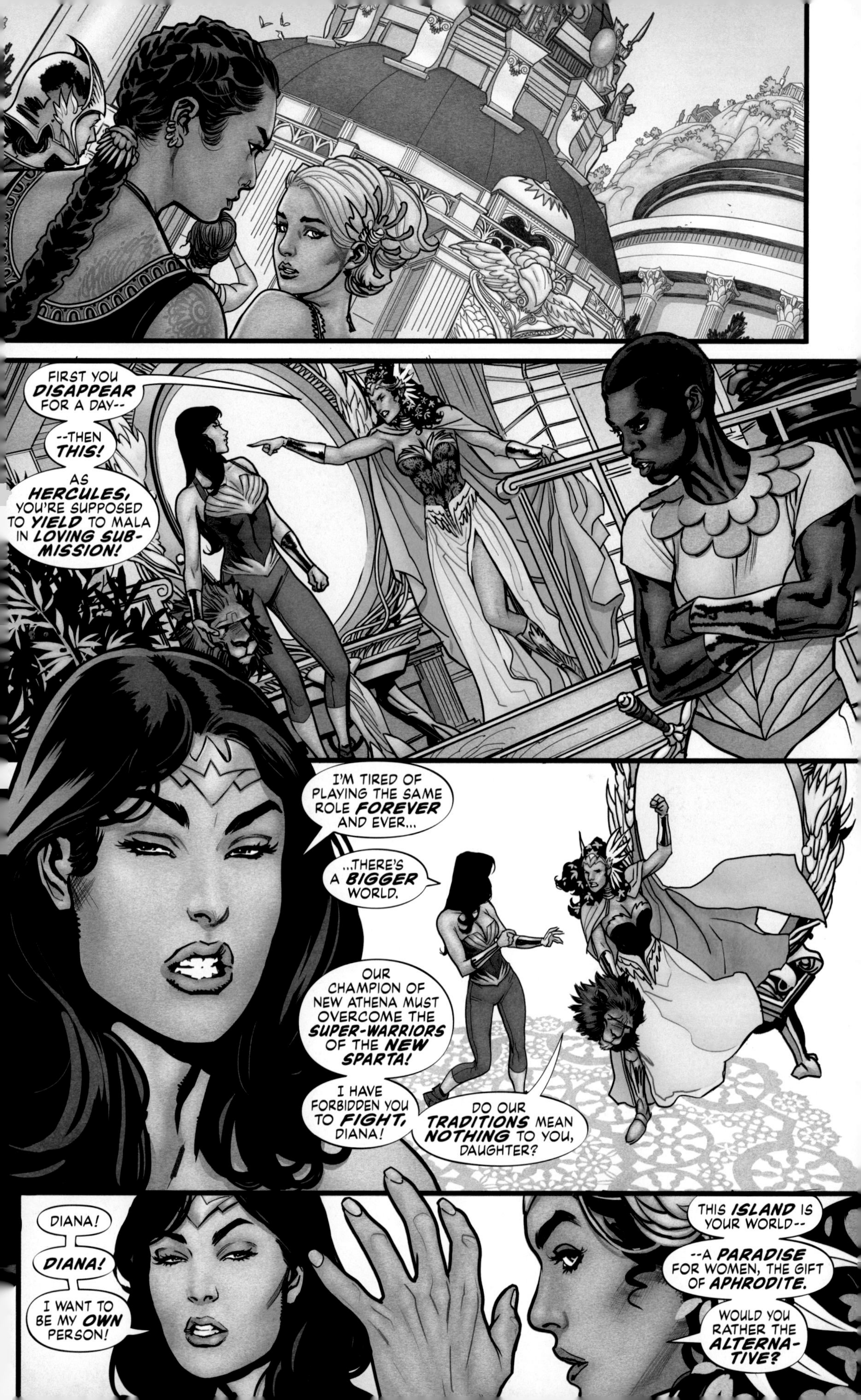
FIRST YOU DISAPPEAR FOR A DAY--
--THEN THIS!
AS HERCULES, YOU'RE SUPPOSED TO YIELD TO MALA IN LOVING SUB-MISSION!
I'M TIRED OF PLAYING THE SAME ROLE FOREVER AND EVER...
...THERE'S A BIGGER WORLD.
OUR CHAMPION OF NEW ATHENA MUST OVERCOME THE SUPER-WARRIORS OF THE NEW SPARTA!
I HAVE FORBIDDEN YOU TO FIGHT, DIANA!
DO OUR TRADITIONS MEAN NOTHING TO YOU, DAUGHTER?
DIANA!
DIANA!
I WANT TO BE MY OWN PERSON!
THIS ISLAND IS YOUR WORLD--
--A PARADISE FOR WOMEN, THE GIFT OF APHRODITE.
WOULD YOU RATHER THE ALTERNA-TIVE?

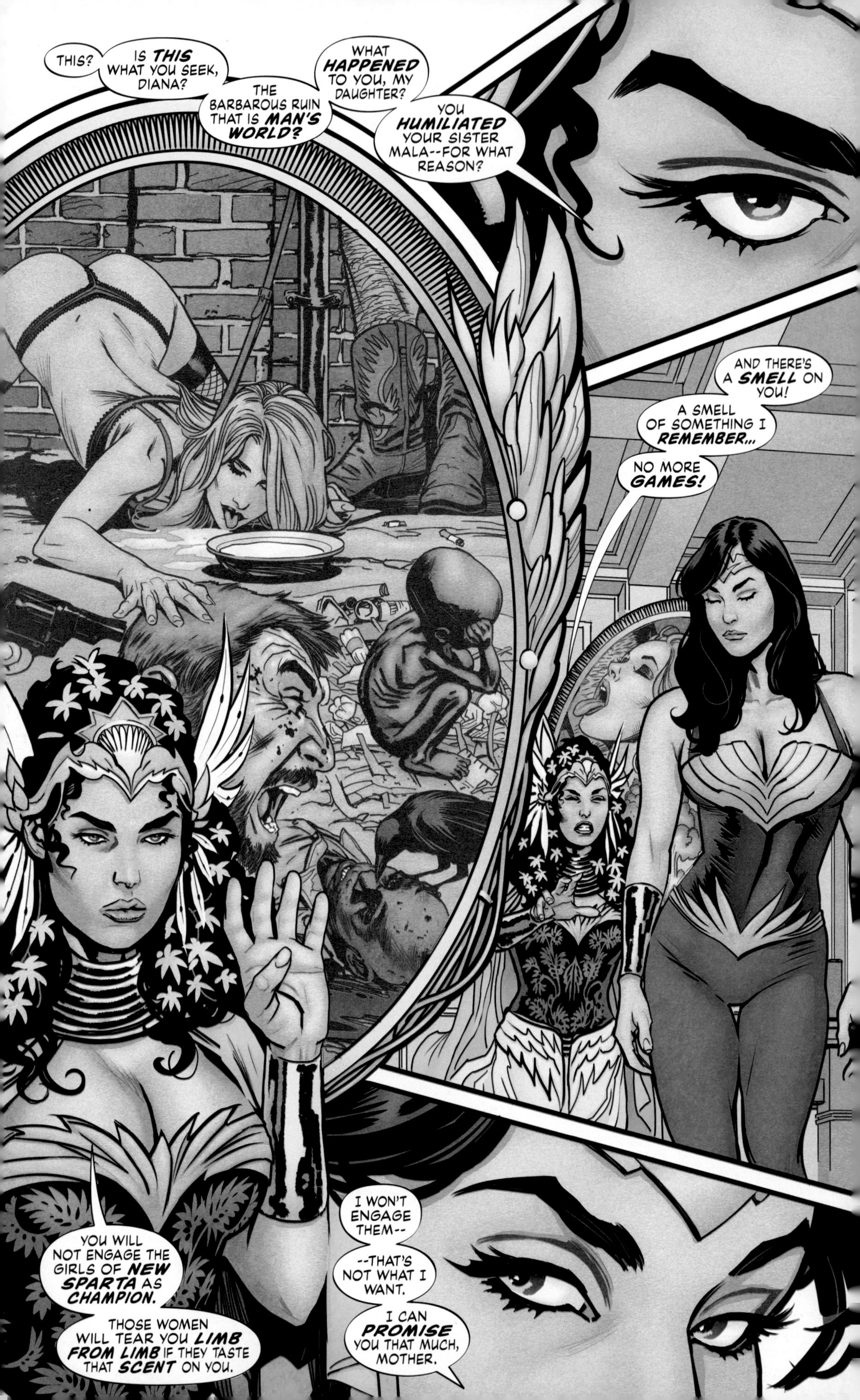
THIS?
IS THIS WHAT YOU SEEK, DIANA?
THE BARBAROUS RUIN THAT IS MAN'S WORLD?
WHAT HAPPENED TO YOU, MY DAUGHTER?
YOU HUMILIATED YOUR SISTER MALA--FOR WHAT REASON?
AND THERE'S A SMELL ON YOU!
A SMELL OF SOMETHING I REMEMBER...
NO MORE GAMES!
YOU WILL NOT ENGAGE THE GIRLS OF NEW SPARTA AS CHAMPION.
THOSE WOMEN WILL TEAR YOU LIMB FROM LIMB IF THEY TASTE THAT SCENT ON YOU.
I WON'T ENGAGE THEM--
--THAT'S NOT WHAT I WANT.
I CAN PROMISE YOU THAT MUCH, MOTHER.

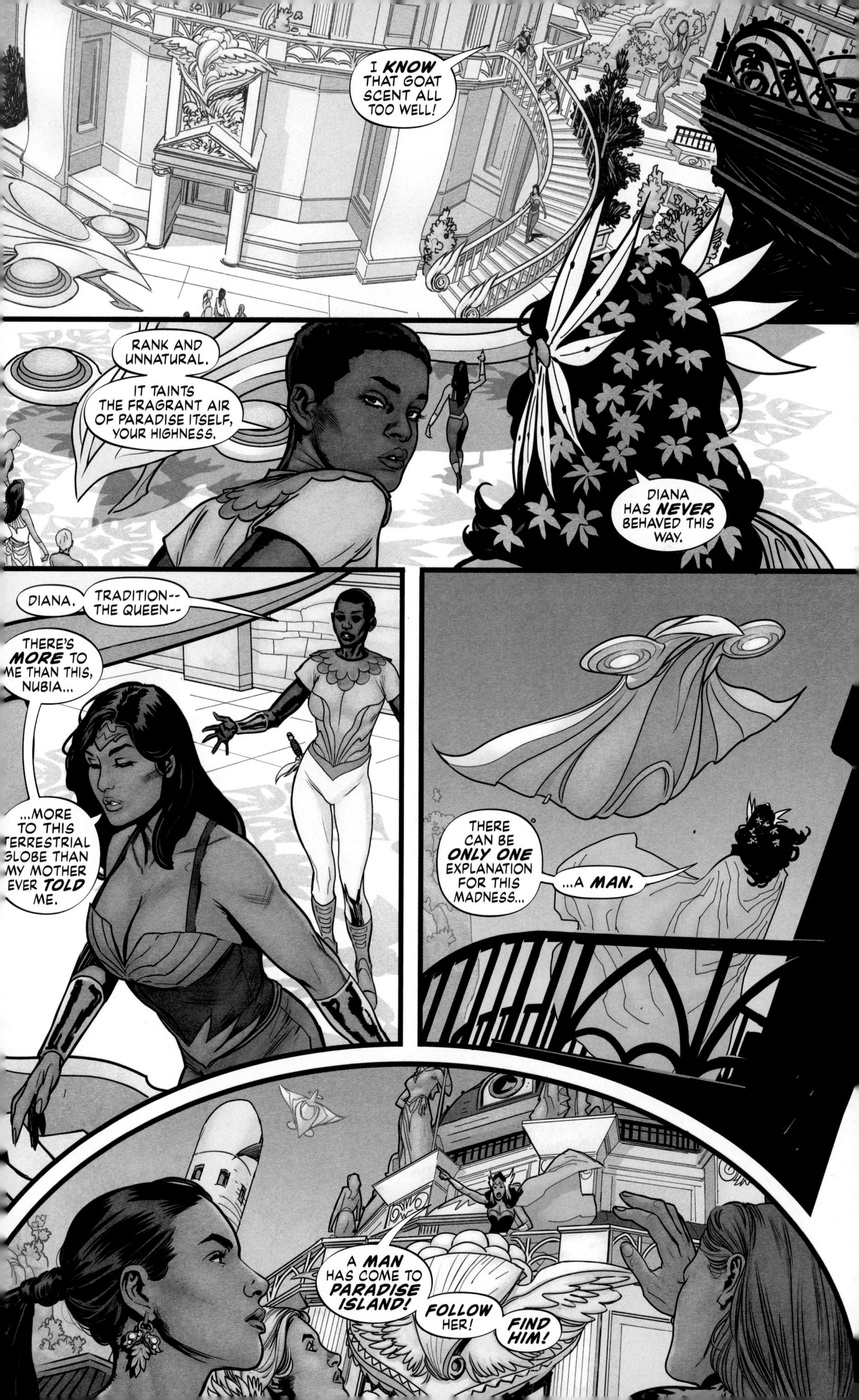

I KNOW THAT GOAT SCENT ALL TOO WELL!
RANK AND UNNATURAL.
IT TAINTS THE FRAGRANT AIR OF PARADISE ITSELF, YOUR HIGHNESS.
DIANA HAS NEVER BEHAVED THIS WAY.
DIANA.
TRADITION-- THE QUEEN--
THERE'S MORE TO ME THAN THIS, NUBIA...
...MORE TO THIS TERRESTRIAL GLOBE THAN MY MOTHER EVER TOLD ME.
THERE CAN BE ONLY ONE EXPLANATION FOR THIS MADNESS...
...A MAN.
A MAN HAS COME TO PARADISE ISLAND!
FOLLOW HER!
FIND HIM!

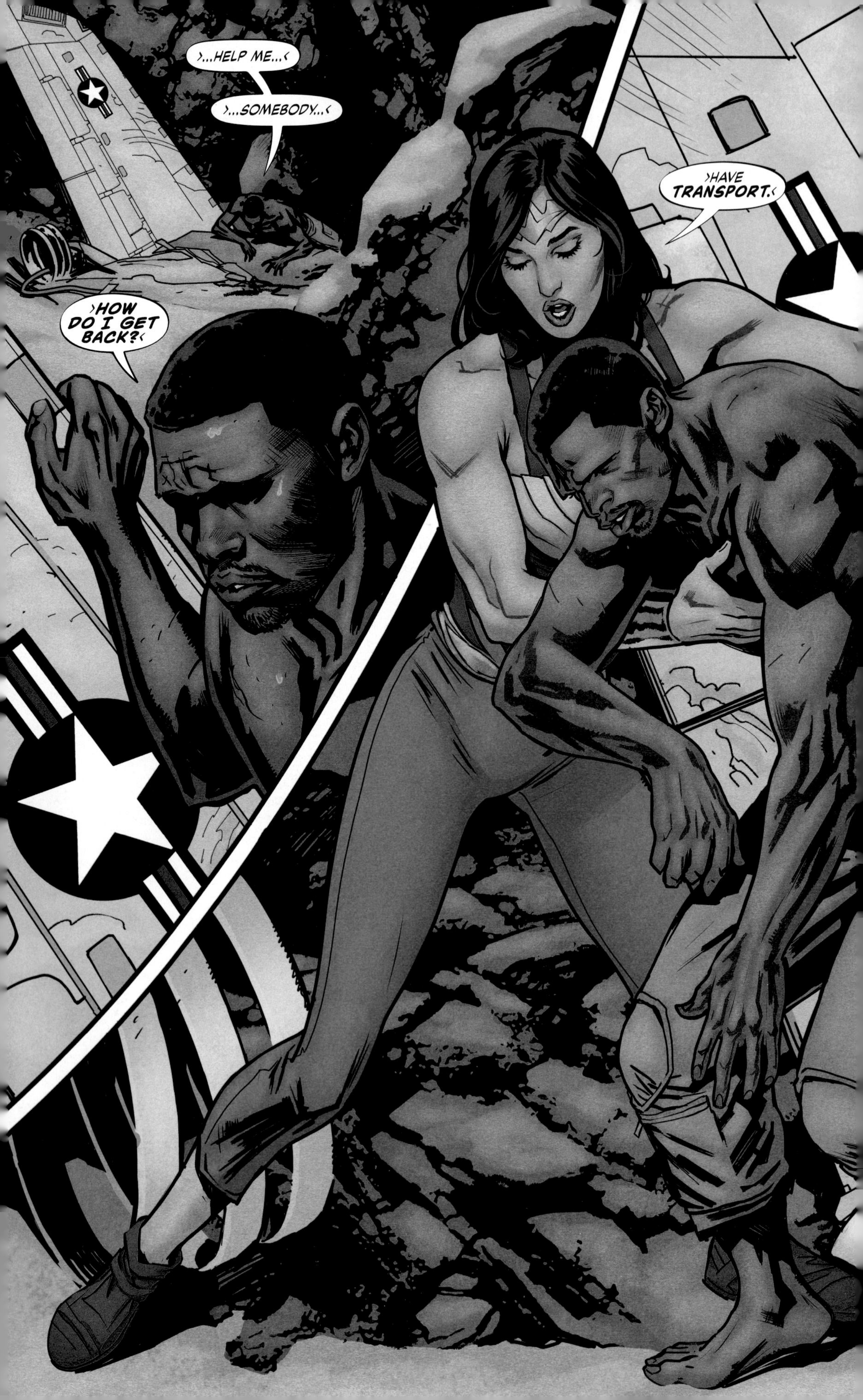
›...HELP ME...‹
›...SOMEBODY...‹
›HOW DO I GET BACK?‹
›HAVE TRANSPORT.‹

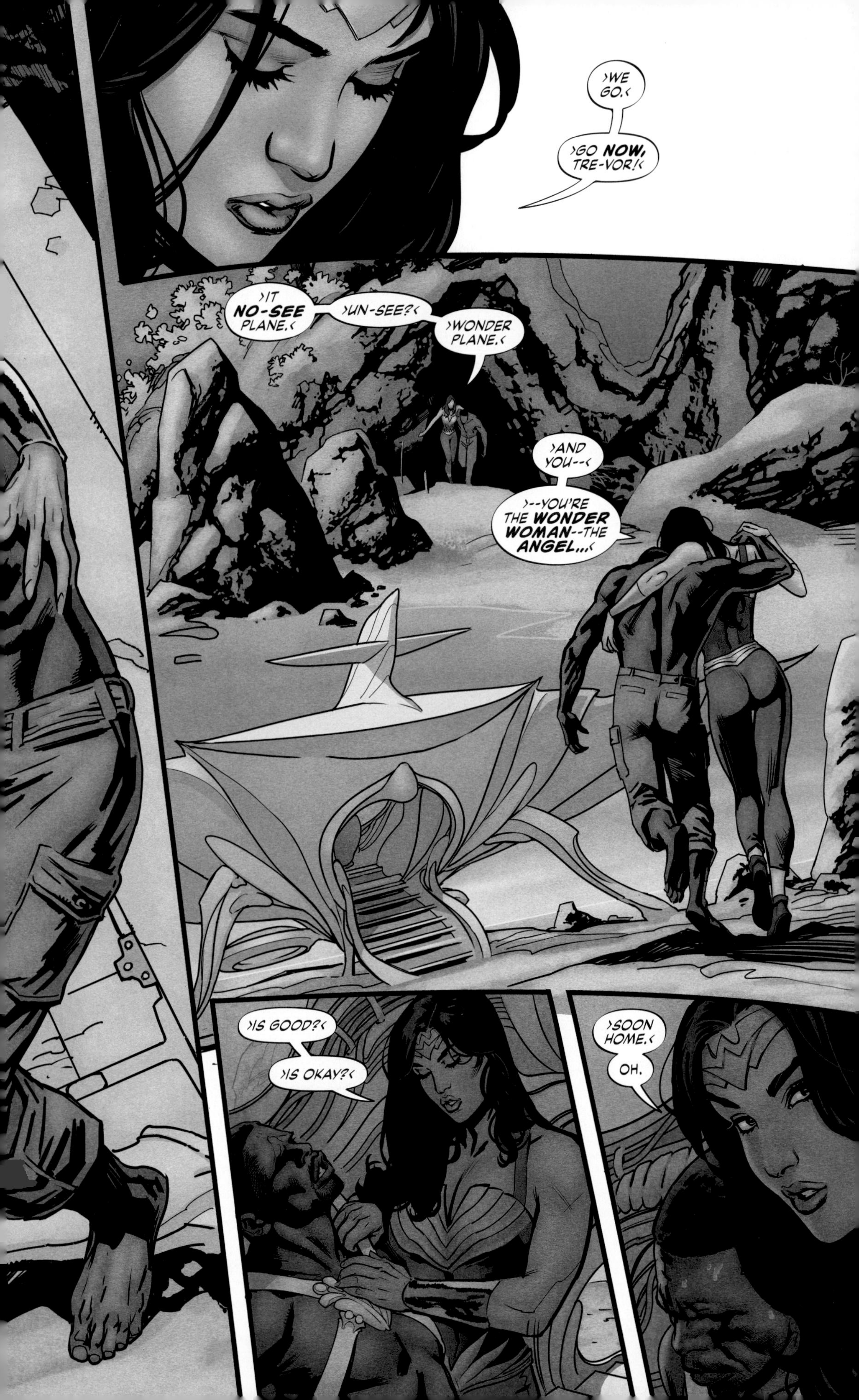
›WE GO.‹
›GO **NOW,** TRE-VOR!‹
›IT **NO-SEE** PLANE.‹
›UN-SEE?‹
›WONDER PLANE.‹
›AND YOU--‹
›--YOU'RE THE **WONDER WOMAN**--THE **ANGEL...**‹
›IS GOOD?‹
›IS OKAY?‹
›SOON HOME.‹
OH.

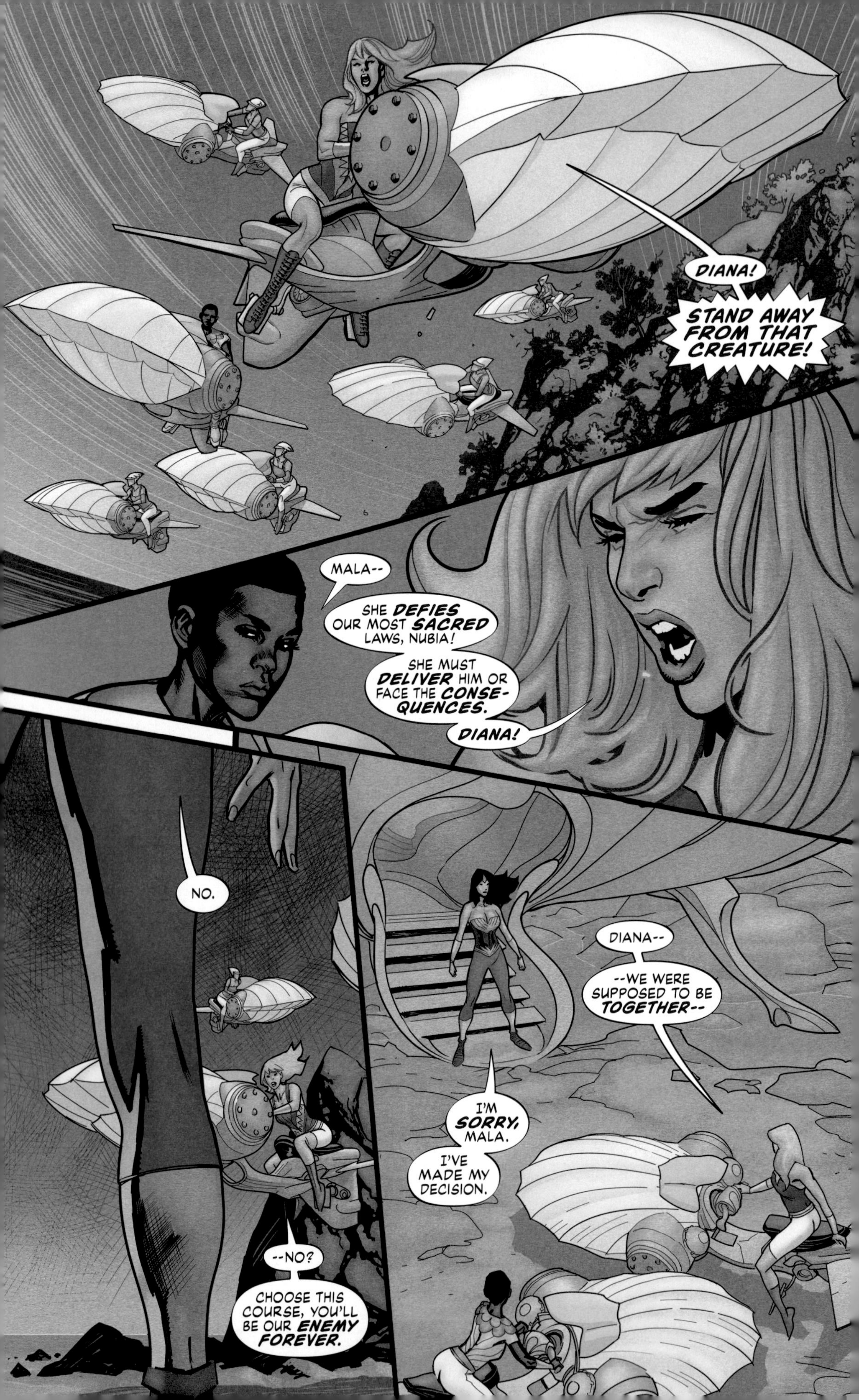
DIANA!
STAND AWAY FROM THAT CREATURE!
MALA--
SHE DEFIES OUR MOST SACRED LAWS, NUBIA!
SHE MUST DELIVER HIM OR FACE THE CONSEQUENCES.
DIANA!
NO.
--NO?
CHOOSE THIS COURSE, YOU'LL BE OUR ENEMY FOREVER.
DIANA--
--WE WERE SUPPOSED TO BE TOGETHER--
I'M SORRY, MALA.
I'VE MADE MY DECISION.

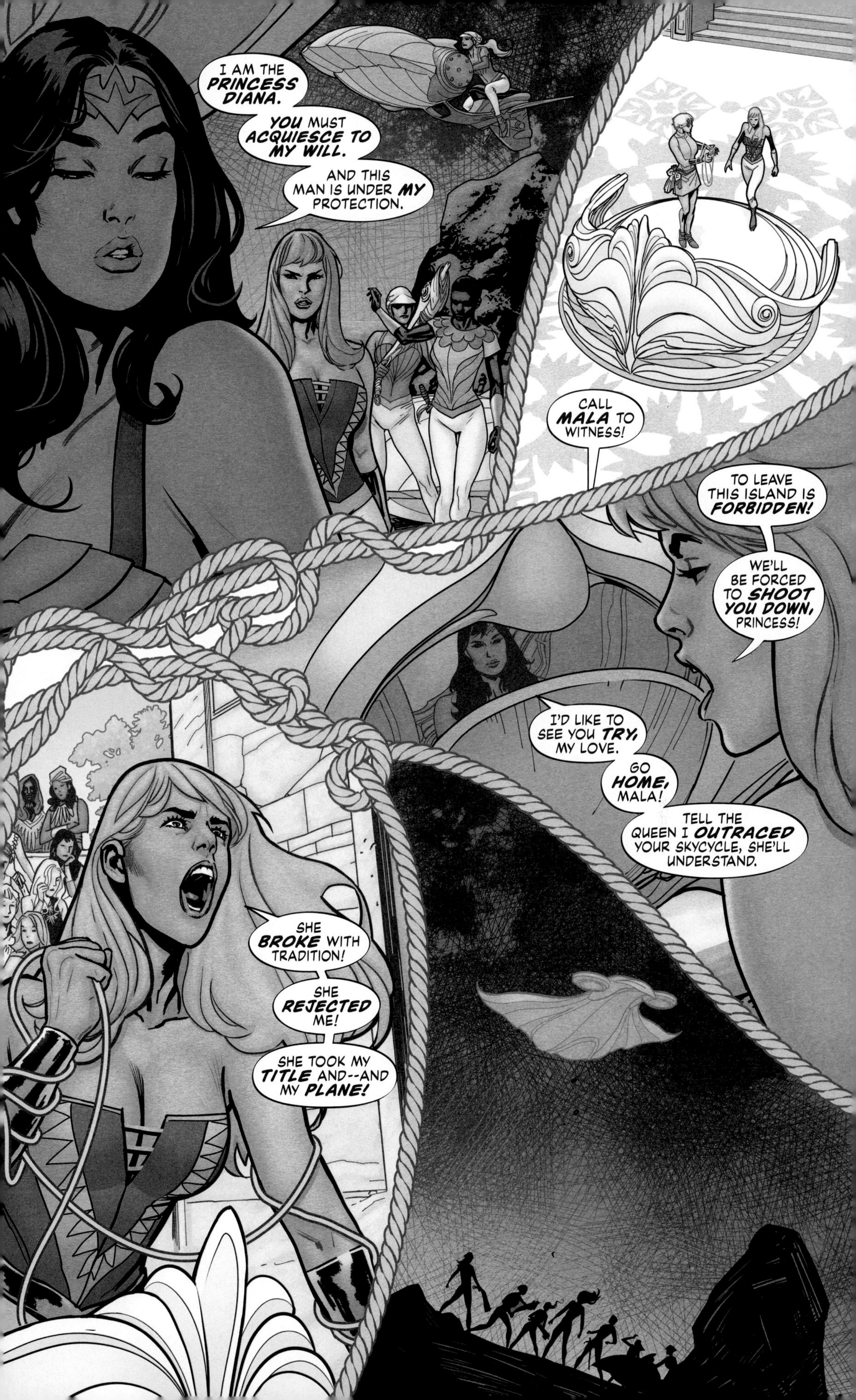
I AM THE PRINCESS DIANA.
YOU MUST ACQUIESCE TO MY WILL.
AND THIS MAN IS UNDER MY PROTECTION.
CALL MALA TO WITNESS!
TO LEAVE THIS ISLAND IS FORBIDDEN!
WE'LL BE FORCED TO SHOOT YOU DOWN, PRINCESS!
I'D LIKE TO SEE YOU TRY, MY LOVE.
GO HOME, MALA!
TELL THE QUEEN I OUTRACED YOUR SKYCYCLE, SHE'LL UNDERSTAND.
SHE BROKE WITH TRADITION!
SHE REJECTED ME!
SHE TOOK MY TITLE AND--AND MY PLANE!

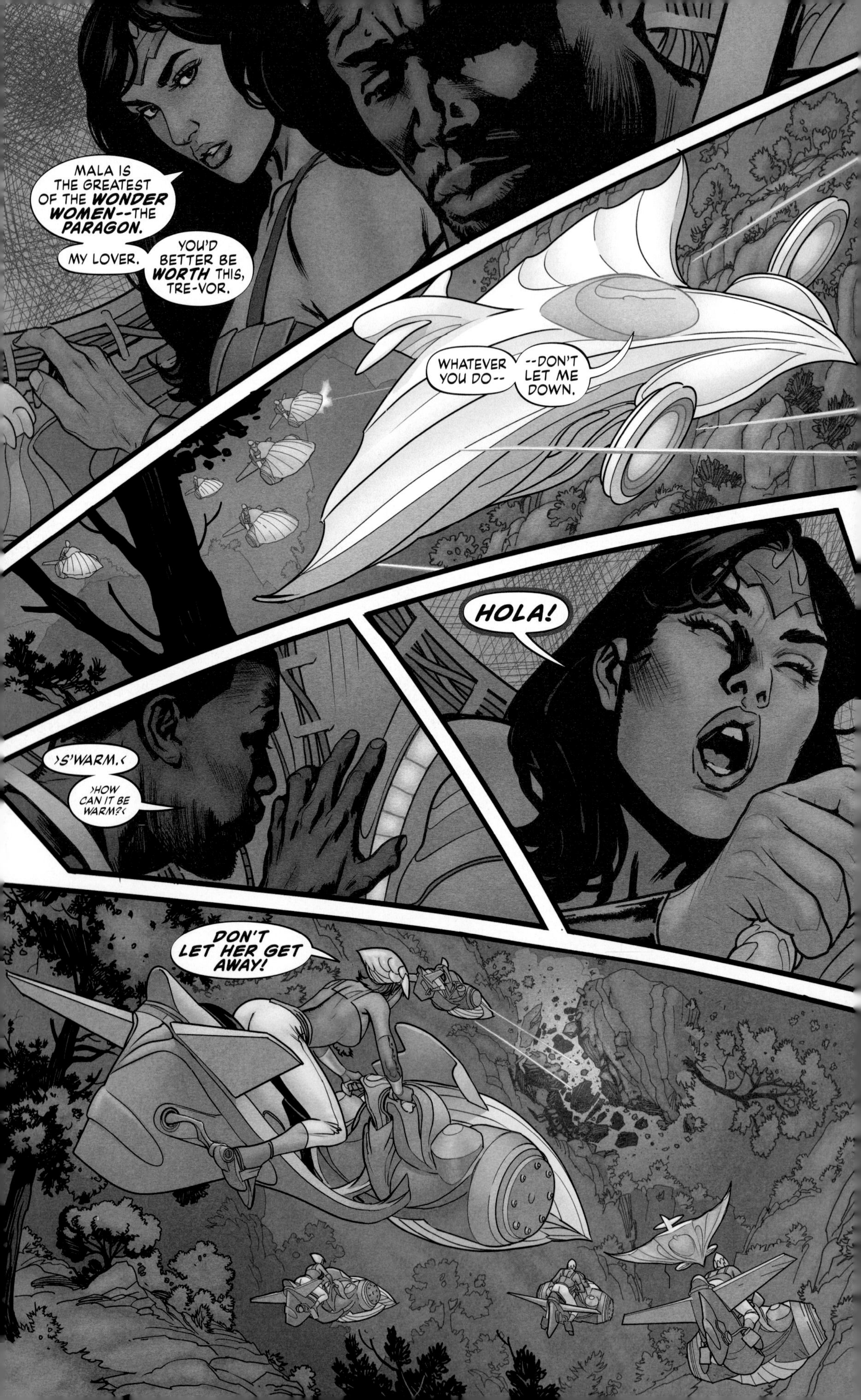
MALA IS THE GREATEST OF THE **WONDER WOMEN**--THE **PARAGON.**
MY LOVER.
YOU'D BETTER BE **WORTH** THIS, TRE-VOR.
WHATEVER YOU DO--
--DON'T LET ME DOWN.
›S'WARM.‹
›HOW CAN IT BE WARM?‹
HOLA!
DON'T LET HER GET AWAY!

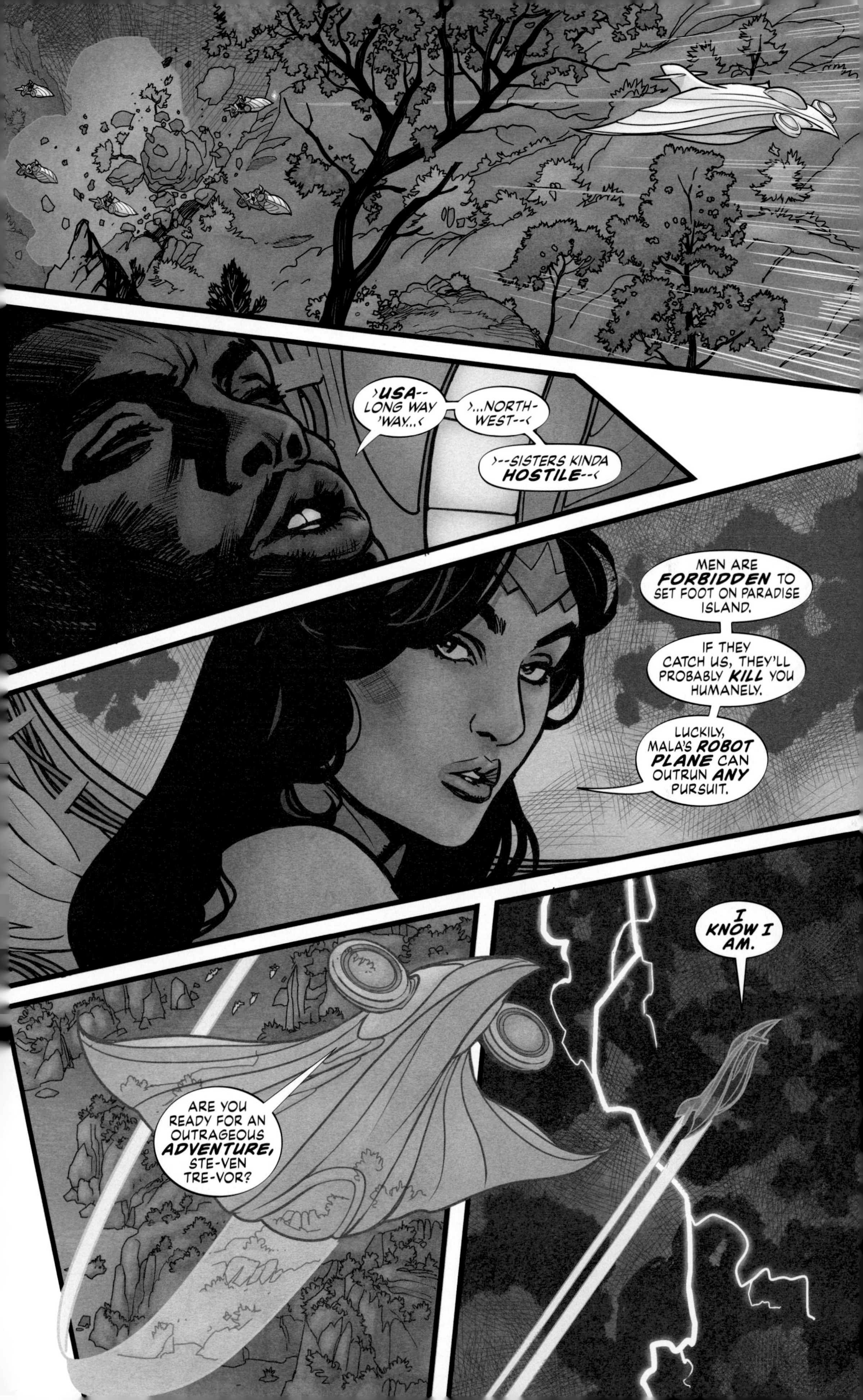
›USA-- LONG WAY 'WAY...‹
›...NORTH-WEST--‹
›--SISTERS KINDA HOSTILE--‹
MEN ARE FORBIDDEN TO SET FOOT ON PARADISE ISLAND.
IF THEY CATCH US, THEY'LL PROBABLY KILL YOU HUMANELY.
LUCKILY, MALA'S ROBOT PLANE CAN OUTRUN ANY PURSUIT.
ARE YOU READY FOR AN OUTRAGEOUS ADVENTURE, STE-VEN TRE-VOR?
I KNOW I AM.

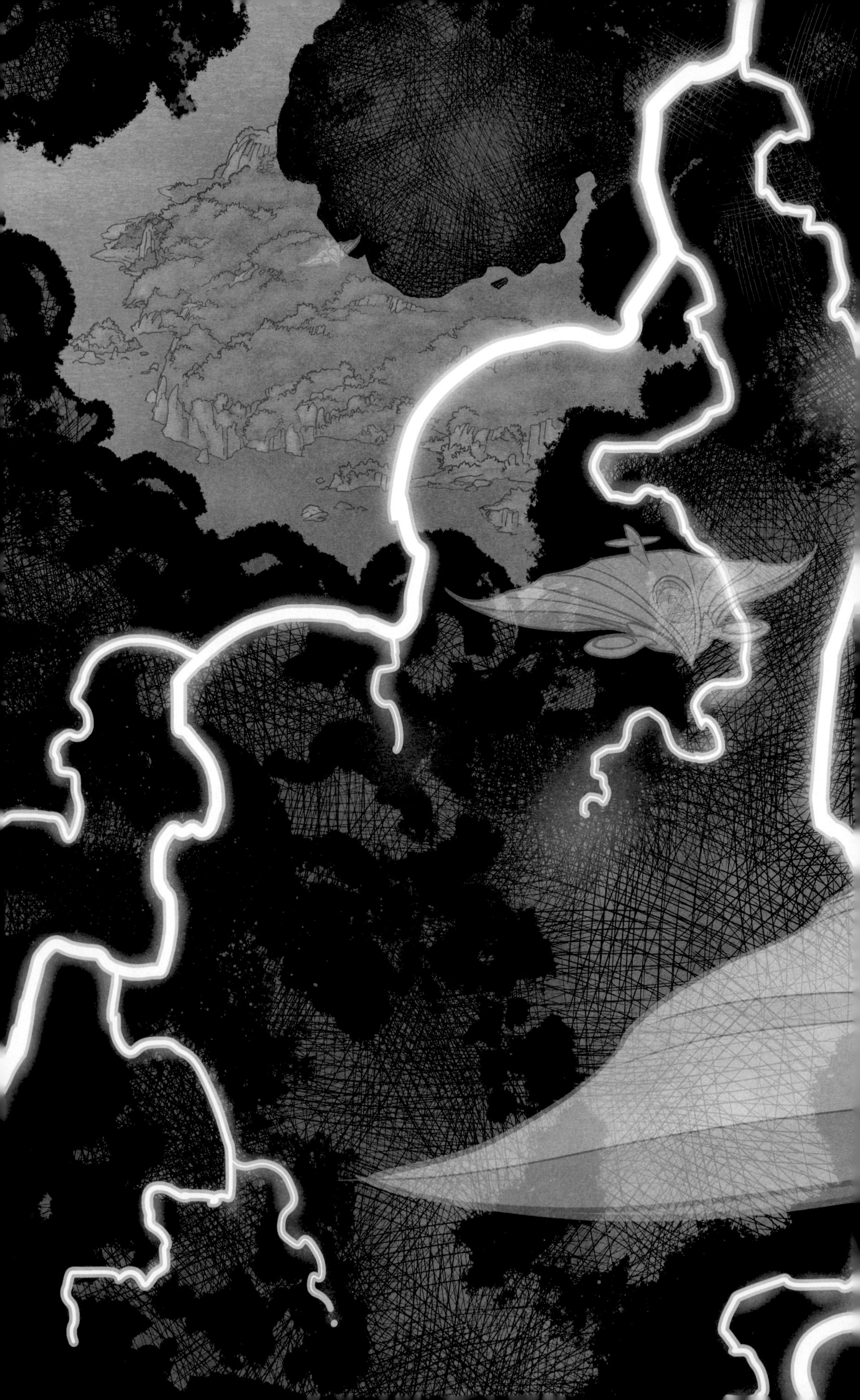

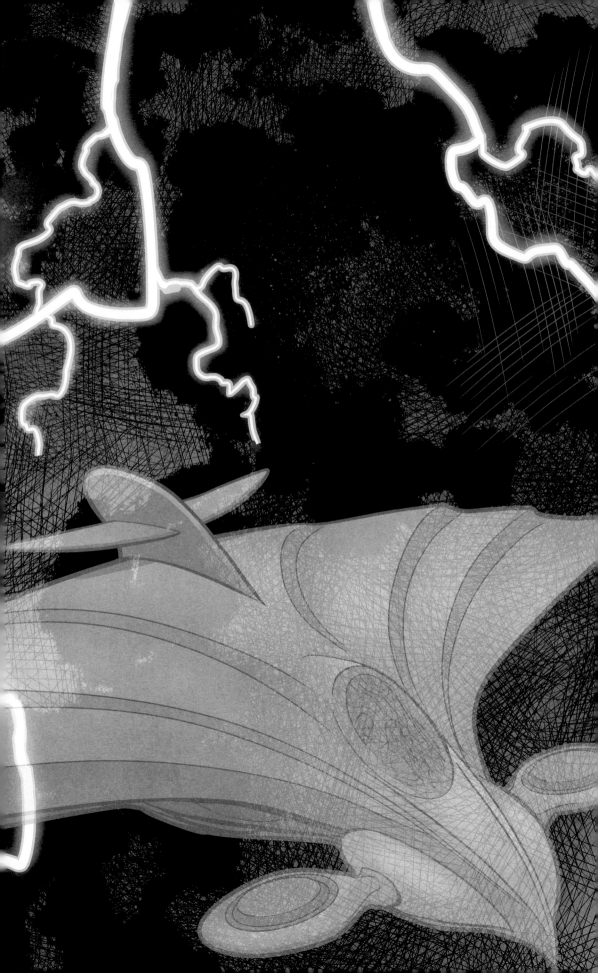

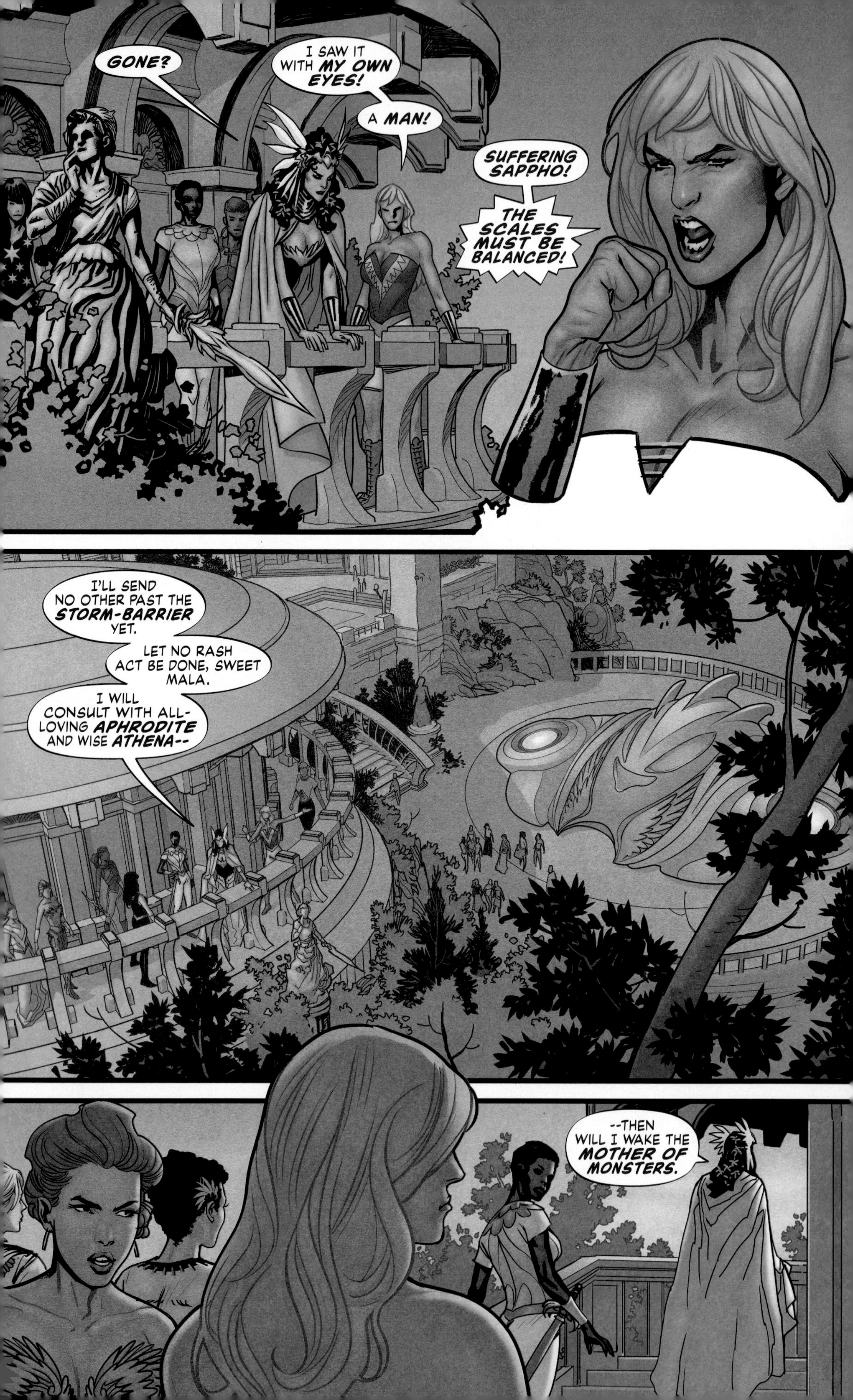
GONE?
I SAW IT WITH MY OWN EYES!
A MAN!
SUFFERING SAPPHO!
THE SCALES MUST BE BALANCED!
I'LL SEND NO OTHER PAST THE STORM-BARRIER YET.
LET NO RASH ACT BE DONE, SWEET MALA.
I WILL CONSULT WITH ALL-LOVING APHRODITE AND WISE ATHENA--
--THEN WILL I WAKE THE MOTHER OF MONSTERS.

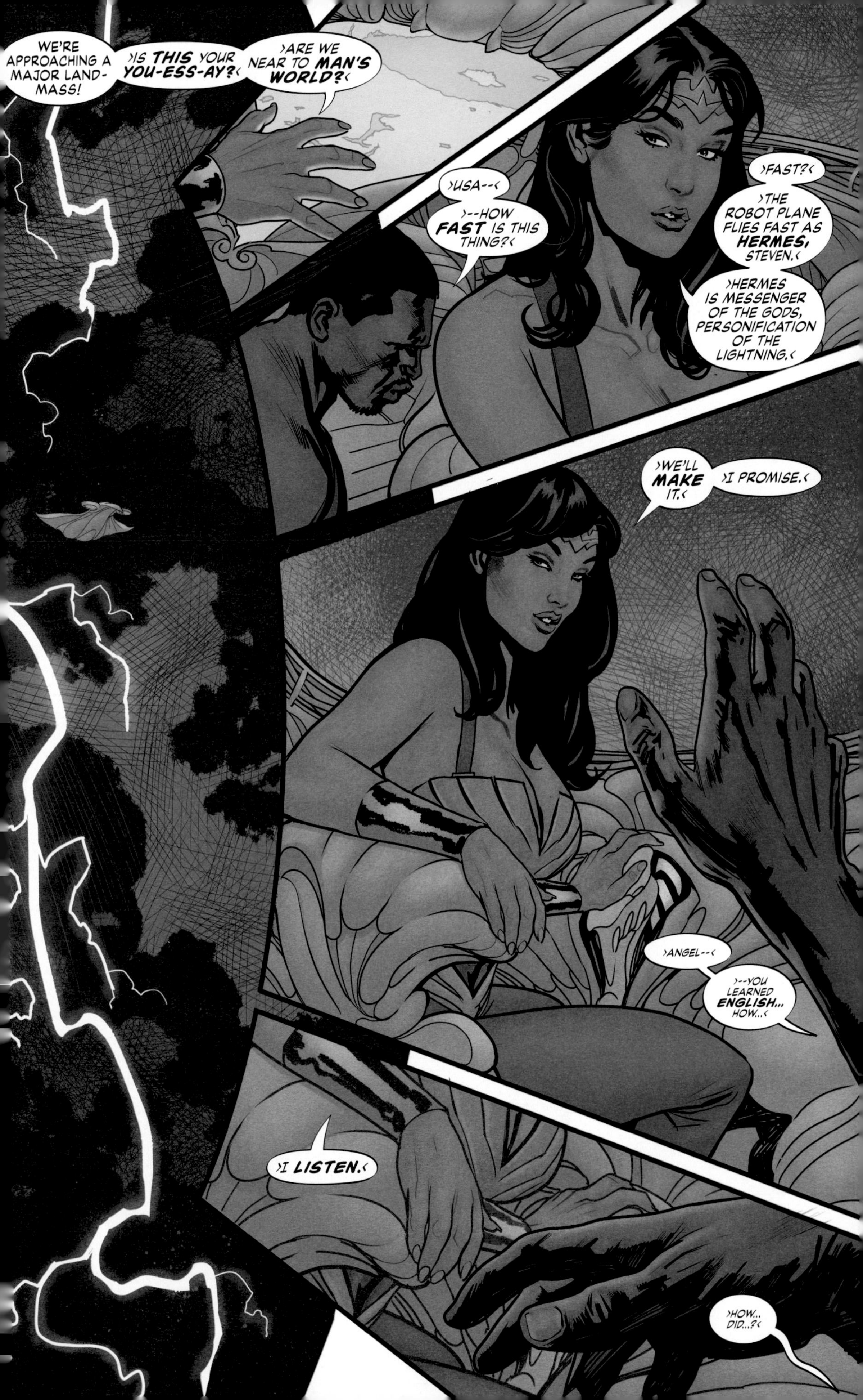

WE'RE APPROACHING A MAJOR LAND-MASS!
›IS THIS YOUR YOU-ESS-AY?‹
›ARE WE NEAR TO MAN'S WORLD?‹
›USA--‹
›--HOW FAST IS THIS THING?‹
›FAST?‹
›THE ROBOT PLANE FLIES FAST AS HERMES, STEVEN.‹
›HERMES IS MESSENGER OF THE GODS, PERSONIFICATION OF THE LIGHTNING.‹
›WE'LL MAKE IT.‹
›I PROMISE.‹
›ANGEL--‹
›--YOU LEARNED ENGLISH... HOW...‹
›I LISTEN.‹
›HOW... DID...?‹

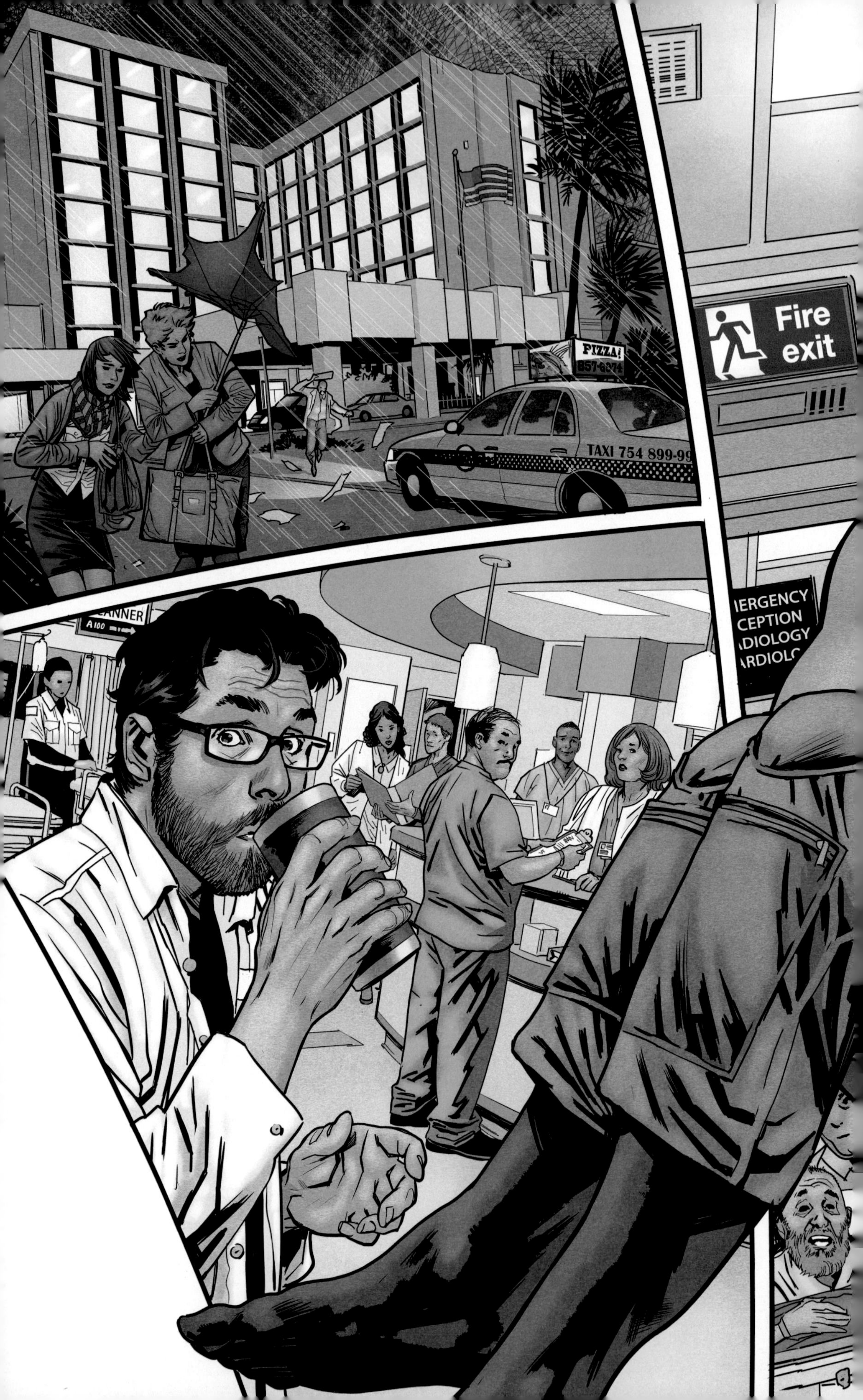

PIZZA!
857-6274
TAXI 754 899-99
Fire exit
ANNER
A100
IERGENCY
CEPTION
ADIOLOGY
ARDIOLO

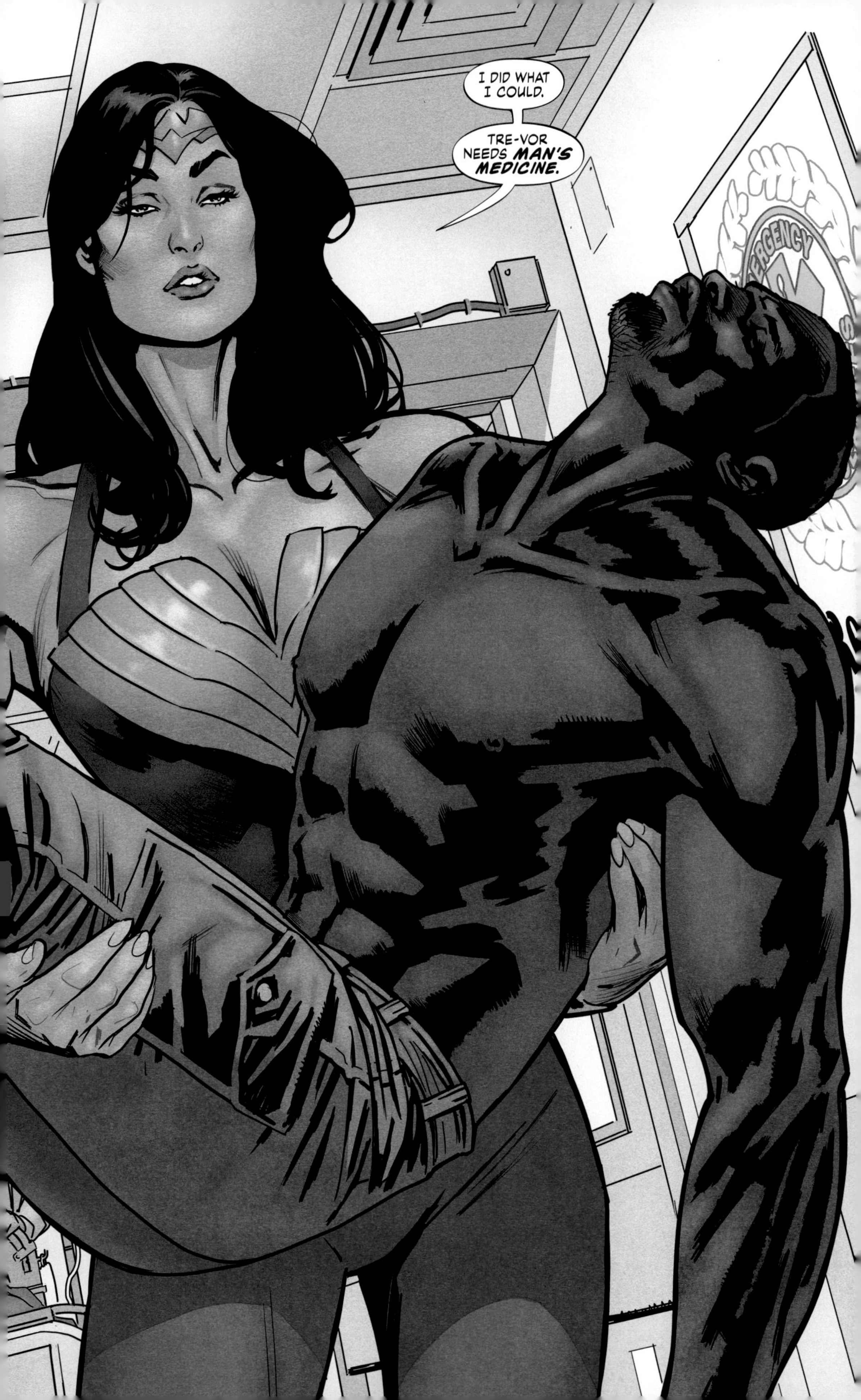
I DID WHAT I COULD.
TRE-VOR NEEDS **MAN'S MEDICINE.**

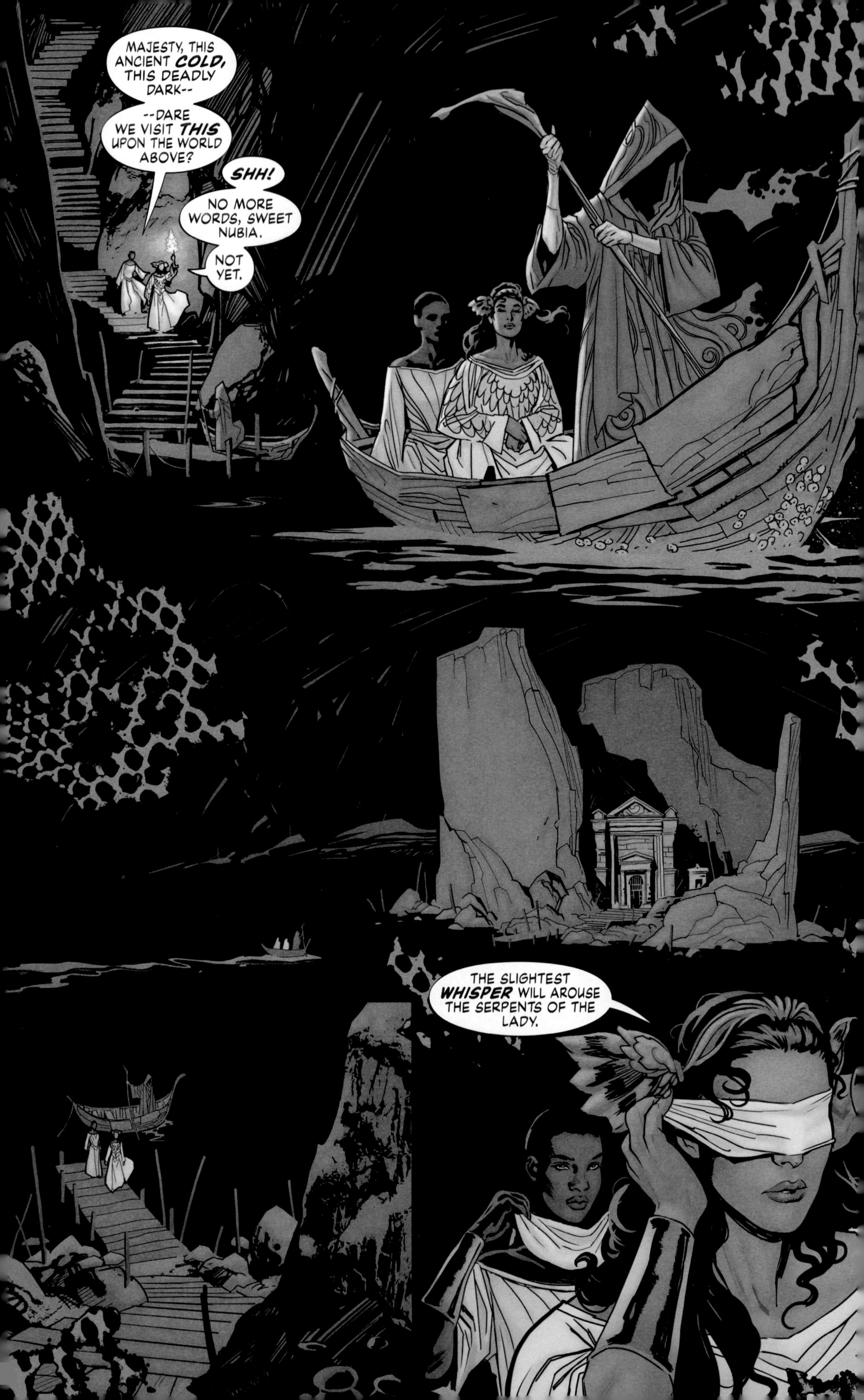
MAJESTY, THIS ANCIENT COLD, THIS DEADLY DARK--
--DARE WE VISIT THIS UPON THE WORLD ABOVE?
SHH!
NO MORE WORDS, SWEET NUBIA.
NOT YET.
THE SLIGHTEST WHISPER WILL AROUSE THE SERPENTS OF THE LADY.

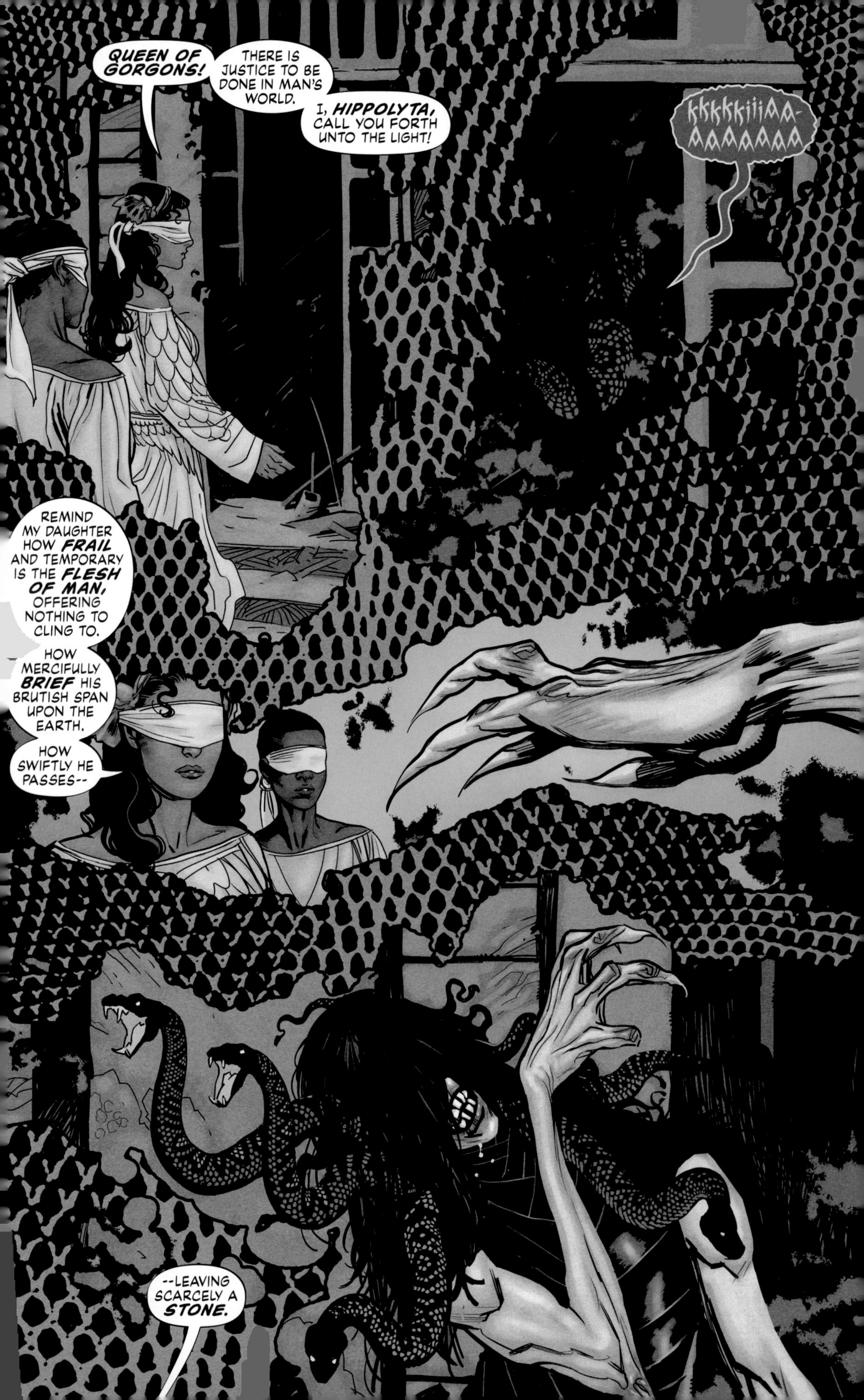
QUEEN OF GORGONS!
THERE IS JUSTICE TO BE DONE IN MAN'S WORLD.
I, HIPPOLYTA, CALL YOU FORTH UNTO THE LIGHT!
KKKKKIIIAA-AAAAAAA
REMIND MY DAUGHTER HOW FRAIL AND TEMPORARY IS THE FLESH OF MAN, OFFERING NOTHING TO CLING TO.
HOW MERCIFULLY BRIEF HIS BRUTISH SPAN UPON THE EARTH.
HOW SWIFTLY HE PASSES--
--LEAVING SCARCELY A STONE.

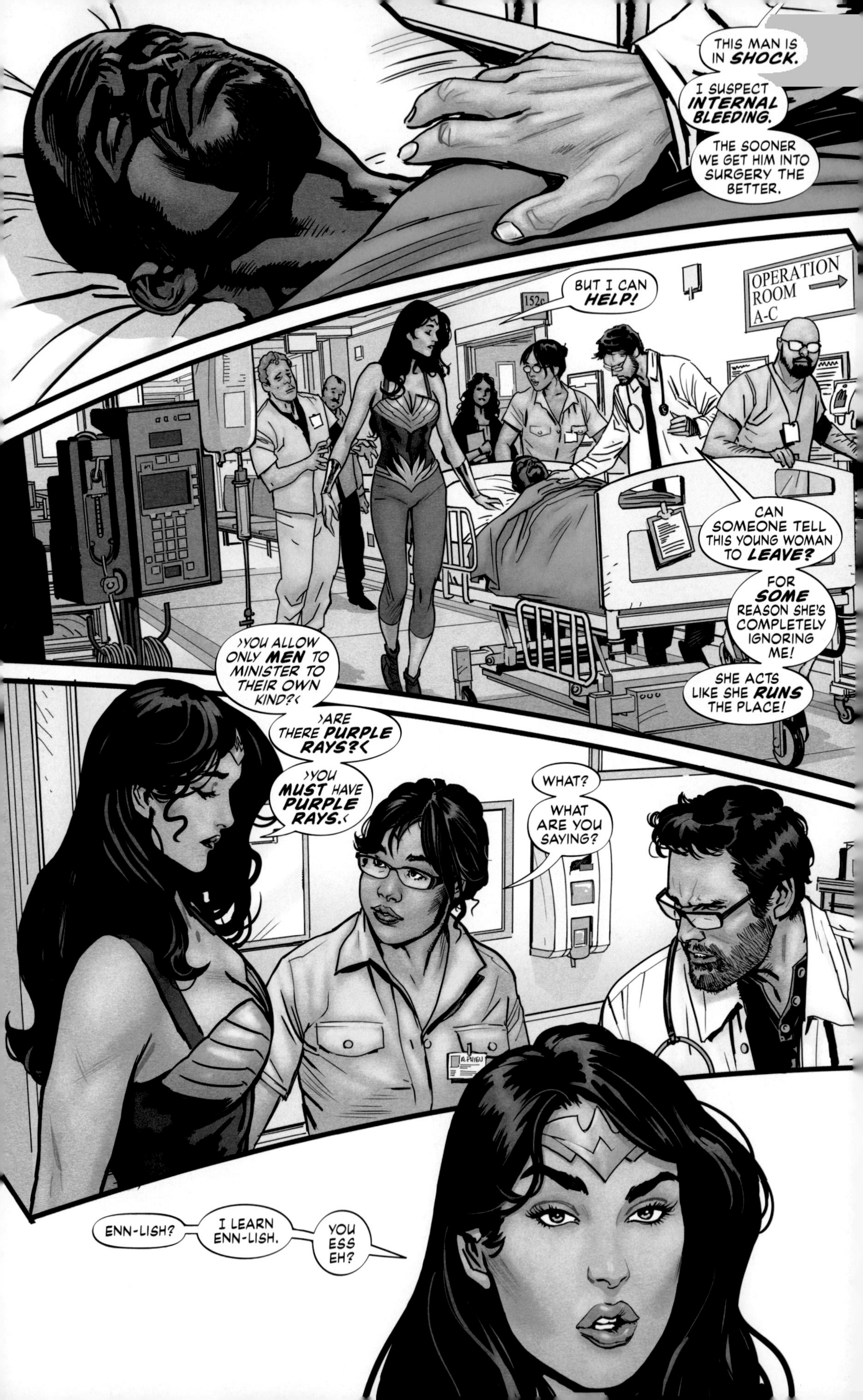

THIS MAN IS IN SHOCK.
I SUSPECT INTERNAL BLEEDING.
THE SOONER WE GET HIM INTO SURGERY THE BETTER.
BUT I CAN HELP!
OPERATION ROOM A-C
152c
CAN SOMEONE TELL THIS YOUNG WOMAN TO LEAVE?
FOR SOME REASON SHE'S COMPLETELY IGNORING ME!
SHE ACTS LIKE SHE RUNS THE PLACE!
›YOU ALLOW ONLY MEN TO MINISTER TO THEIR OWN KIND?‹
›ARE THERE PURPLE RAYS?‹
›YOU MUST HAVE PURPLE RAYS.‹
WHAT?
WHAT ARE YOU SAYING?
ENN-LISH?
I LEARN ENN-LISH.
YOU ESS EH?

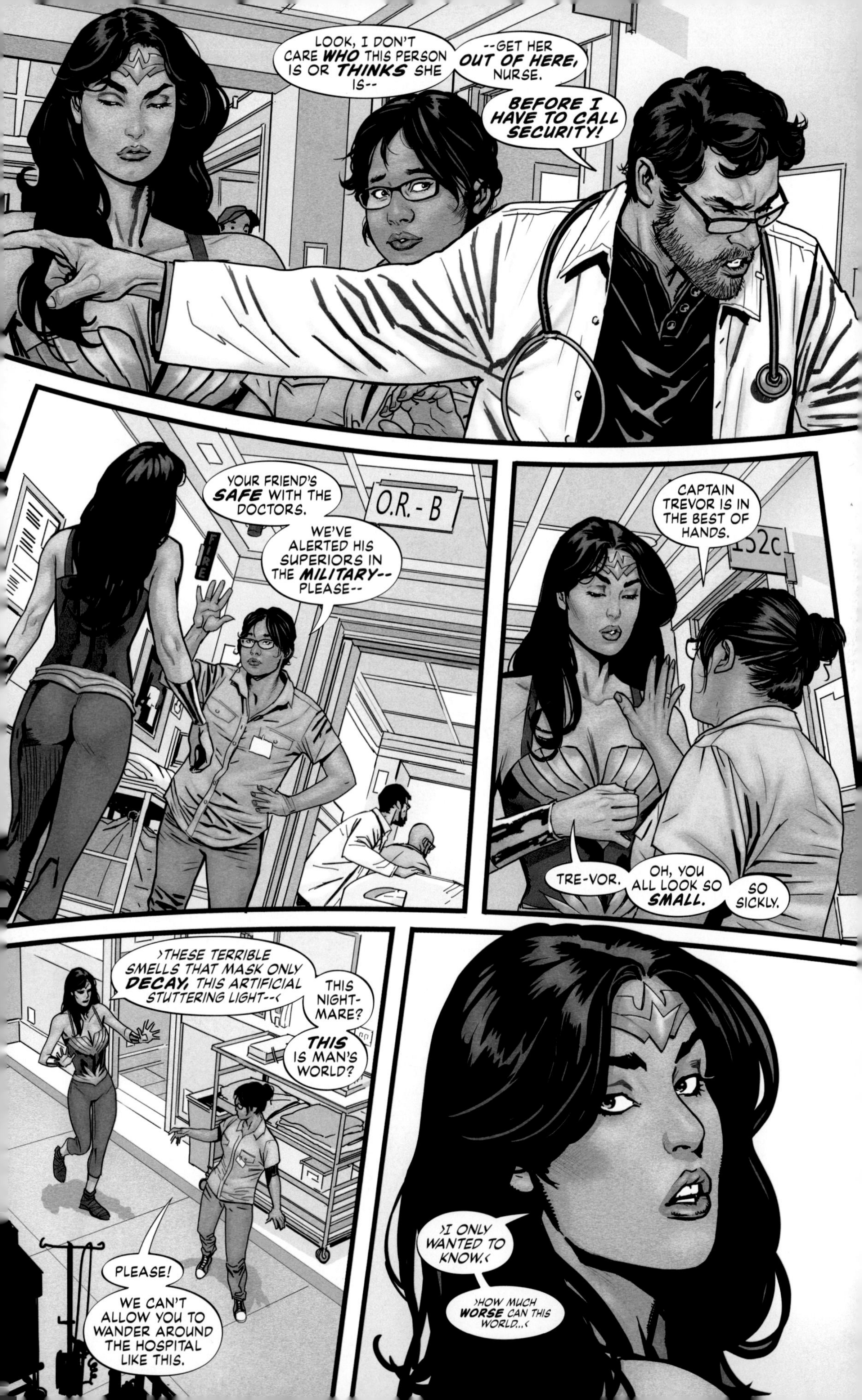
LOOK, I DON'T CARE **WHO** THIS PERSON IS OR **THINKS** SHE IS--
--GET HER **OUT OF HERE,** NURSE.
BEFORE I HAVE TO CALL SECURITY!
YOUR FRIEND'S **SAFE** WITH THE DOCTORS.
WE'VE ALERTED HIS SUPERIORS IN THE **MILITARY--** PLEASE--
O.R. - B
FIRE
CAPTAIN TREVOR IS IN THE BEST OF HANDS.
152c
TRE-VOR.
OH, YOU ALL LOOK SO **SMALL.**
SO SICKLY.
›THESE TERRIBLE SMELLS THAT MASK ONLY **DECAY,** THIS ARTIFICIAL STUTTERING LIGHT--‹
THIS NIGHT-MARE?
THIS IS MAN'S WORLD?
PLEASE!
WE CAN'T ALLOW YOU TO WANDER AROUND THE HOSPITAL LIKE THIS.
›I ONLY WANTED TO KNOW.‹
›HOW MUCH **WORSE** CAN THIS WORLD...‹

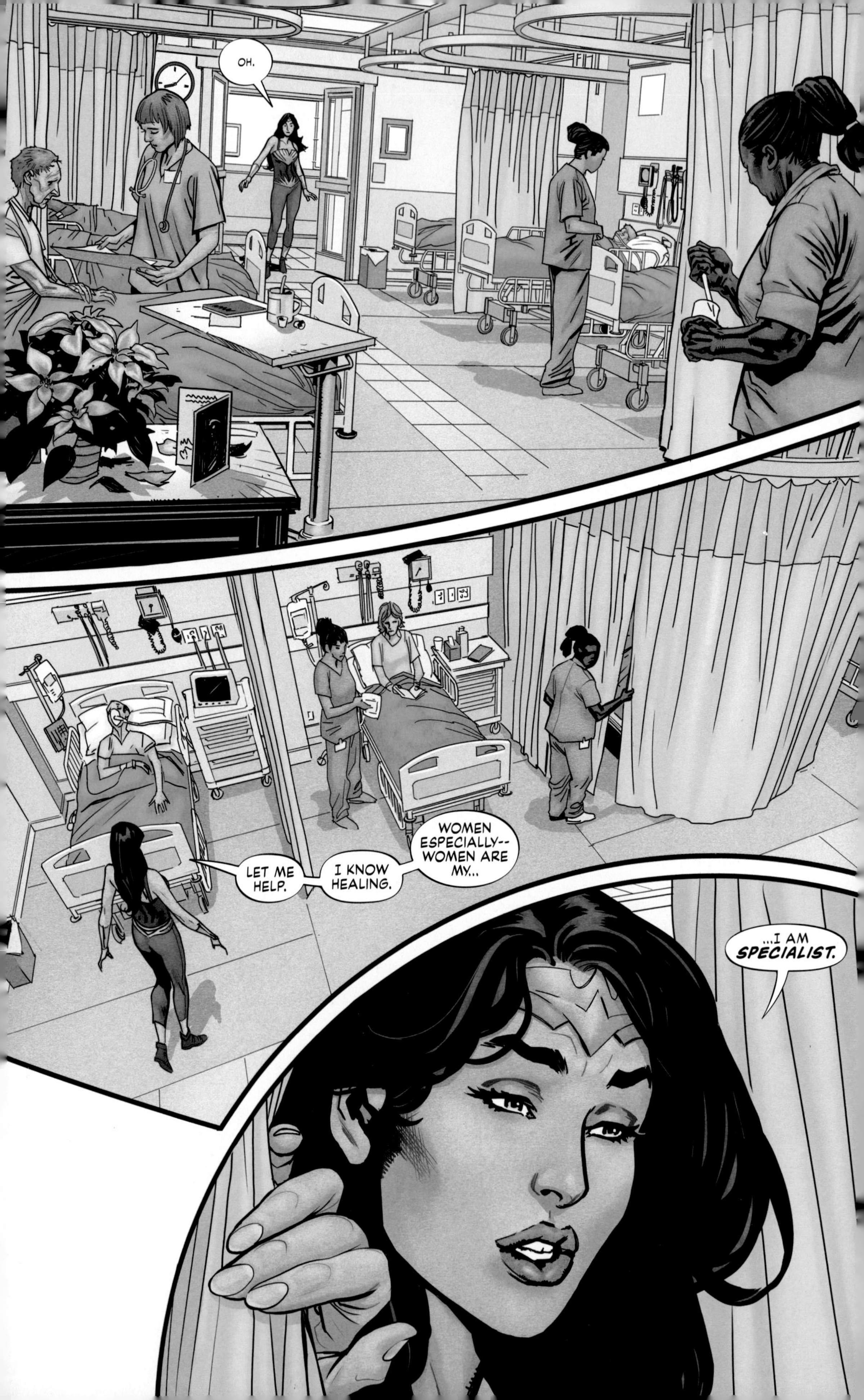
OH.
LET ME HELP.
I KNOW HEALING.
WOMEN ESPECIALLY-- WOMEN ARE MY...
...I AM SPECIALIST.

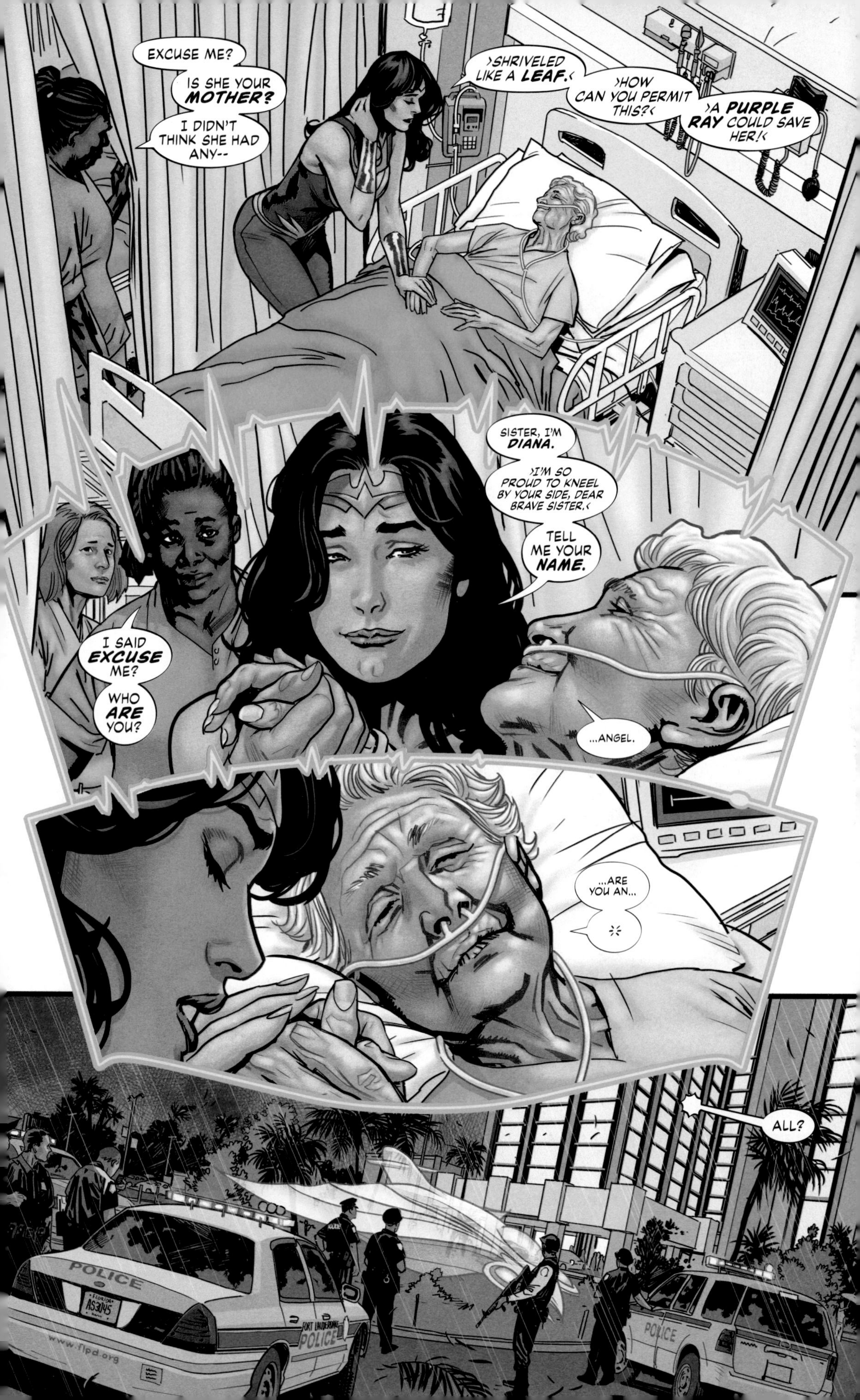
EXCUSE ME?
IS SHE YOUR MOTHER?
I DIDN'T THINK SHE HAD ANY--
›SHRIVELED LIKE A LEAF.‹
›HOW CAN YOU PERMIT THIS?‹
›A PURPLE RAY COULD SAVE HER!‹
SISTER, I'M DIANA.
›I'M SO PROUD TO KNEEL BY YOUR SIDE, DEAR BRAVE SISTER.‹
TELL ME YOUR NAME.
I SAID EXCUSE ME?
WHO ARE YOU?
...ANGEL.
...ARE YOU AN...
ALL?
POLICE
FORT LAUDERDALE POLICE
www.flpd.org
POLICE

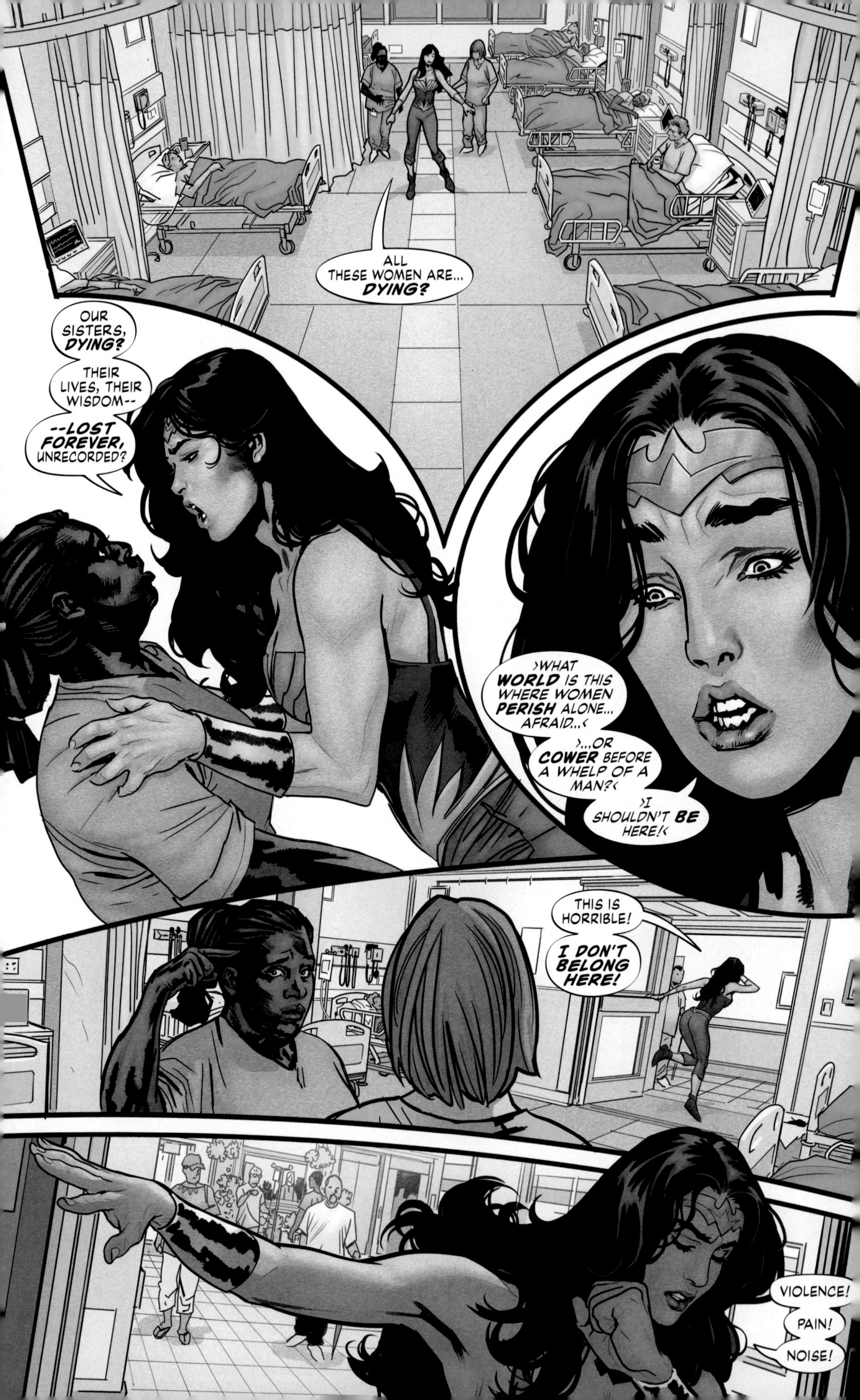
ALL THESE WOMEN ARE... DYING?
OUR SISTERS, DYING?
THEIR LIVES, THEIR WISDOM--
--LOST FOREVER, UNRECORDED?
›WHAT WORLD IS THIS WHERE WOMEN PERISH ALONE... AFRAID...‹
›...OR COWER BEFORE A WHELP OF A MAN?‹
›I SHOULDN'T BE HERE!‹
THIS IS HORRIBLE!
I DON'T BELONG HERE!
VIOLENCE!
PAIN!
NOISE!

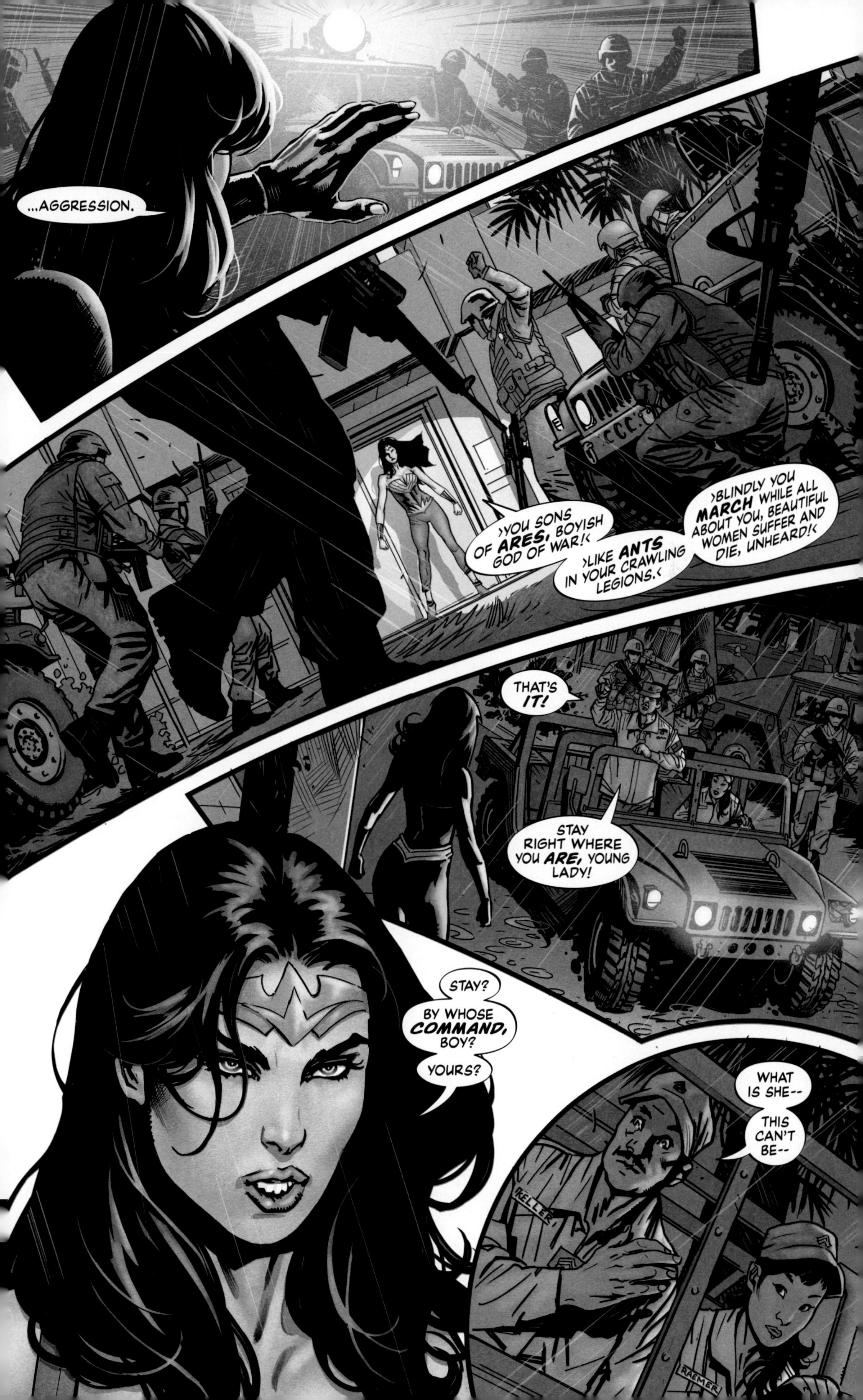
...AGGRESSION.
›YOU SONS OF ARES, BOYISH GOD OF WAR!‹
›LIKE ANTS IN YOUR CRAWLING LEGIONS.‹
›BLINDLY YOU MARCH WHILE ALL ABOUT YOU, BEAUTIFUL WOMEN SUFFER AND DIE, UNHEARD!‹
THAT'S IT!
STAY RIGHT WHERE YOU ARE, YOUNG LADY!
STAY?
BY WHOSE COMMAND, BOY?
YOURS?
WHAT IS SHE--
THIS CAN'T BE--
KELLER
RAEMER

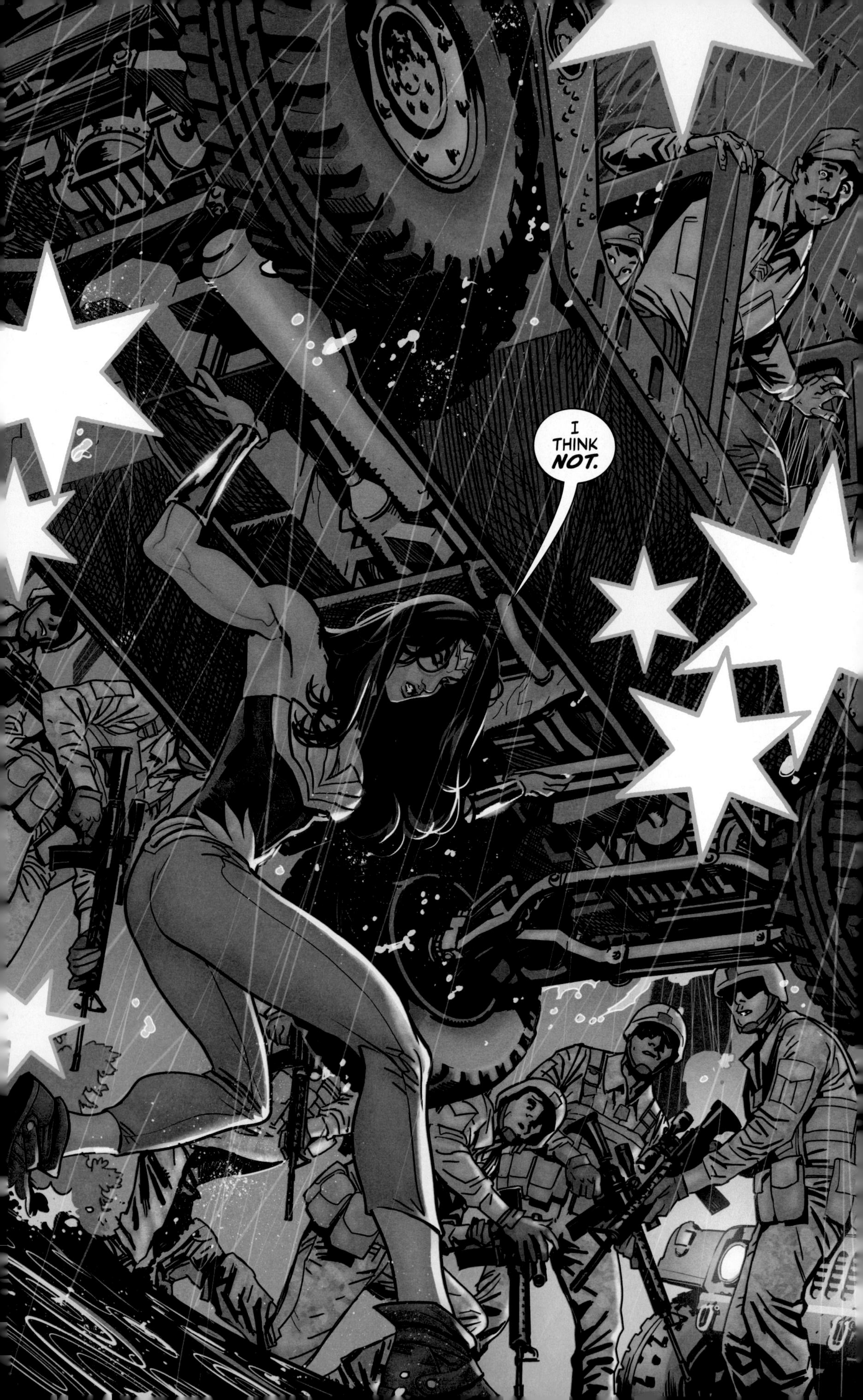
I THINK NOT.

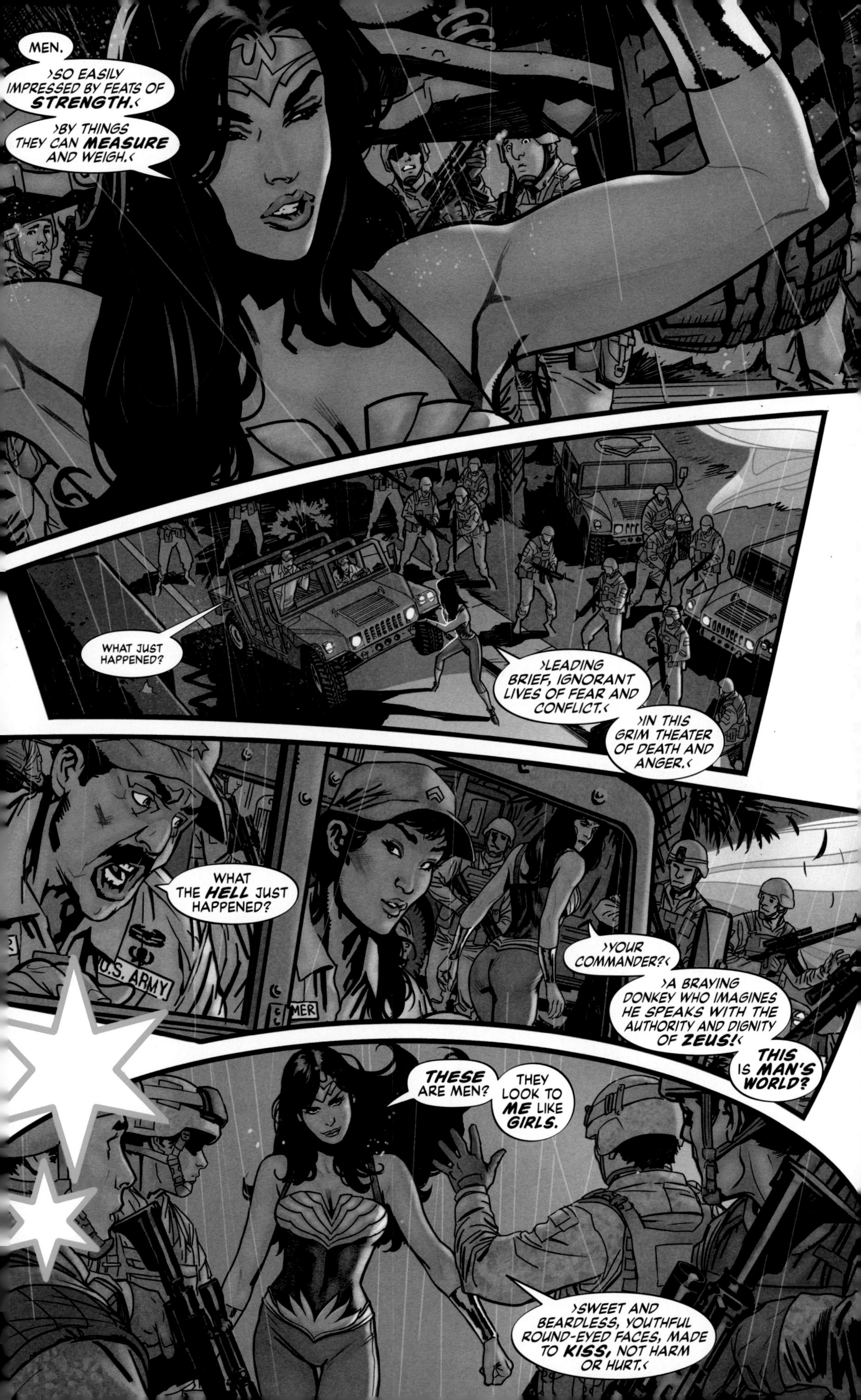
MEN.
›SO EASILY IMPRESSED BY FEATS OF STRENGTH.‹
›BY THINGS THEY CAN MEASURE AND WEIGH.‹
WHAT JUST HAPPENED?
›LEADING BRIEF, IGNORANT LIVES OF FEAR AND CONFLICT.‹
›IN THIS GRIM THEATER OF DEATH AND ANGER.‹
WHAT THE HELL JUST HAPPENED?
U.S. ARMY
›YOUR COMMANDER?‹
›A BRAYING DONKEY WHO IMAGINES HE SPEAKS WITH THE AUTHORITY AND DIGNITY OF ZEUS!‹
THIS IS MAN'S WORLD?
THESE ARE MEN?
THEY LOOK TO ME LIKE GIRLS.
›SWEET AND BEARDLESS, YOUTHFUL ROUND-EYED FACES, MADE TO KISS, NOT HARM OR HURT.‹

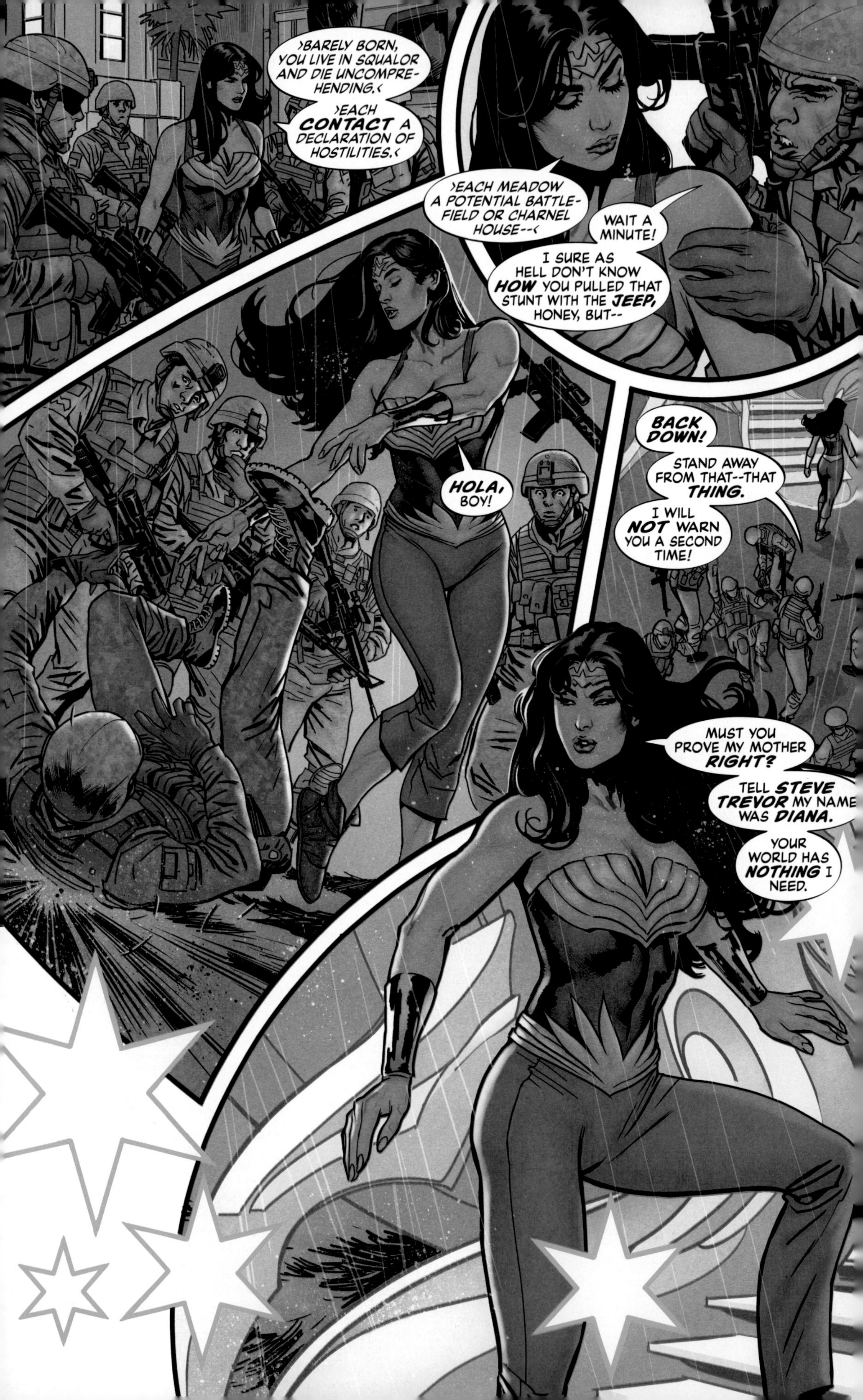
›BARELY BORN, YOU LIVE IN SQUALOR AND DIE UNCOMPRE-HENDING.‹
›EACH CONTACT A DECLARATION OF HOSTILITIES.‹
›EACH MEADOW A POTENTIAL BATTLE-FIELD OR CHARNEL HOUSE--‹
WAIT A MINUTE!
I SURE AS HELL DON'T KNOW HOW YOU PULLED THAT STUNT WITH THE JEEP, HONEY, BUT--
HOLA, BOY!
BACK DOWN!
STAND AWAY FROM THAT--THAT THING.
I WILL NOT WARN YOU A SECOND TIME!
MUST YOU PROVE MY MOTHER RIGHT?
TELL STEVE TREVOR MY NAME WAS DIANA.
YOUR WORLD HAS NOTHING I NEED.

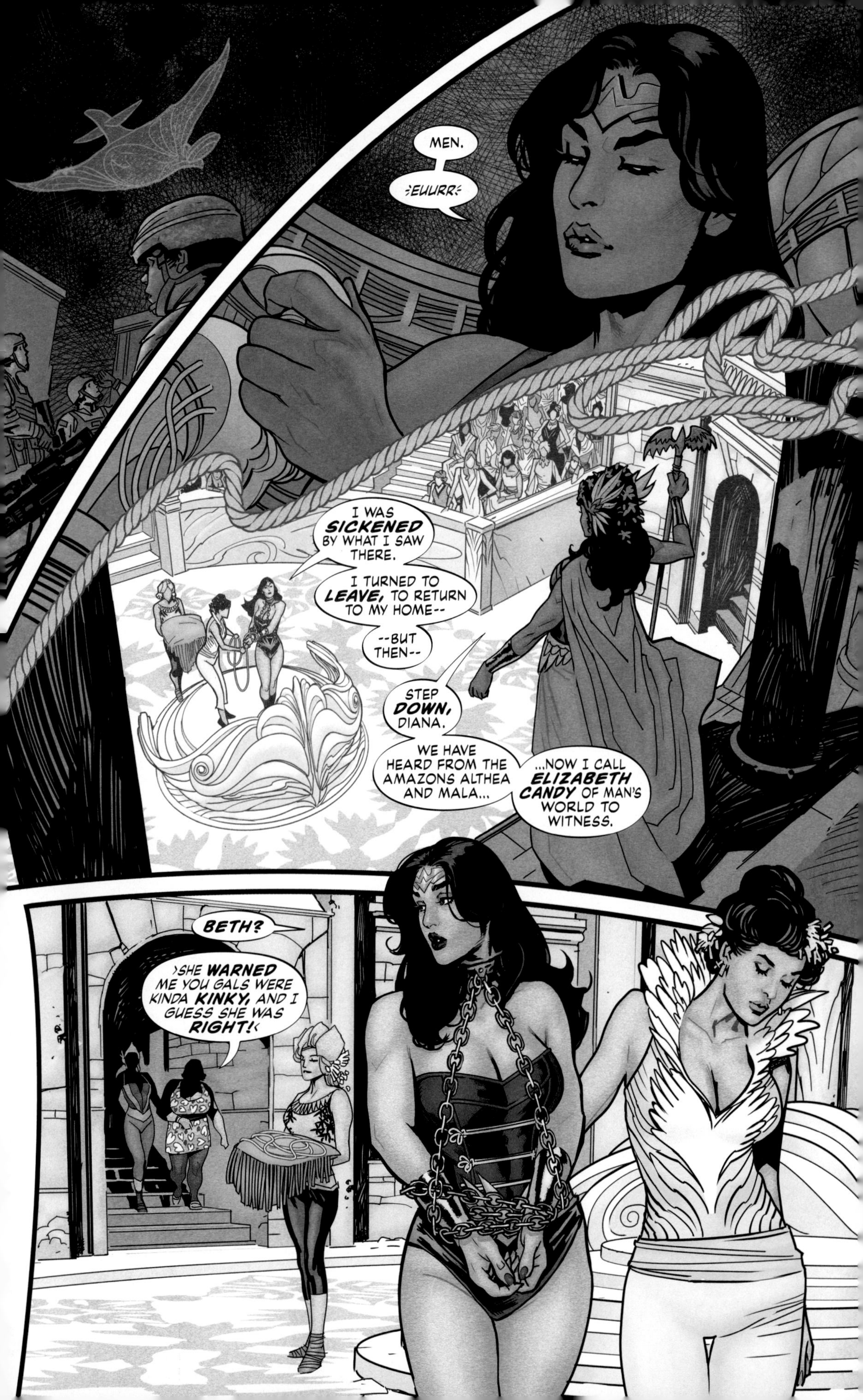
MEN.
›EUURR‹
I WAS SICKENED BY WHAT I SAW THERE.
I TURNED TO LEAVE, TO RETURN TO MY HOME--
--BUT THEN--
STEP DOWN, DIANA.
WE HAVE HEARD FROM THE AMAZONS ALTHEA AND MALA...
...NOW I CALL ELIZABETH CANDY OF MAN'S WORLD TO WITNESS.
BETH?
›SHE WARNED ME YOU GALS WERE KINDA KINKY, AND I GUESS SHE WAS RIGHT!‹

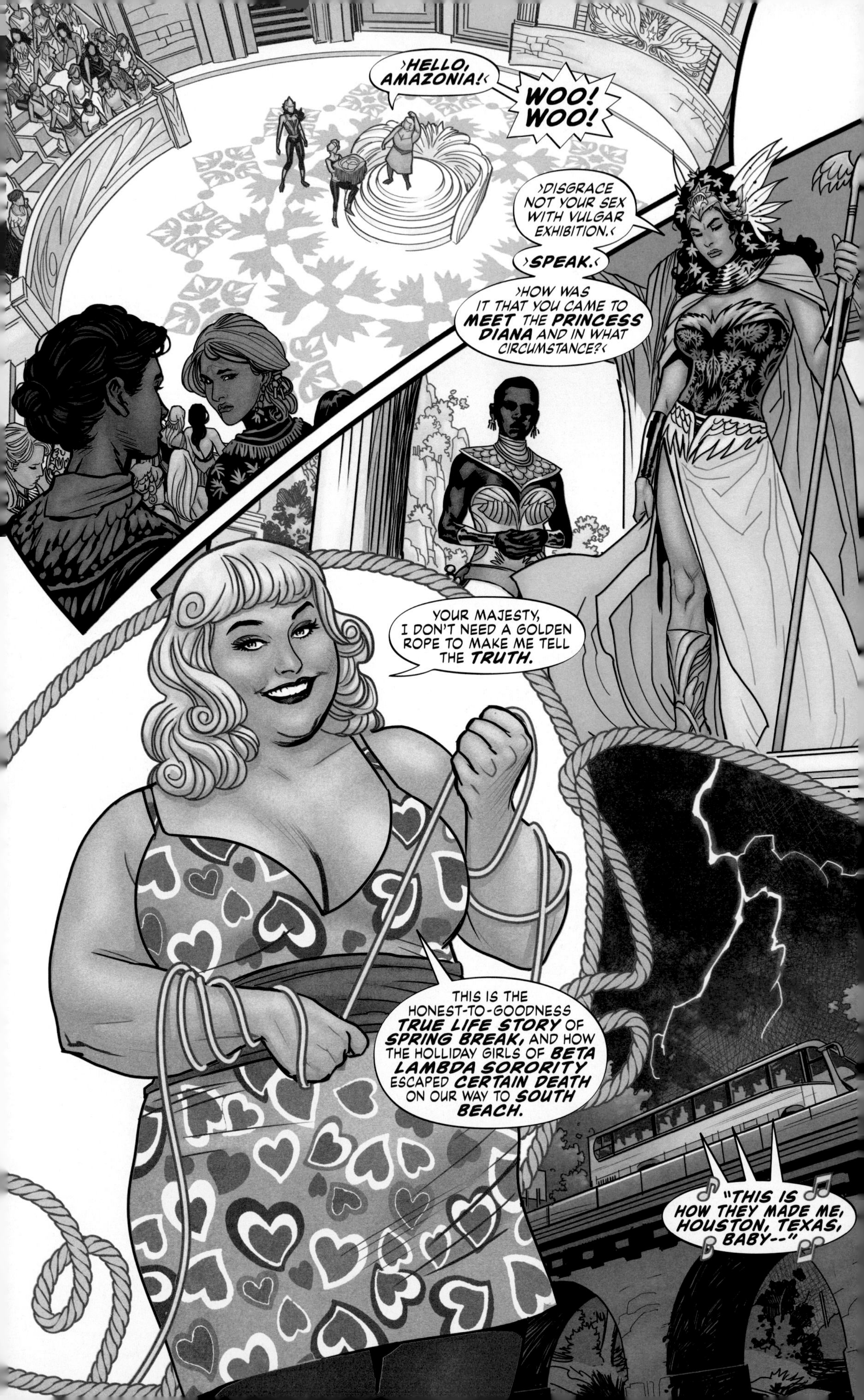
›HELLO, AMAZONIA!‹
WOO! WOO!
›DISGRACE NOT YOUR SEX WITH VULGAR EXHIBITION.‹
›SPEAK.‹
›HOW WAS IT THAT YOU CAME TO MEET THE PRINCESS DIANA AND IN WHAT CIRCUMSTANCE?‹
YOUR MAJESTY, I DON'T NEED A GOLDEN ROPE TO MAKE ME TELL THE TRUTH.
THIS IS THE HONEST-TO-GOODNESS TRUE LIFE STORY OF SPRING BREAK, AND HOW THE HOLLIDAY GIRLS OF BETA LAMBDA SORORITY ESCAPED CERTAIN DEATH ON OUR WAY TO SOUTH BEACH.
"THIS IS HOW THEY MADE ME, HOUSTON, TEXAS, BABY--"

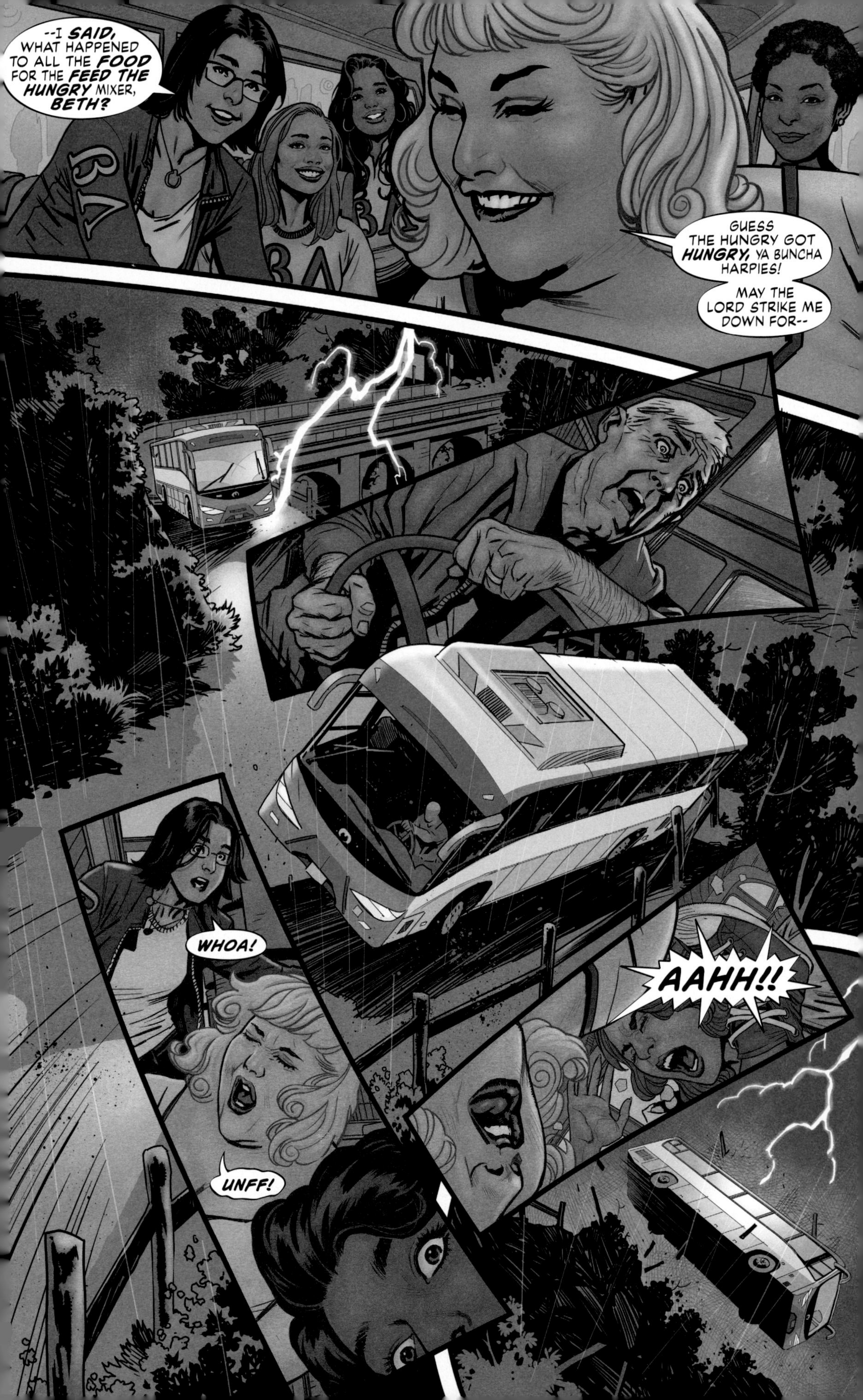
--I SAID, WHAT HAPPENED TO ALL THE FOOD FOR THE FEED THE HUNGRY MIXER, BETH?
GUESS THE HUNGRY GOT HUNGRY, YA BUNCHA HARPIES!
MAY THE LORD STRIKE ME DOWN FOR--
WHOA!
UNFF!
AAHH!!

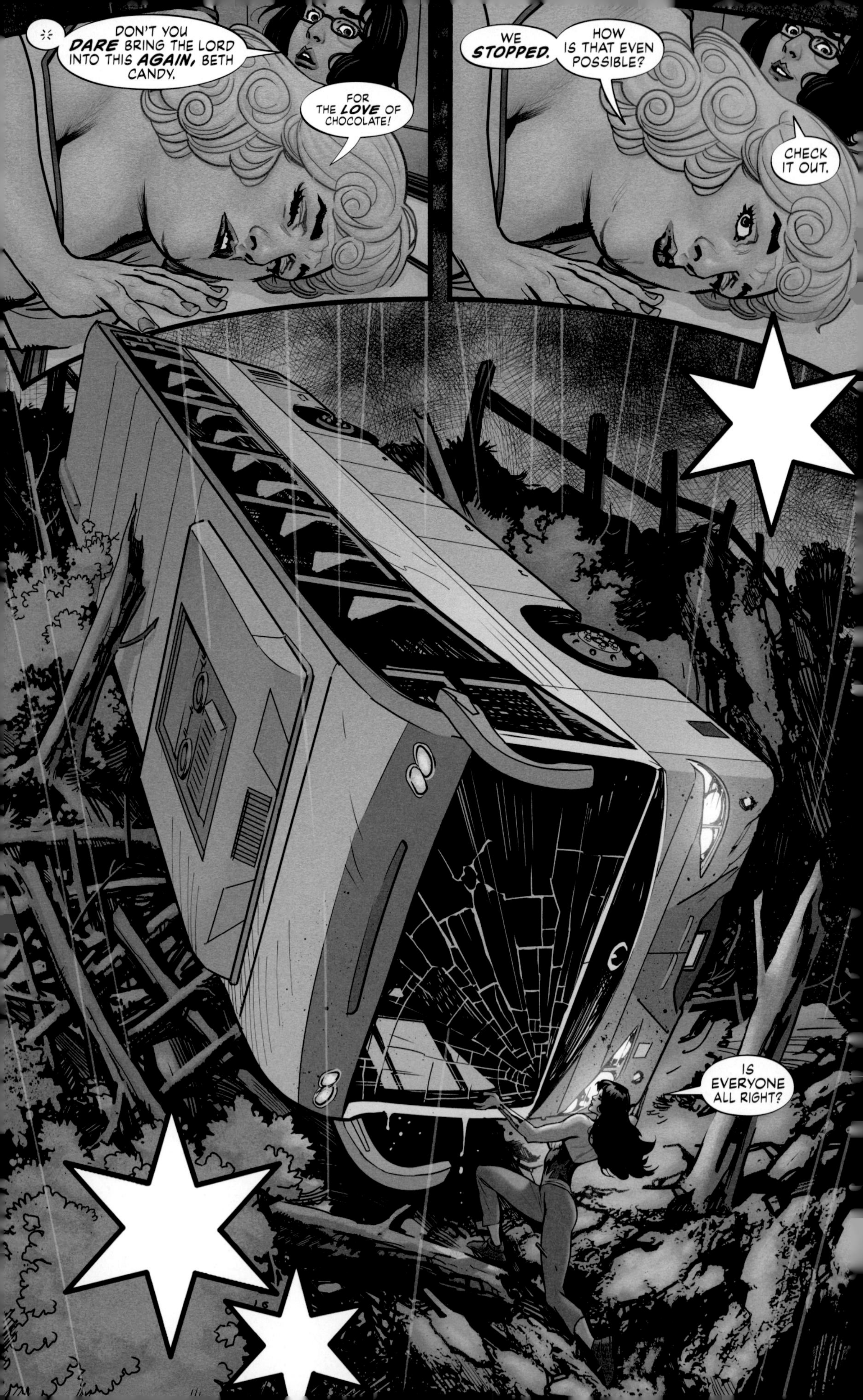
DON'T YOU DARE BRING THE LORD INTO THIS AGAIN, BETH CANDY.
FOR THE LOVE OF CHOCOLATE!
WE STOPPED.
HOW IS THAT EVEN POSSIBLE?
CHECK IT OUT.
IS EVERYONE ALL RIGHT?

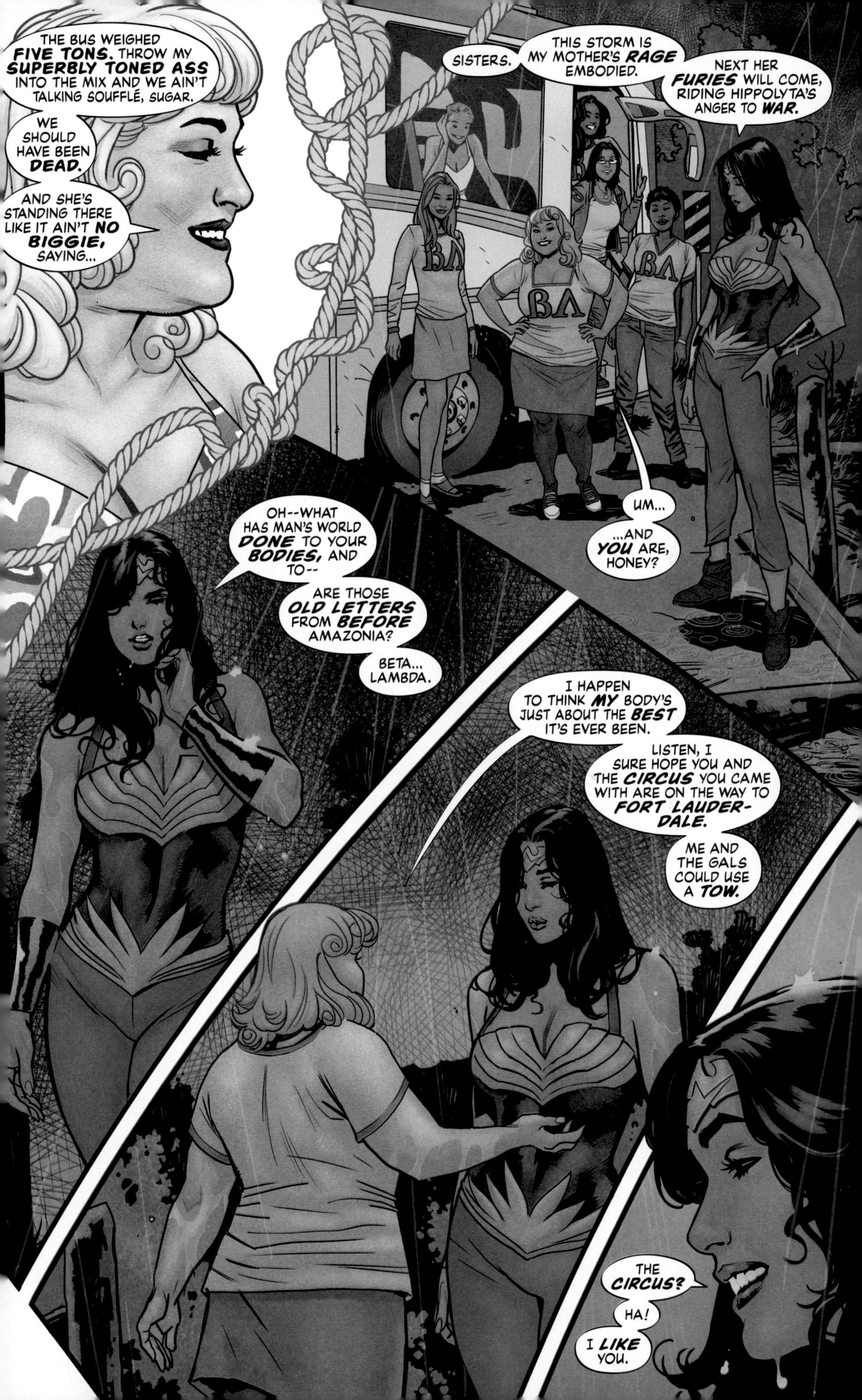
THE BUS WEIGHED FIVE TONS. THROW MY SUPERBLY TONED ASS INTO THE MIX AND WE AIN'T TALKING SOUFFLÉ, SUGAR.
WE SHOULD HAVE BEEN DEAD.
AND SHE'S STANDING THERE LIKE IT AIN'T NO BIGGIE, SAYING...
SISTERS.
THIS STORM IS MY MOTHER'S RAGE EMBODIED.
NEXT HER FURIES WILL COME, RIDING HIPPOLYTA'S ANGER TO WAR.
UM...
...AND YOU ARE, HONEY?
OH--WHAT HAS MAN'S WORLD DONE TO YOUR BODIES, AND TO--
ARE THOSE OLD LETTERS FROM BEFORE AMAZONIA?
BETA... LAMBDA.
I HAPPEN TO THINK MY BODY'S JUST ABOUT THE BEST IT'S EVER BEEN.
LISTEN, I SURE HOPE YOU AND THE CIRCUS YOU CAME WITH ARE ON THE WAY TO FORT LAUDER-DALE.
ME AND THE GALS COULD USE A TOW.
THE CIRCUS?
HA!
I LIKE YOU.

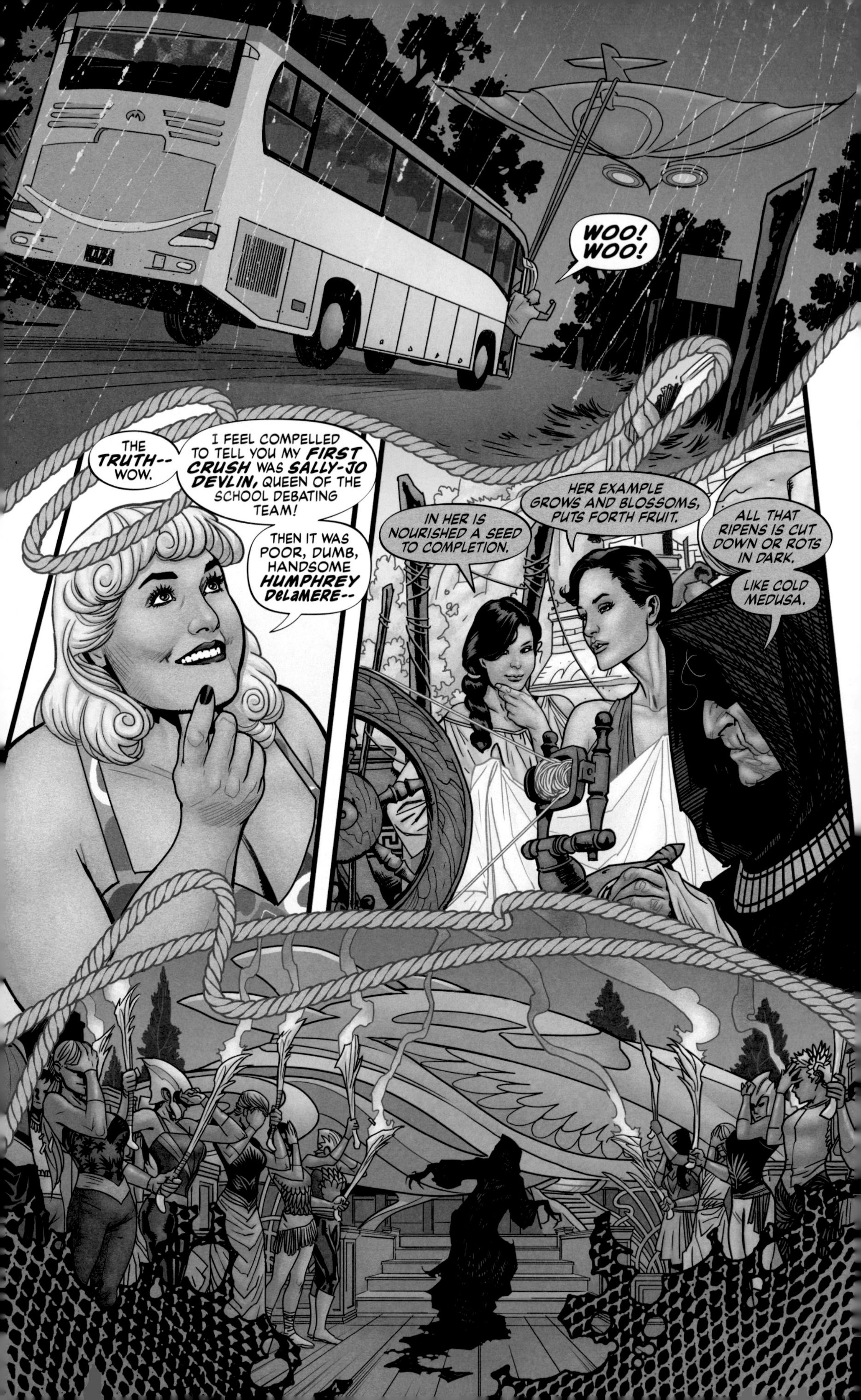
WOO! WOO!
THE TRUTH-- WOW.
I FEEL COMPELLED TO TELL YOU MY FIRST CRUSH WAS SALLY-JO DEVLIN, QUEEN OF THE SCHOOL DEBATING TEAM!
THEN IT WAS POOR, DUMB, HANDSOME HUMPHREY DeLAMERE--
IN HER IS NOURISHED A SEED TO COMPLETION.
HER EXAMPLE GROWS AND BLOSSOMS, PUTS FORTH FRUIT.
ALL THAT RIPENS IS CUT DOWN OR ROTS IN DARK.
LIKE COLD MEDUSA.

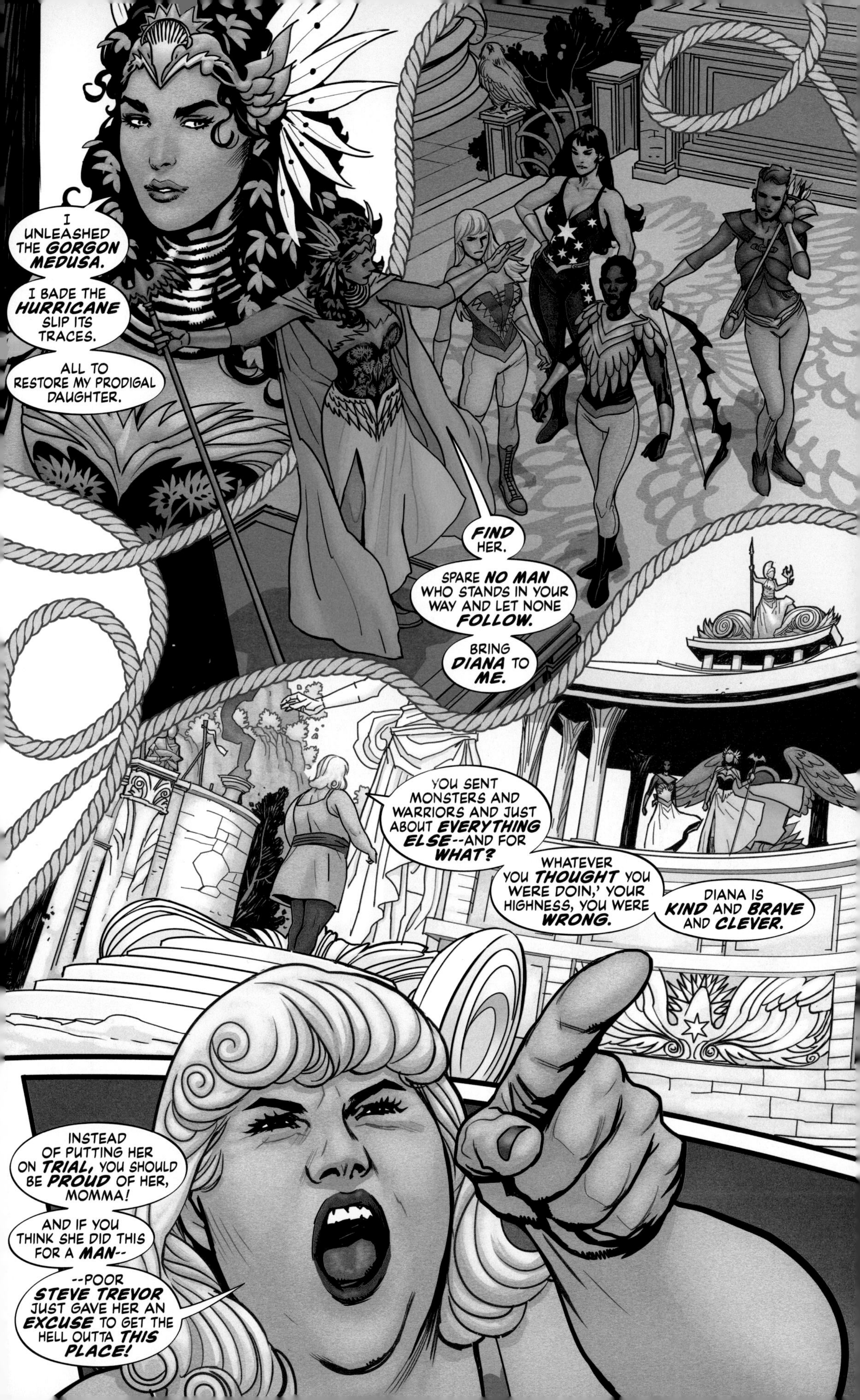

I UNLEASHED THE GORGON MEDUSA.
I BADE THE HURRICANE SLIP ITS TRACES.
ALL TO RESTORE MY PRODIGAL DAUGHTER.
FIND HER.
SPARE NO MAN WHO STANDS IN YOUR WAY AND LET NONE FOLLOW.
BRING DIANA TO ME.
YOU SENT MONSTERS AND WARRIORS AND JUST ABOUT EVERYTHING ELSE--AND FOR WHAT?
WHATEVER YOU THOUGHT YOU WERE DOIN,' YOUR HIGHNESS, YOU WERE WRONG.
DIANA IS KIND AND BRAVE AND CLEVER.
INSTEAD OF PUTTING HER ON TRIAL, YOU SHOULD BE PROUD OF HER, MOMMA!
AND IF YOU THINK SHE DID THIS FOR A MAN--
--POOR STEVE TREVOR JUST GAVE HER AN EXCUSE TO GET THE HELL OUTTA THIS PLACE!

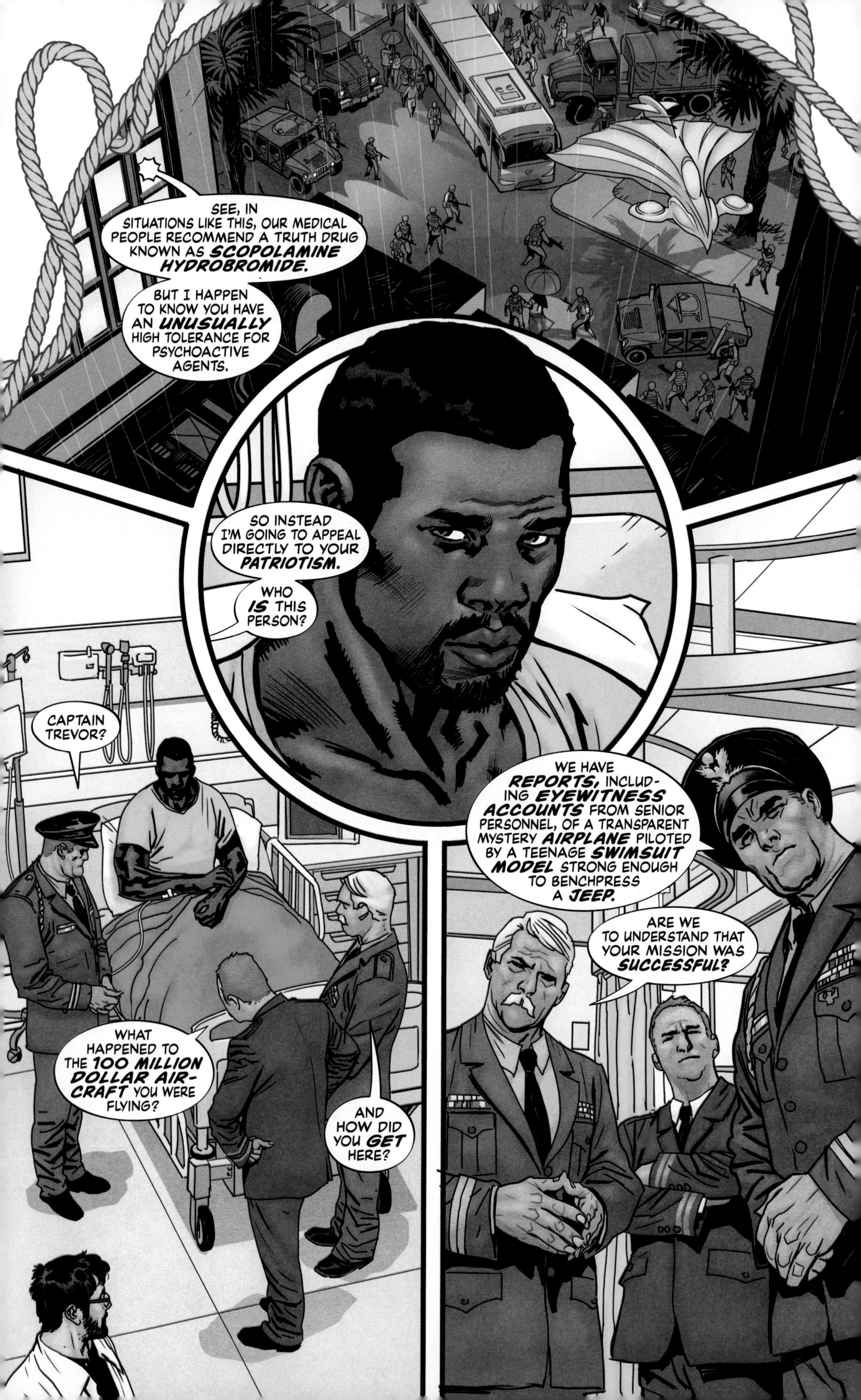
SEE, IN SITUATIONS LIKE THIS, OUR MEDICAL PEOPLE RECOMMEND A TRUTH DRUG KNOWN AS SCOPOLAMINE HYDROBROMIDE.
BUT I HAPPEN TO KNOW YOU HAVE AN UNUSUALLY HIGH TOLERANCE FOR PSYCHOACTIVE AGENTS.
SO INSTEAD I'M GOING TO APPEAL DIRECTLY TO YOUR PATRIOTISM.
WHO IS THIS PERSON?
CAPTAIN TREVOR?
WHAT HAPPENED TO THE 100 MILLION DOLLAR AIR-CRAFT YOU WERE FLYING?
AND HOW DID YOU GET HERE?
WE HAVE REPORTS, INCLUDING EYEWITNESS ACCOUNTS FROM SENIOR PERSONNEL, OF A TRANSPARENT MYSTERY AIRPLANE PILOTED BY A TEENAGE SWIMSUIT MODEL STRONG ENOUGH TO BENCHPRESS A JEEP.
ARE WE TO UNDERSTAND THAT YOUR MISSION WAS SUCCESSFUL?

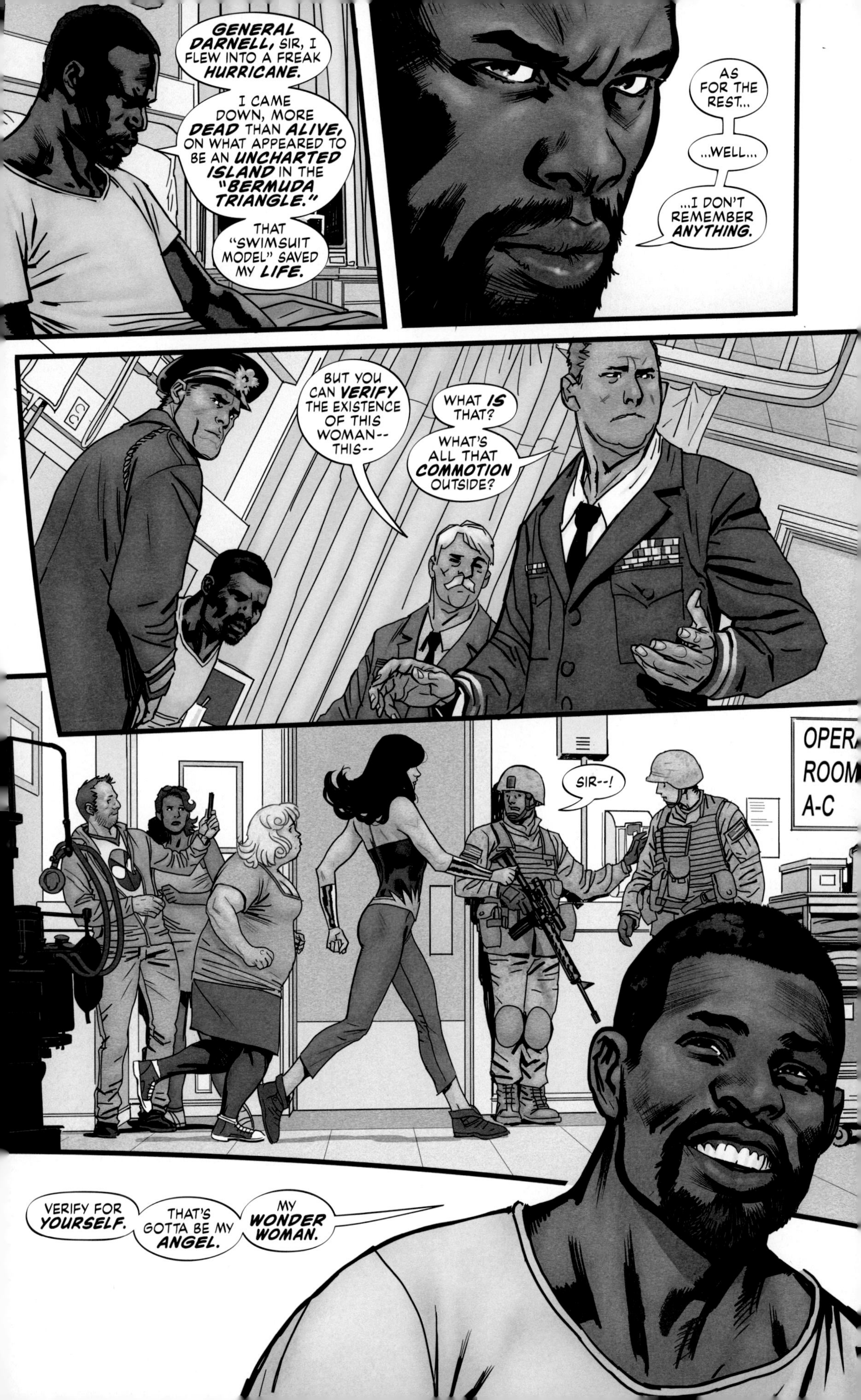
GENERAL DARNELL, SIR, I FLEW INTO A FREAK HURRICANE.
I CAME DOWN, MORE DEAD THAN ALIVE, ON WHAT APPEARED TO BE AN UNCHARTED ISLAND IN THE "BERMUDA TRIANGLE."
THAT "SWIMSUIT MODEL" SAVED MY LIFE.
AS FOR THE REST...
...WELL...
...I DON'T REMEMBER ANYTHING.
BUT YOU CAN VERIFY THE EXISTENCE OF THIS WOMAN-- THIS--
WHAT IS THAT?
WHAT'S ALL THAT COMMOTION OUTSIDE?
OPER
ROOM
A-C
SIR--!
VERIFY FOR YOURSELF.
THAT'S GOTTA BE MY ANGEL.
MY WONDER WOMAN.

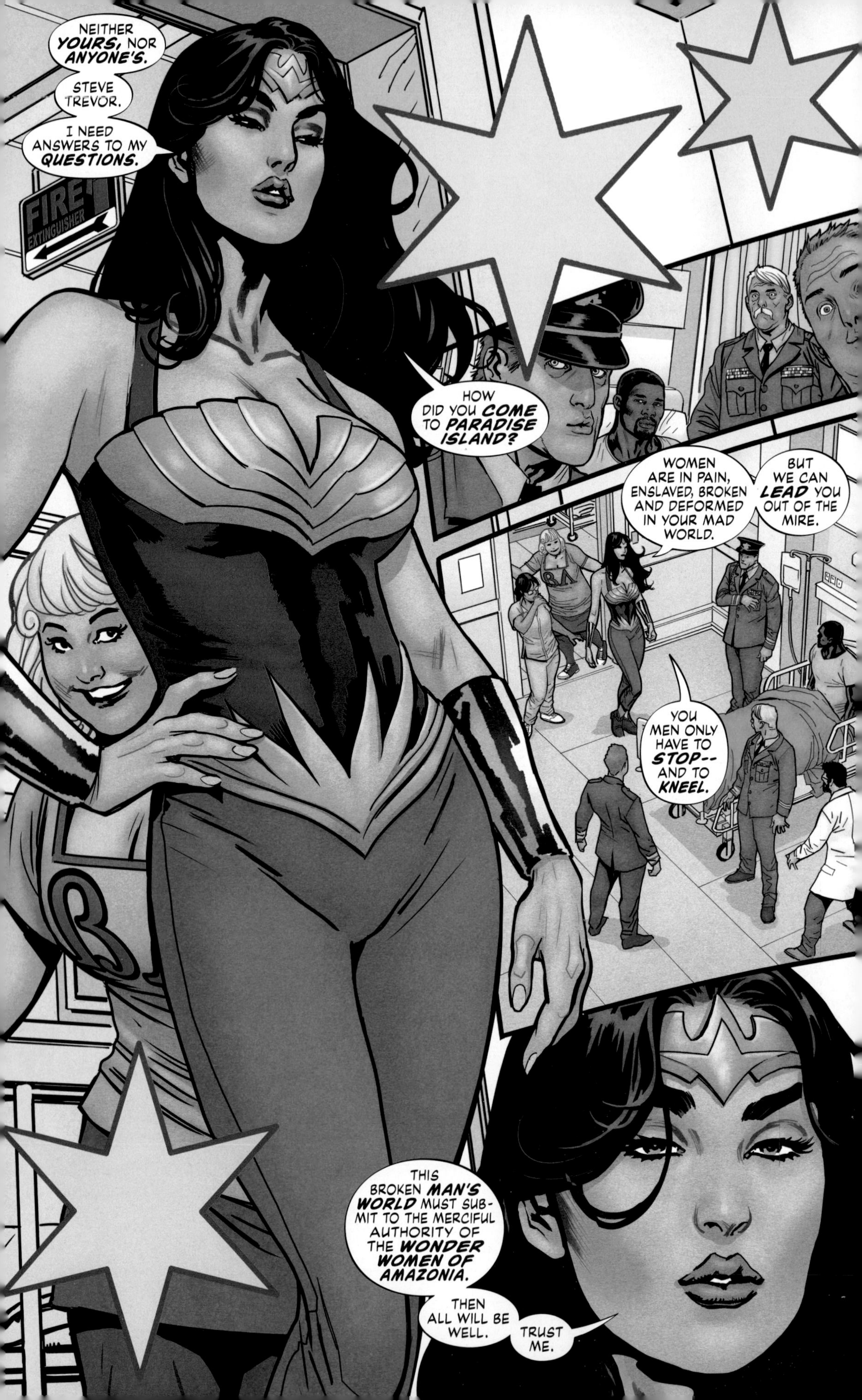
NEITHER YOURS, NOR ANYONE'S.
STEVE TREVOR.
I NEED ANSWERS TO MY QUESTIONS.
FIRE EXTINGUISHER
HOW DID YOU COME TO PARADISE ISLAND?
WOMEN ARE IN PAIN, ENSLAVED, BROKEN AND DEFORMED IN YOUR MAD WORLD.
BUT WE CAN LEAD YOU OUT OF THE MIRE.
YOU MEN ONLY HAVE TO STOP-- AND TO KNEEL.
THIS BROKEN MAN'S WORLD MUST SUB-MIT TO THE MERCIFUL AUTHORITY OF THE WONDER WOMEN OF AMAZONIA.
THEN ALL WILL BE WELL.
TRUST ME.

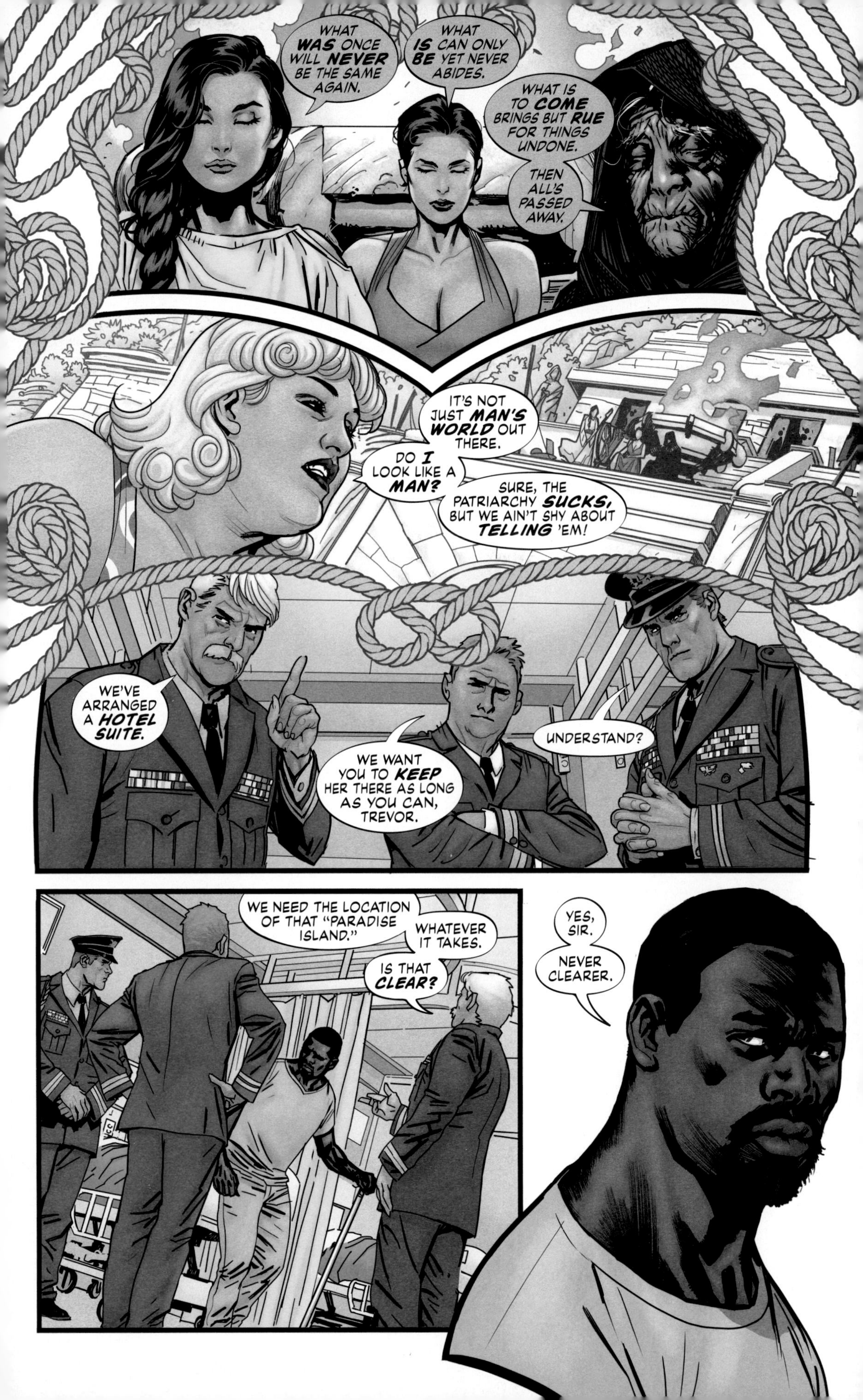
WHAT WAS ONCE WILL NEVER BE THE SAME AGAIN.
WHAT IS CAN ONLY BE YET NEVER ABIDES.
WHAT IS TO COME BRINGS BUT RUE FOR THINGS UNDONE.
THEN ALL'S PASSED AWAY.
IT'S NOT JUST MAN'S WORLD OUT THERE.
DO I LOOK LIKE A MAN?
SURE, THE PATRIARCHY SUCKS, BUT WE AIN'T SHY ABOUT TELLING 'EM!
WE'VE ARRANGED A HOTEL SUITE.
WE WANT YOU TO KEEP HER THERE AS LONG AS YOU CAN, TREVOR.
UNDERSTAND?
WE NEED THE LOCATION OF THAT "PARADISE ISLAND."
WHATEVER IT TAKES.
IS THAT CLEAR?
YES, SIR.
NEVER CLEARER.

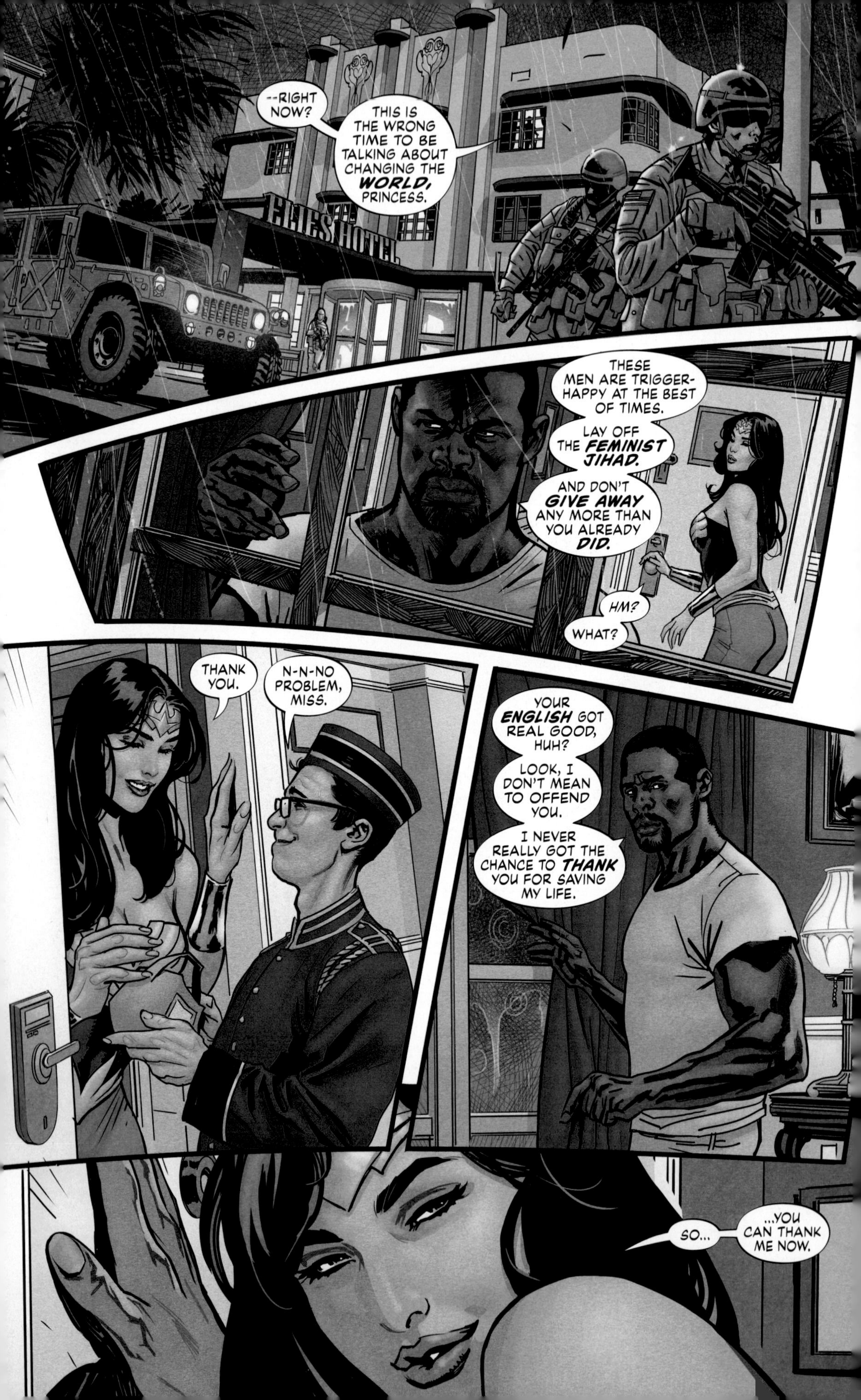

--RIGHT NOW?
THIS IS THE WRONG TIME TO BE TALKING ABOUT CHANGING THE WORLD, PRINCESS.
THESE MEN ARE TRIGGER-HAPPY AT THE BEST OF TIMES.
LAY OFF THE FEMINIST JIHAD.
AND DON'T GIVE AWAY ANY MORE THAN YOU ALREADY DID.
HM?
WHAT?
THANK YOU.
N-N-NO PROBLEM, MISS.
YOUR ENGLISH GOT REAL GOOD, HUH?
LOOK, I DON'T MEAN TO OFFEND YOU.
I NEVER REALLY GOT THE CHANCE TO THANK YOU FOR SAVING MY LIFE.
SO...
...YOU CAN THANK ME NOW.

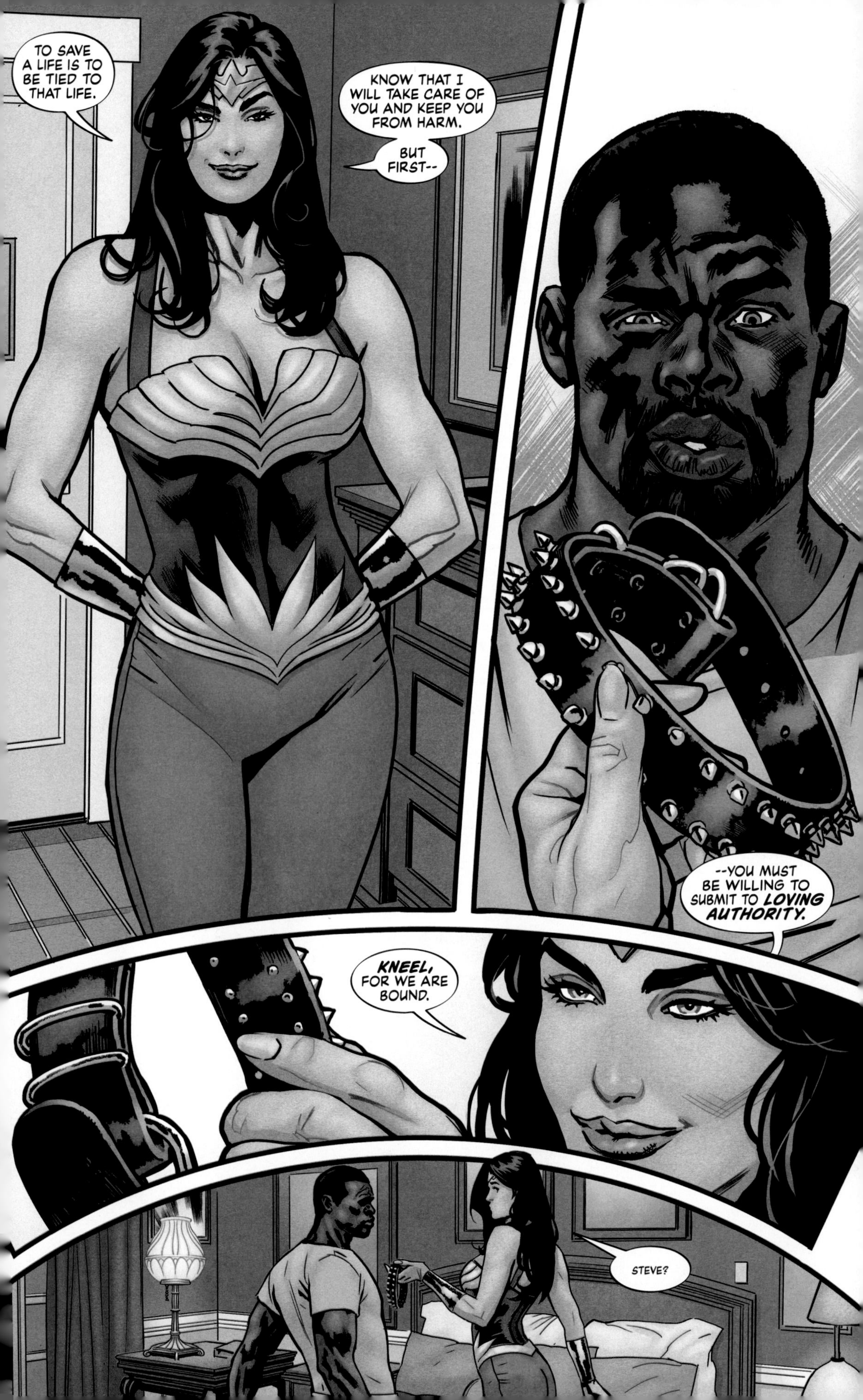
TO SAVE A LIFE IS TO BE TIED TO THAT LIFE.
KNOW THAT I WILL TAKE CARE OF YOU AND KEEP YOU FROM HARM.
BUT FIRST--
--YOU MUST BE WILLING TO SUBMIT TO LOVING AUTHORITY.
KNEEL, FOR WE ARE BOUND.
STEVE?

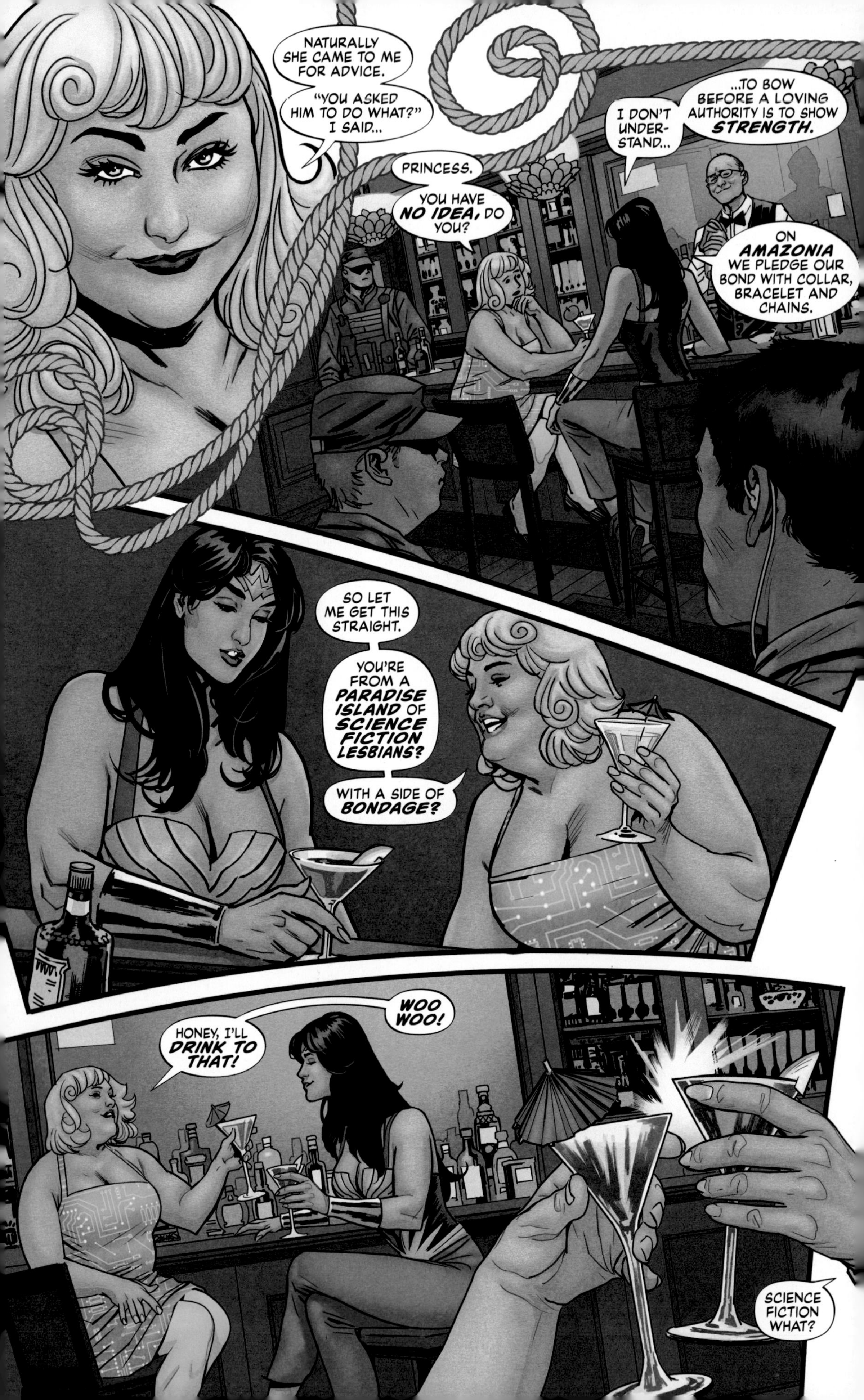
NATURALLY SHE CAME TO ME FOR ADVICE.
"YOU ASKED HIM TO DO WHAT?" I SAID...
PRINCESS.
YOU HAVE NO IDEA, DO YOU?
I DON'T UNDER-STAND...
...TO BOW BEFORE A LOVING AUTHORITY IS TO SHOW STRENGTH.
ON AMAZONIA WE PLEDGE OUR BOND WITH COLLAR, BRACELET AND CHAINS.
SO LET ME GET THIS STRAIGHT.
YOU'RE FROM A PARADISE ISLAND OF SCIENCE FICTION LESBIANS?
WITH A SIDE OF BONDAGE?
HONEY, I'LL DRINK TO THAT!
WOO WOO!
SCIENCE FICTION WHAT?

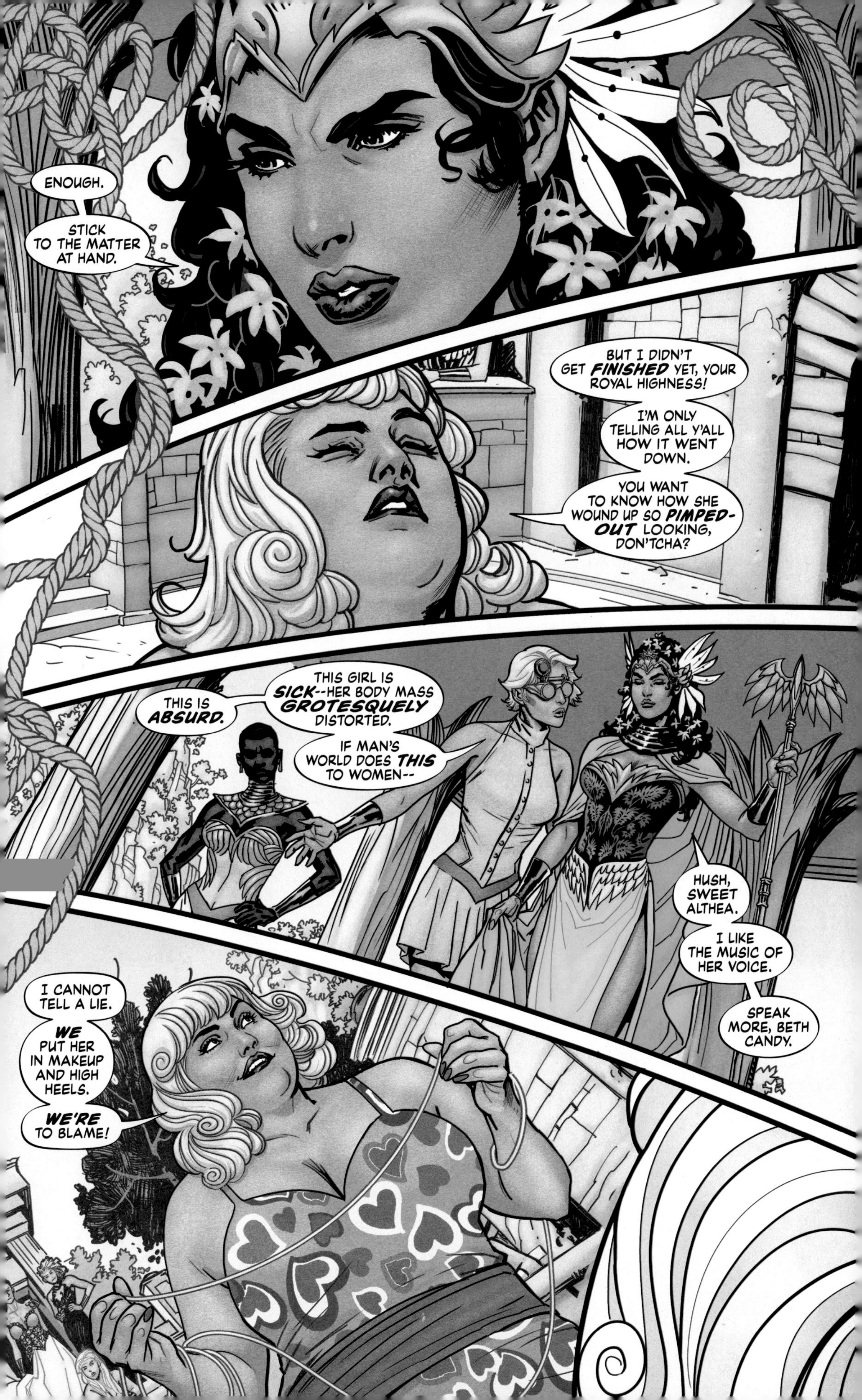
ENOUGH.
STICK TO THE MATTER AT HAND.
BUT I DIDN'T GET FINISHED YET, YOUR ROYAL HIGHNESS!
I'M ONLY TELLING ALL Y'ALL HOW IT WENT DOWN.
YOU WANT TO KNOW HOW SHE WOUND UP SO PIMPED-OUT LOOKING, DON'TCHA?
THIS IS ABSURD.
THIS GIRL IS SICK--HER BODY MASS GROTESQUELY DISTORTED.
IF MAN'S WORLD DOES THIS TO WOMEN--
HUSH, SWEET ALTHEA.
I LIKE THE MUSIC OF HER VOICE.
SPEAK MORE, BETH CANDY.
I CANNOT TELL A LIE.
WE PUT HER IN MAKEUP AND HIGH HEELS.
WE'RE TO BLAME!

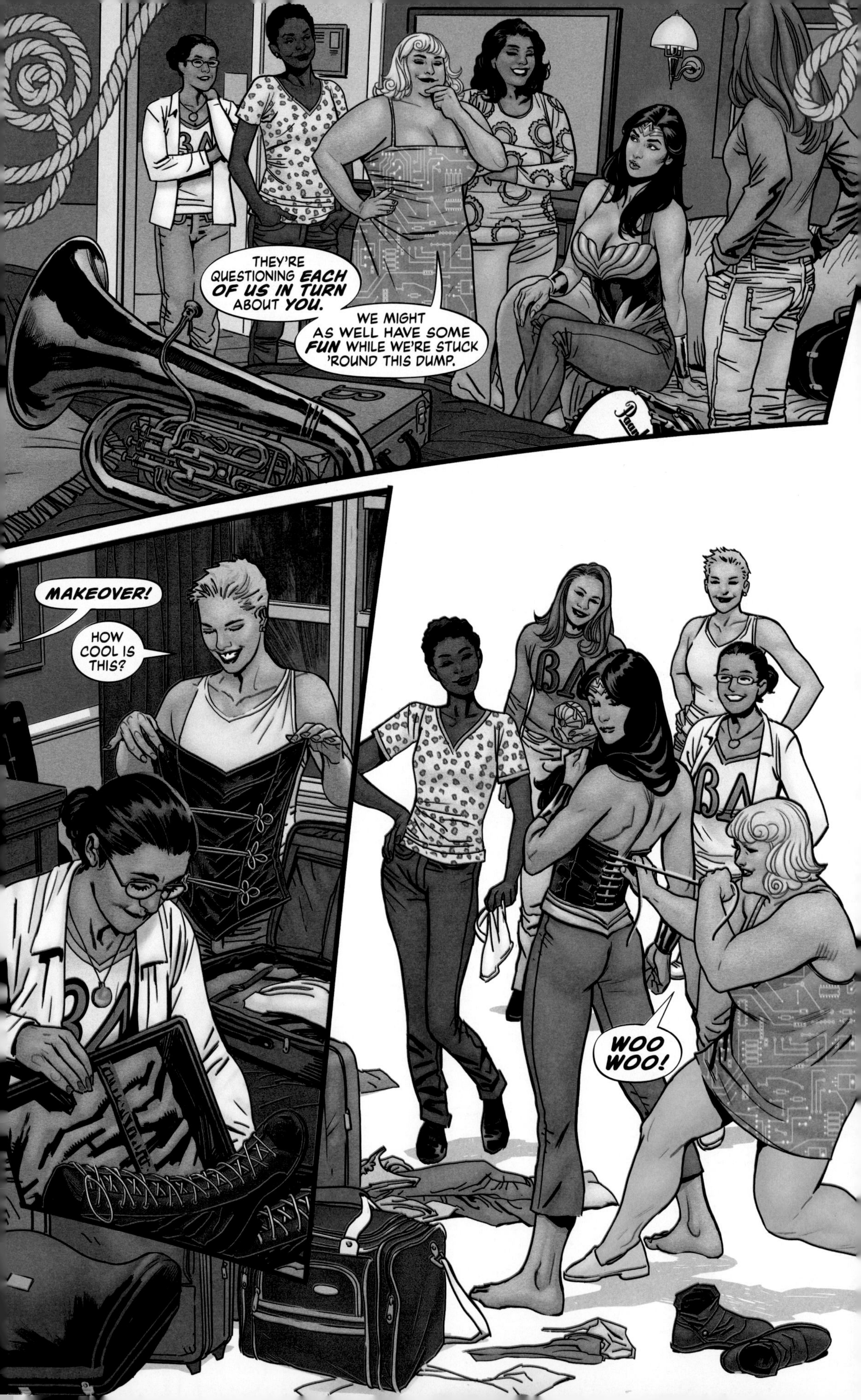
THEY'RE QUESTIONING EACH OF US IN TURN ABOUT YOU.
WE MIGHT AS WELL HAVE SOME FUN WHILE WE'RE STUCK 'ROUND THIS DUMP.
MAKEOVER!
HOW COOL IS THIS?
WOO WOO!

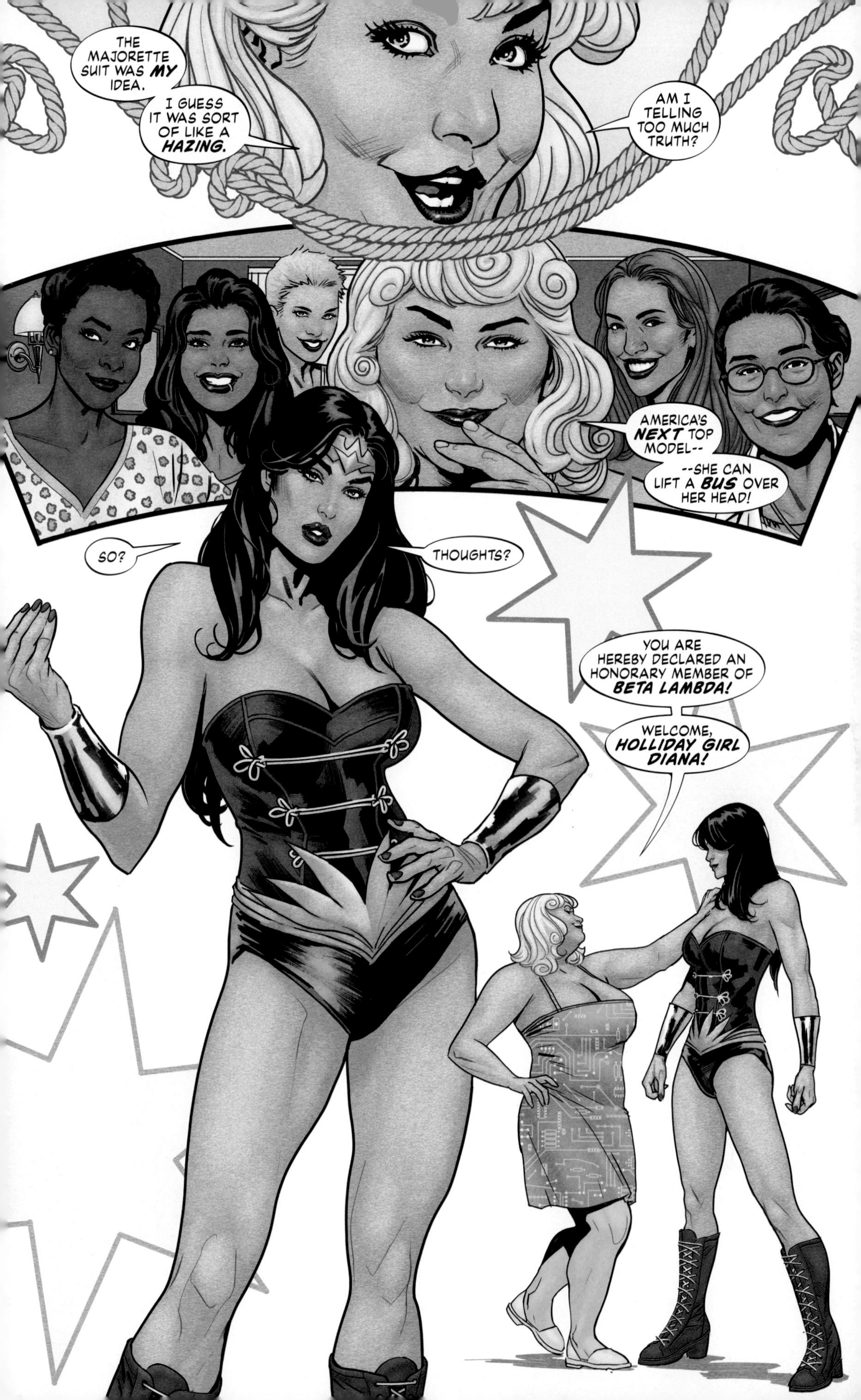
THE MAJORETTE SUIT WAS MY IDEA.
I GUESS IT WAS SORT OF LIKE A HAZING.
AM I TELLING TOO MUCH TRUTH?
AMERICA'S NEXT TOP MODEL--
--SHE CAN LIFT A BUS OVER HER HEAD!
SO?
THOUGHTS?
YOU ARE HEREBY DECLARED AN HONORARY MEMBER OF BETA LAMBDA!
WELCOME, HOLLIDAY GIRL DIANA!

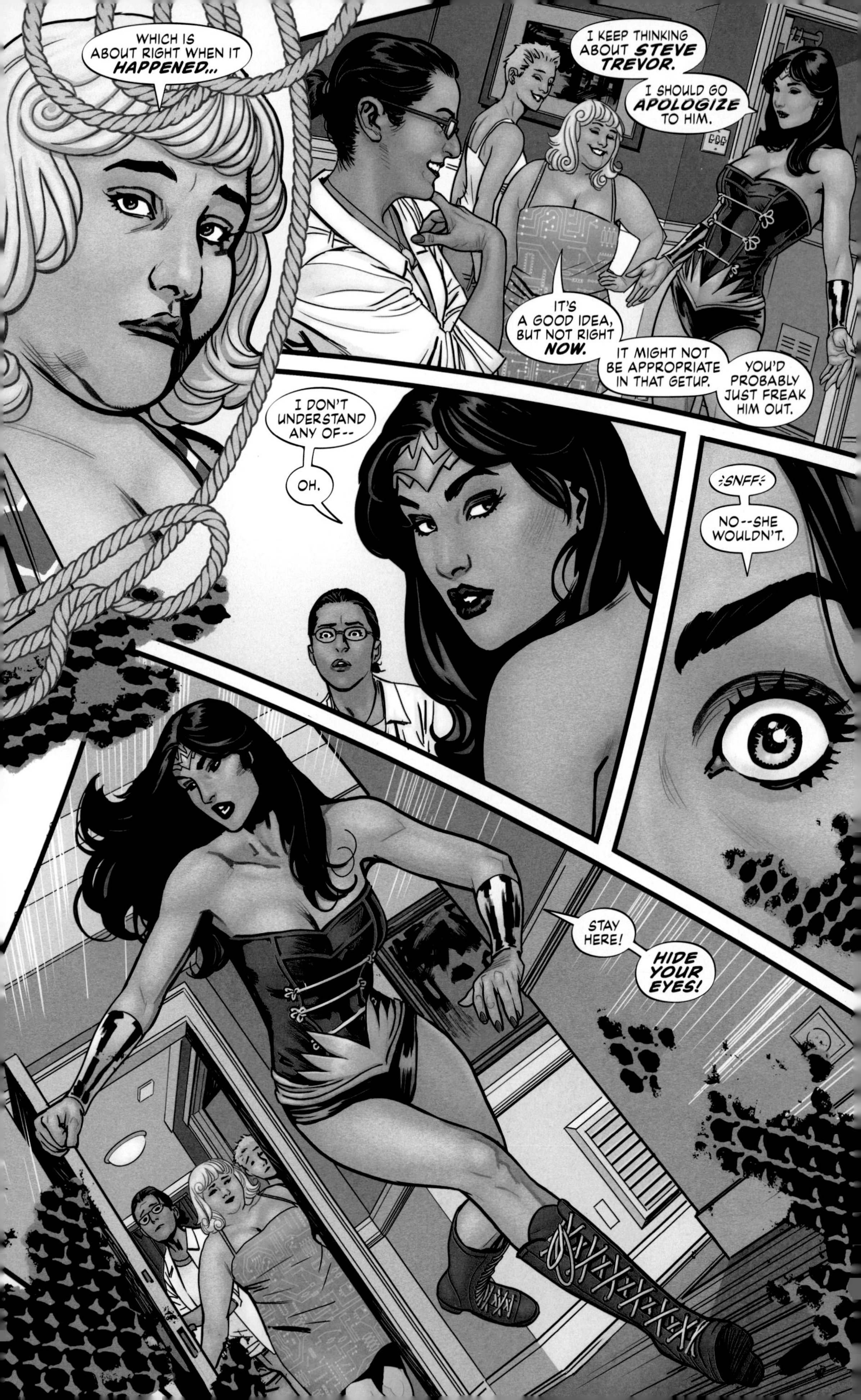
WHICH IS ABOUT RIGHT WHEN IT HAPPENED...
I KEEP THINKING ABOUT STEVE TREVOR.
I SHOULD GO APOLOGIZE TO HIM.
IT'S A GOOD IDEA, BUT NOT RIGHT NOW.
IT MIGHT NOT BE APPROPRIATE IN THAT GETUP.
YOU'D PROBABLY JUST FREAK HIM OUT.
I DON'T UNDERSTAND ANY OF--
OH.
SNFF
NO--SHE WOULDN'T.
STAY HERE!
HIDE YOUR EYES!

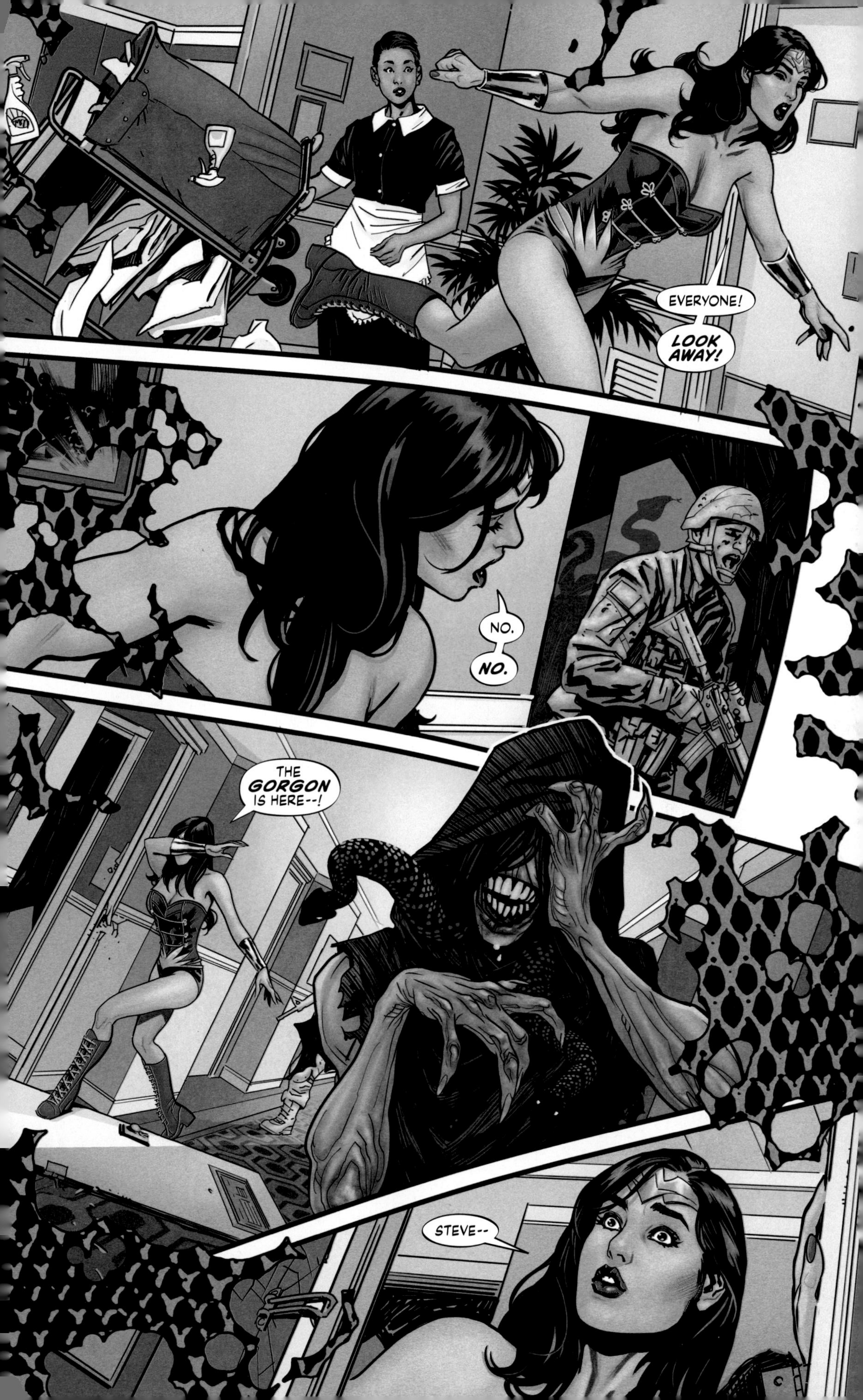
EVERYONE!
LOOK AWAY!
NO.
NO.
THE GORGON IS HERE--!
STEVE--

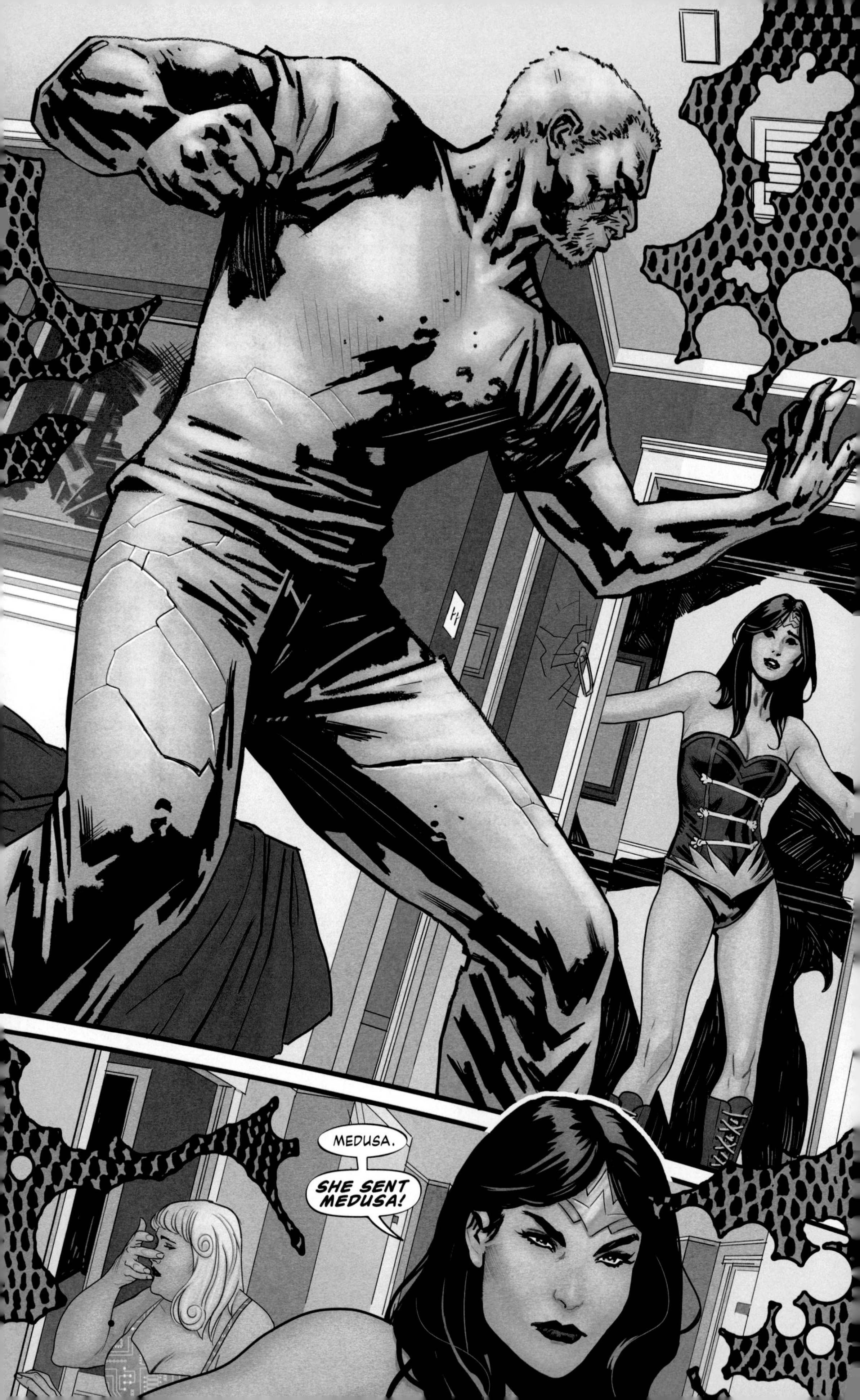
MEDUSA.
SHE SENT MEDUSA!

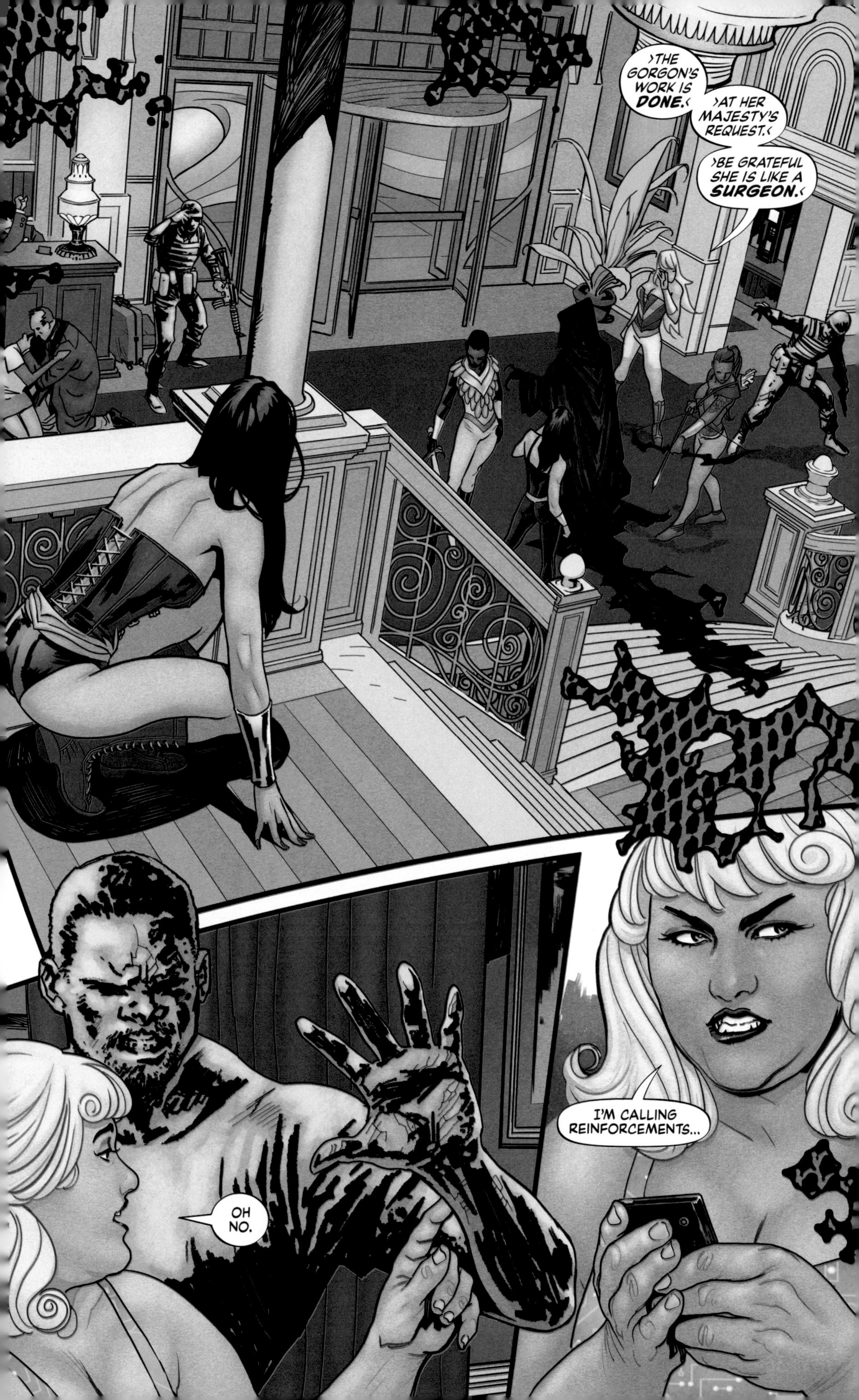
›THE GORGON'S WORK IS DONE.‹
›AT HER MAJESTY'S REQUEST.‹
›BE GRATEFUL SHE IS LIKE A SURGEON.‹
I'M CALLING REINFORCEMENTS...
OH NO.

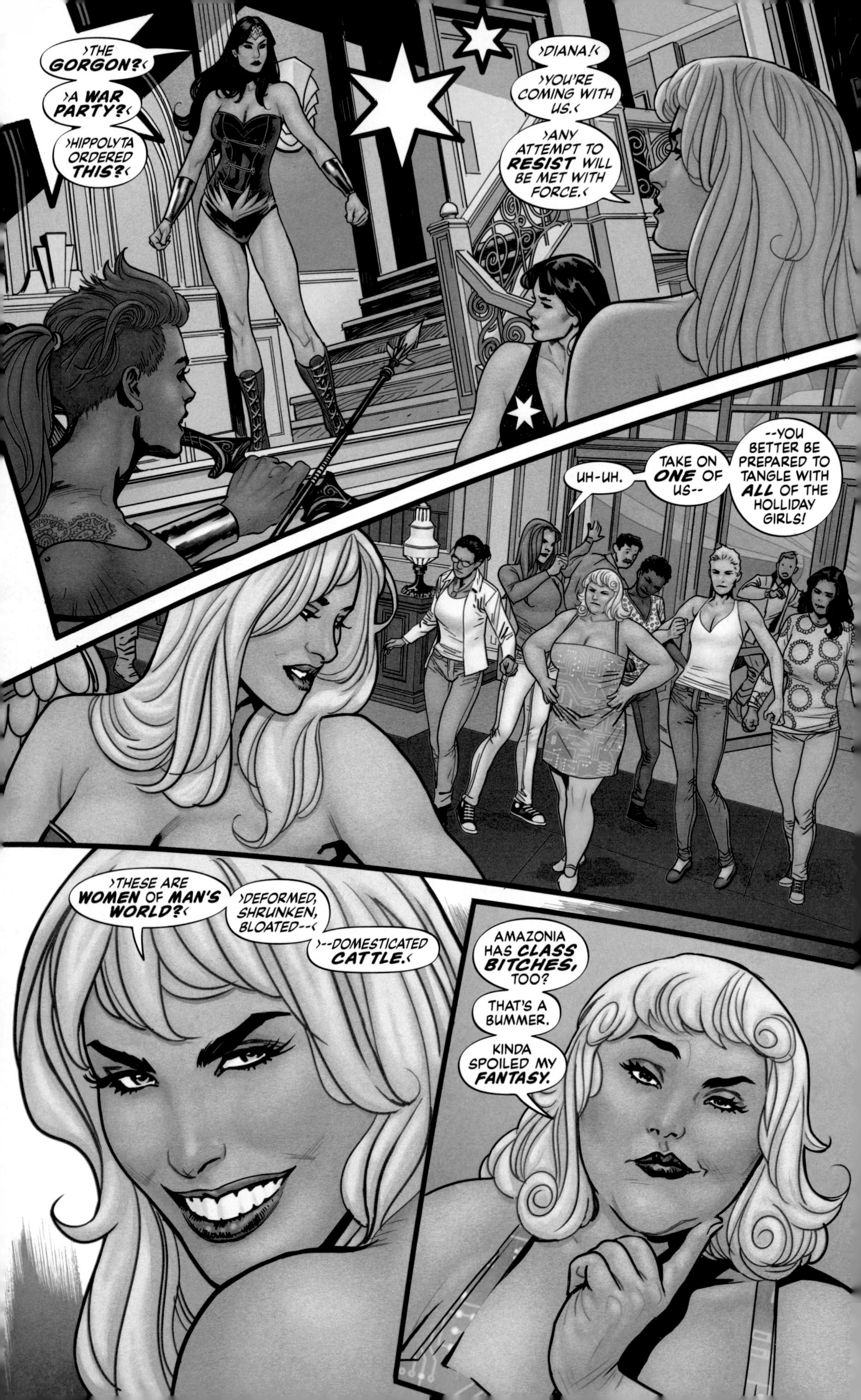
›THE GORGON?‹
›A WAR PARTY?‹
›HIPPOLYTA ORDERED THIS?‹
›DIANA!‹
›YOU'RE COMING WITH US.‹
›ANY ATTEMPT TO RESIST WILL BE MET WITH FORCE.‹
UH-UH.
TAKE ON ONE OF US--
--YOU BETTER BE PREPARED TO TANGLE WITH ALL OF THE HOLLIDAY GIRLS!
›THESE ARE WOMEN OF MAN'S WORLD?‹
›DEFORMED, SHRUNKEN, BLOATED--‹
›--DOMESTICATED CATTLE.‹
AMAZONIA HAS CLASS BITCHES, TOO?
THAT'S A BUMMER.
KINDA SPOILED MY FANTASY.

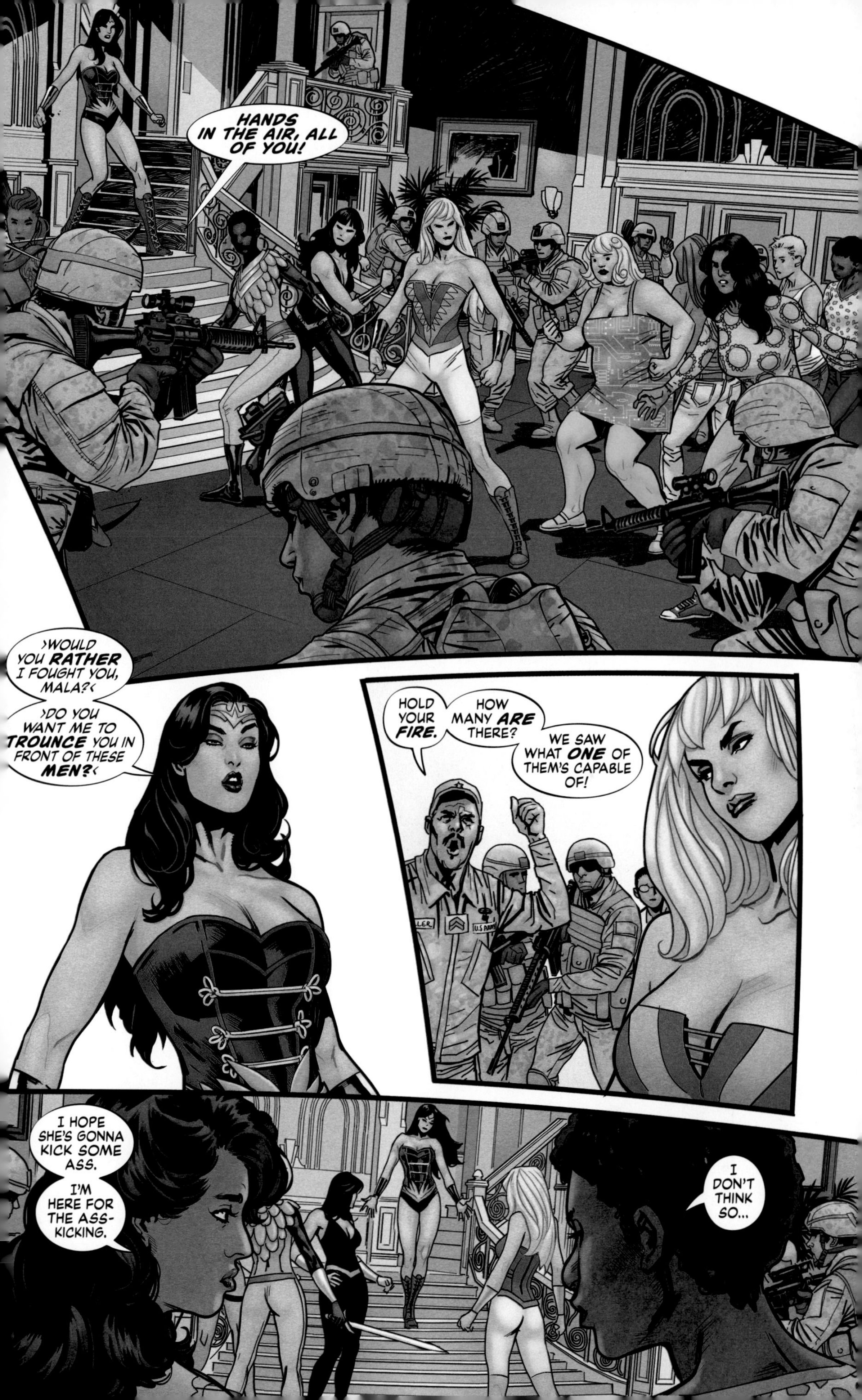
HANDS IN THE AIR, ALL OF YOU!
›WOULD YOU RATHER I FOUGHT YOU, MALA?‹
›DO YOU WANT ME TO TROUNCE YOU IN FRONT OF THESE MEN?‹
HOLD YOUR FIRE.
HOW MANY ARE THERE?
WE SAW WHAT ONE OF THEM'S CAPABLE OF!
I HOPE SHE'S GONNA KICK SOME ASS.
I'M HERE FOR THE ASS-KICKING.
I DON'T THINK SO...

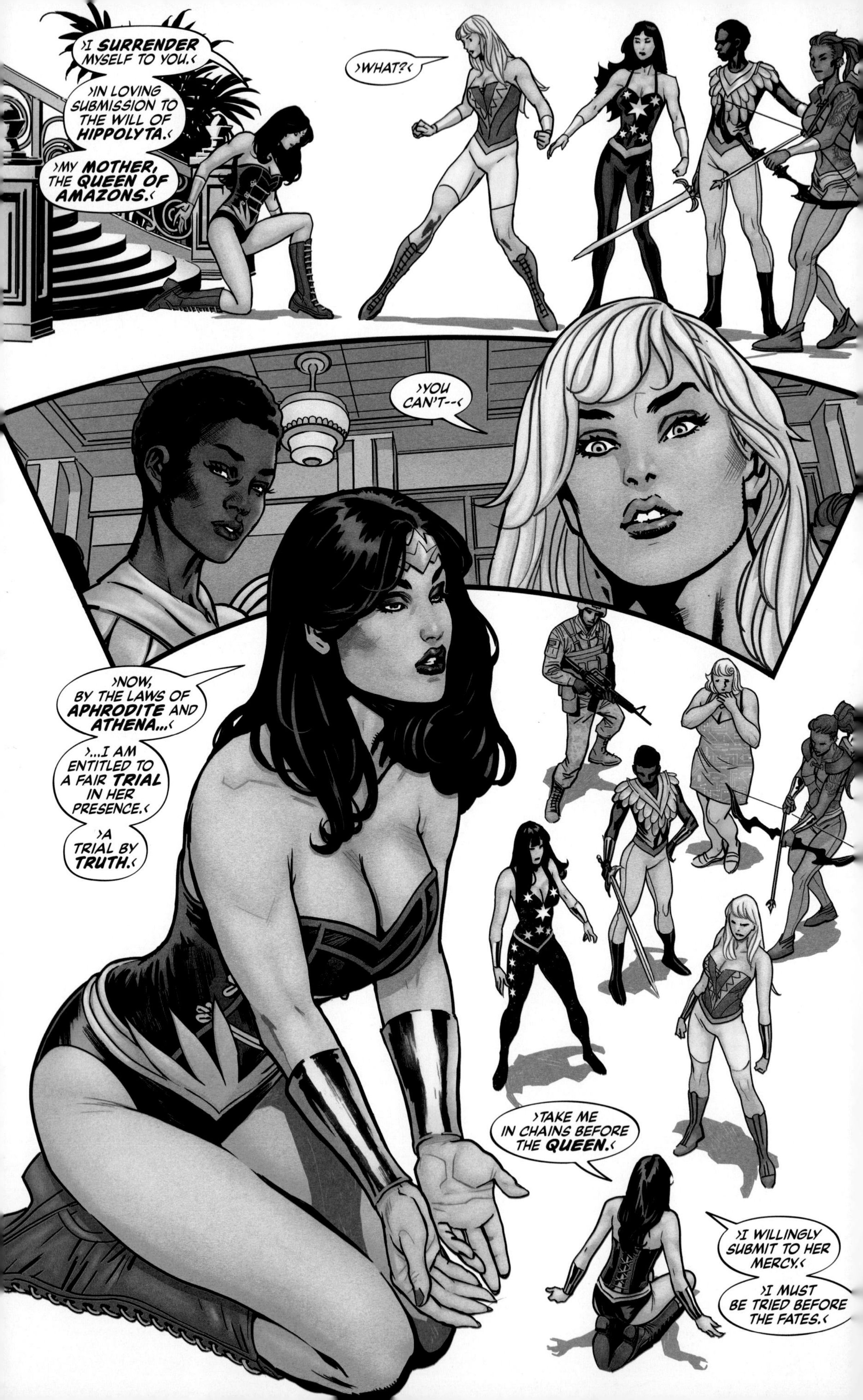
›I SURRENDER MYSELF TO YOU.‹
›IN LOVING SUBMISSION TO THE WILL OF HIPPOLYTA.‹
›MY MOTHER, THE QUEEN OF AMAZONS.‹
›WHAT?‹
›YOU CAN'T--‹
›NOW, BY THE LAWS OF APHRODITE AND ATHENA...‹
›...I AM ENTITLED TO A FAIR TRIAL IN HER PRESENCE.‹
›A TRIAL BY TRUTH.‹
›TAKE ME IN CHAINS BEFORE THE QUEEN.‹
›I WILLINGLY SUBMIT TO HER MERCY.‹
›I MUST BE TRIED BEFORE THE FATES.‹

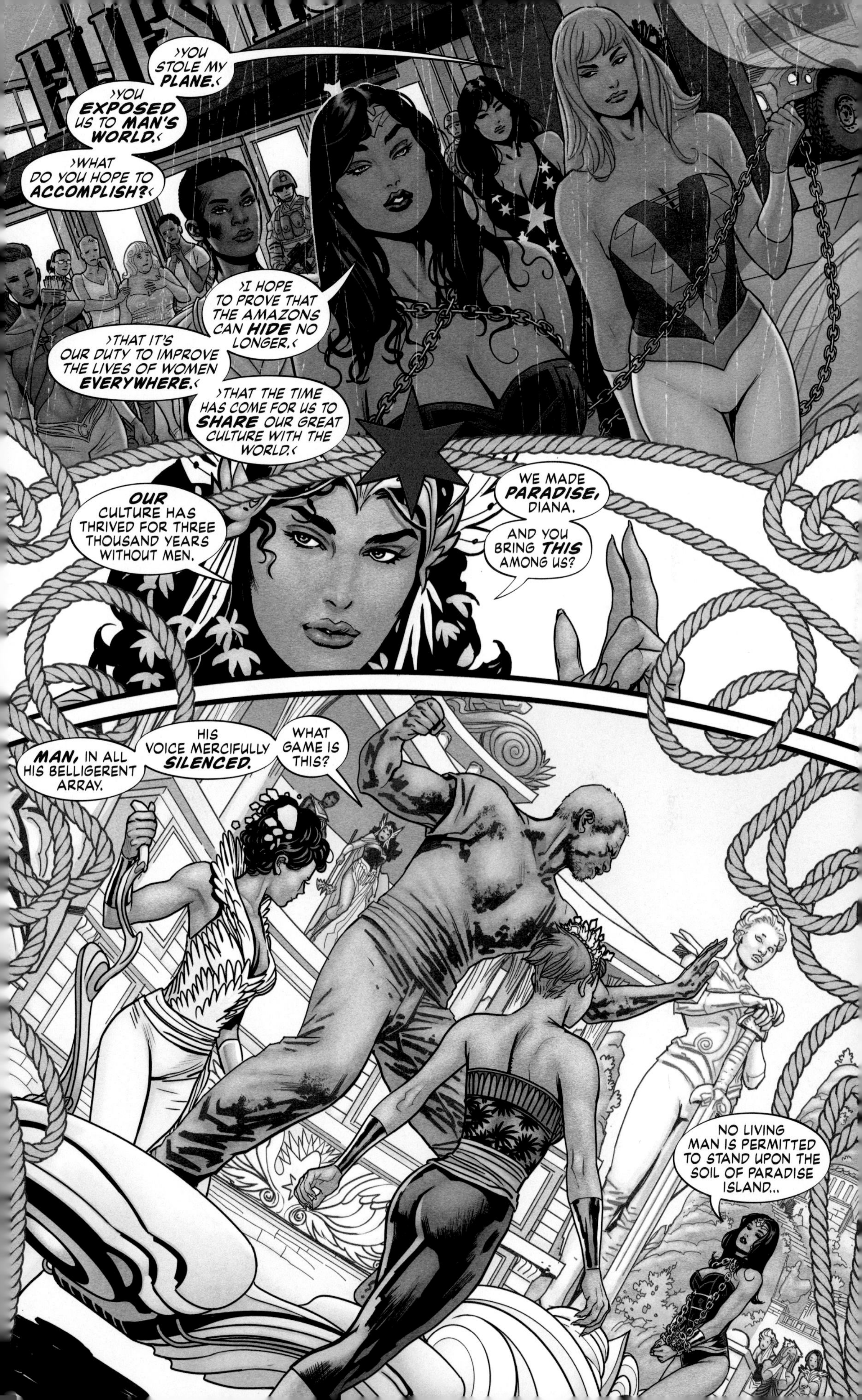
›YOU STOLE MY PLANE.‹
›YOU EXPOSED US TO MAN'S WORLD.‹
›WHAT DO YOU HOPE TO ACCOMPLISH?‹
›I HOPE TO PROVE THAT THE AMAZONS CAN HIDE NO LONGER.‹
›THAT IT'S OUR DUTY TO IMPROVE THE LIVES OF WOMEN EVERYWHERE.‹
›THAT THE TIME HAS COME FOR US TO SHARE OUR GREAT CULTURE WITH THE WORLD.‹
OUR CULTURE HAS THRIVED FOR THREE THOUSAND YEARS WITHOUT MEN.
WE MADE PARADISE, DIANA.
AND YOU BRING THIS AMONG US?
MAN, IN ALL HIS BELLIGERENT ARRAY.
HIS VOICE MERCIFULLY SILENCED.
WHAT GAME IS THIS?
NO LIVING MAN IS PERMITTED TO STAND UPON THE SOIL OF PARADISE ISLAND...

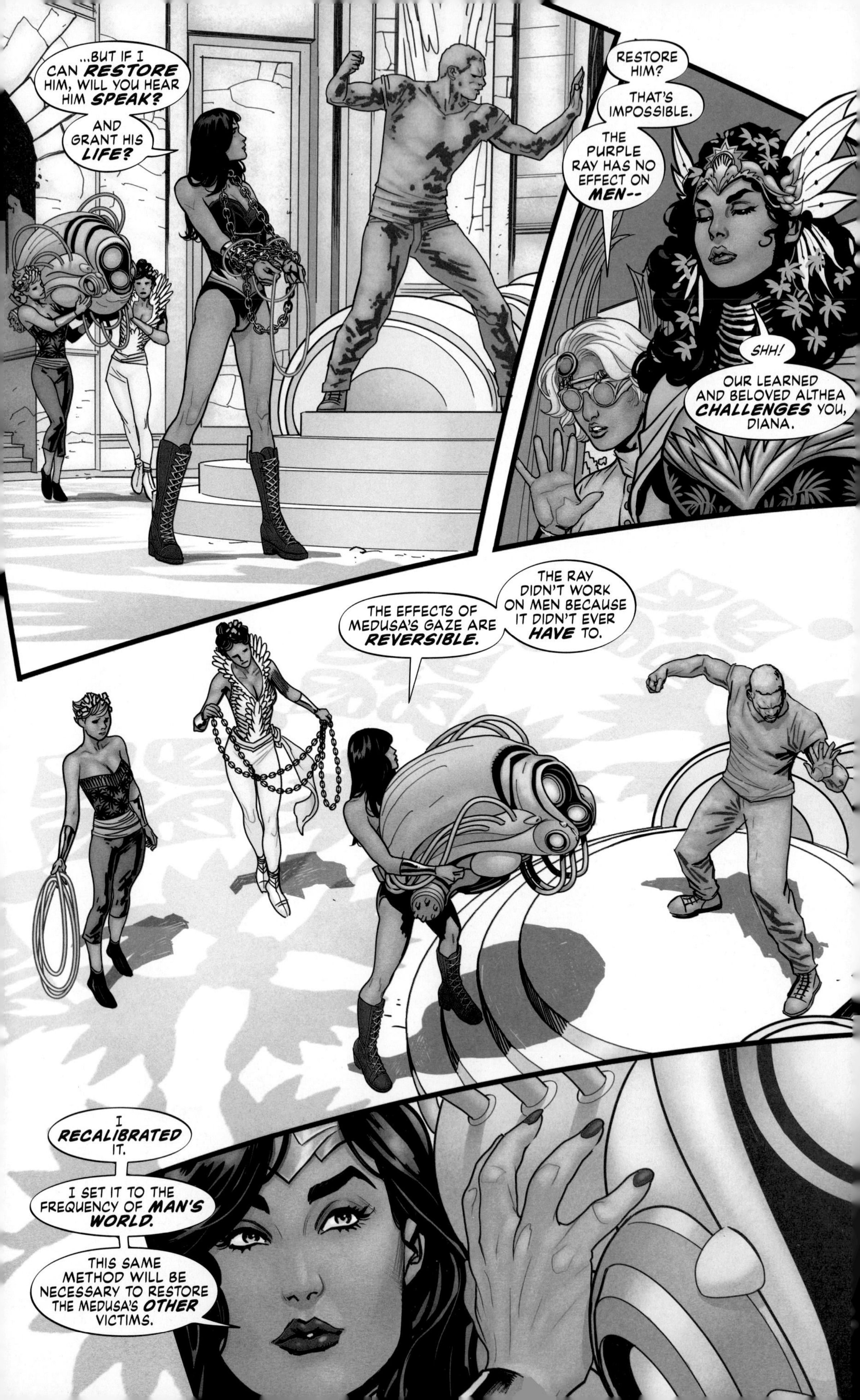

...BUT IF I CAN RESTORE HIM, WILL YOU HEAR HIM SPEAK?
AND GRANT HIS LIFE?
RESTORE HIM?
THAT'S IMPOSSIBLE.
THE PURPLE RAY HAS NO EFFECT ON MEN--
SHH!
OUR LEARNED AND BELOVED ALTHEA CHALLENGES YOU, DIANA.
THE EFFECTS OF MEDUSA'S GAZE ARE REVERSIBLE.
THE RAY DIDN'T WORK ON MEN BECAUSE IT DIDN'T EVER HAVE TO.
I RECALIBRATED IT.
I SET IT TO THE FREQUENCY OF MAN'S WORLD.
THIS SAME METHOD WILL BE NECESSARY TO RESTORE THE MEDUSA'S OTHER VICTIMS.

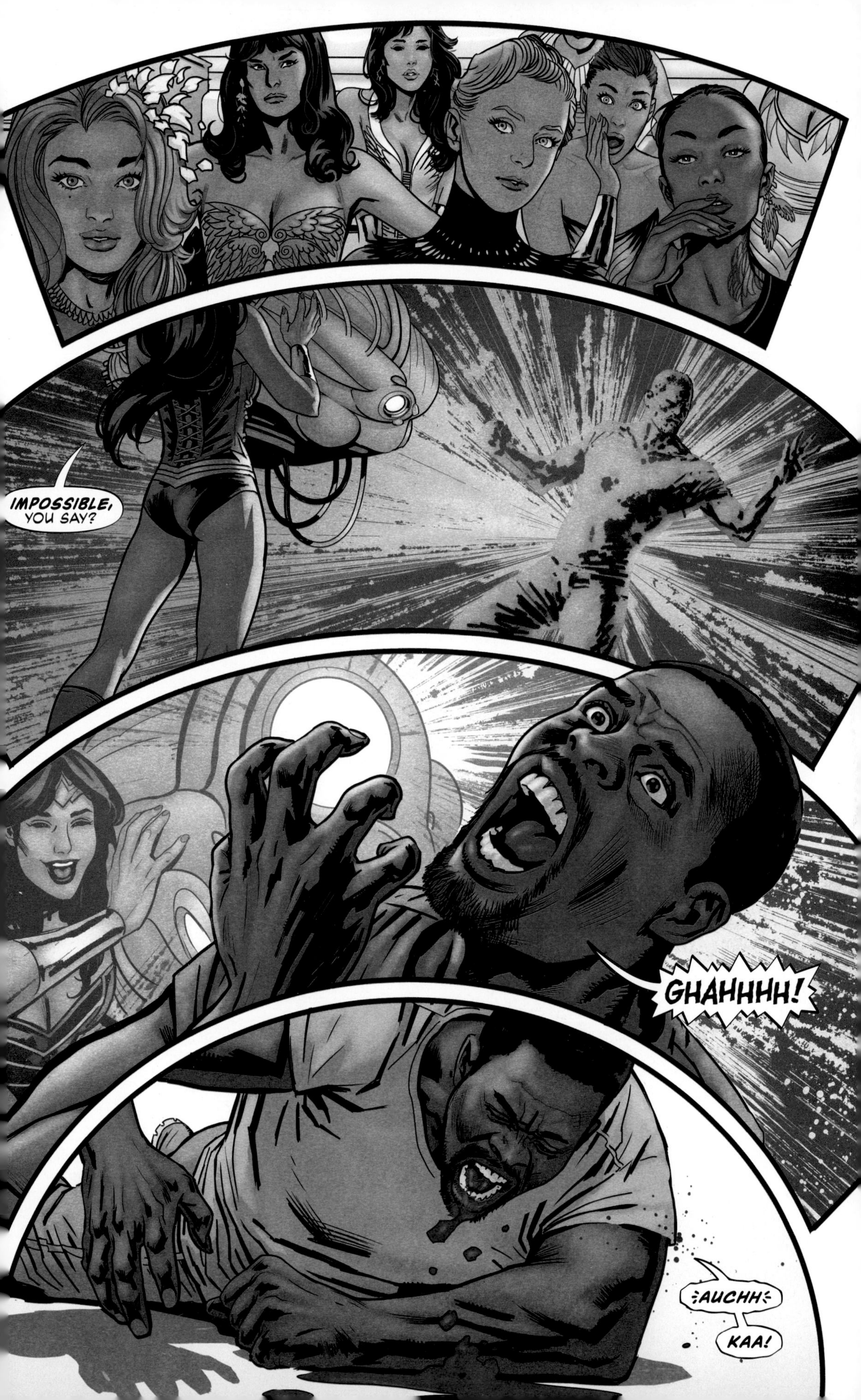
IMPOSSIBLE, YOU SAY?
GHAHHHH!
AUCHH
KAA!

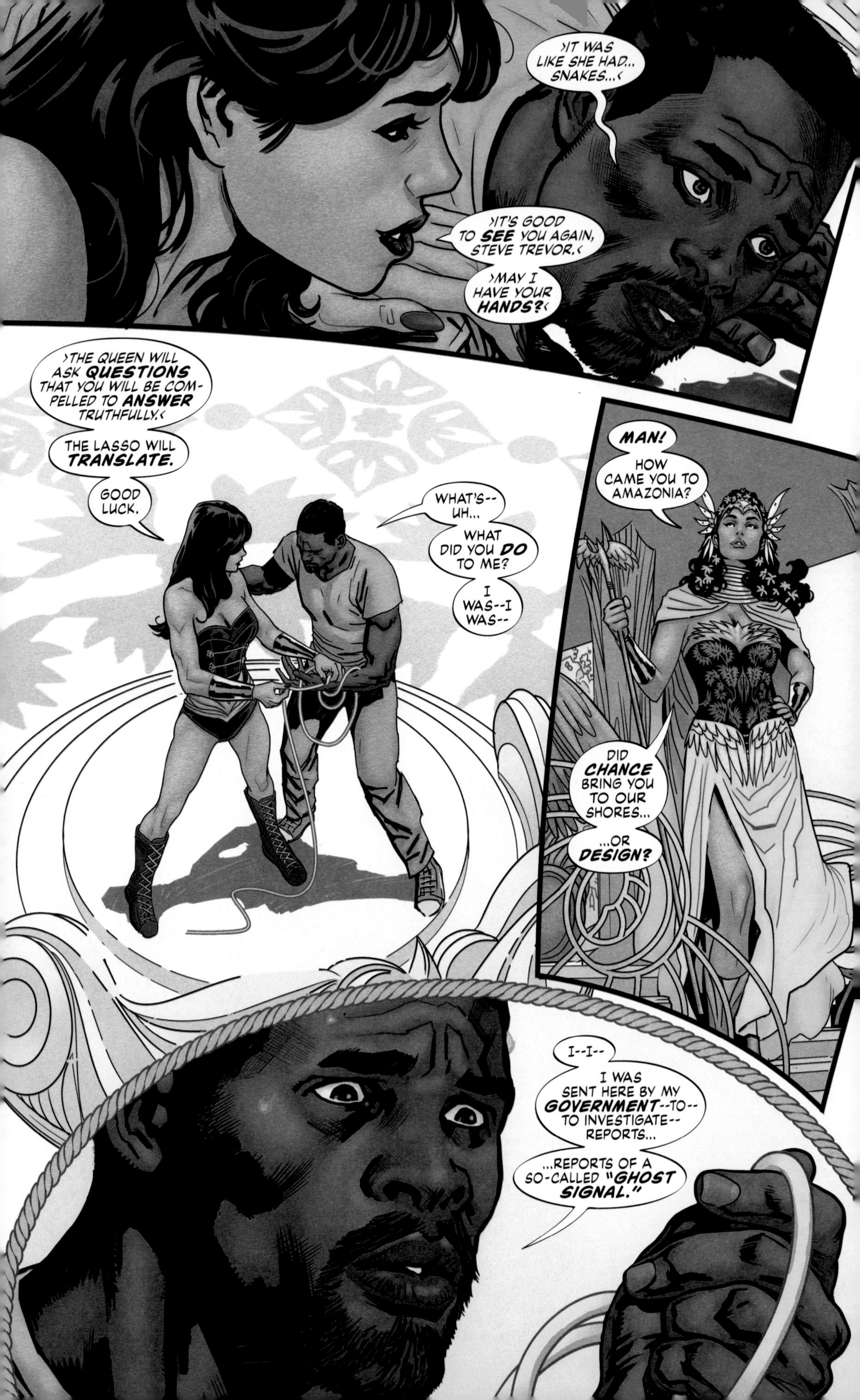
›IT WAS LIKE SHE HAD... SNAKES...‹
›IT'S GOOD TO SEE YOU AGAIN, STEVE TREVOR.‹
›MAY I HAVE YOUR HANDS?‹
›THE QUEEN WILL ASK QUESTIONS THAT YOU WILL BE COMPELLED TO ANSWER TRUTHFULLY.‹
THE LASSO WILL TRANSLATE.
GOOD LUCK.
WHAT'S-- UH...
WHAT DID YOU DO TO ME?
I WAS--I WAS--
MAN!
HOW CAME YOU TO AMAZONIA?
DID CHANCE BRING YOU TO OUR SHORES...
...OR DESIGN?
I--I--
I WAS SENT HERE BY MY GOVERNMENT--TO--TO INVESTIGATE--REPORTS...
...REPORTS OF A SO-CALLED "GHOST SIGNAL."

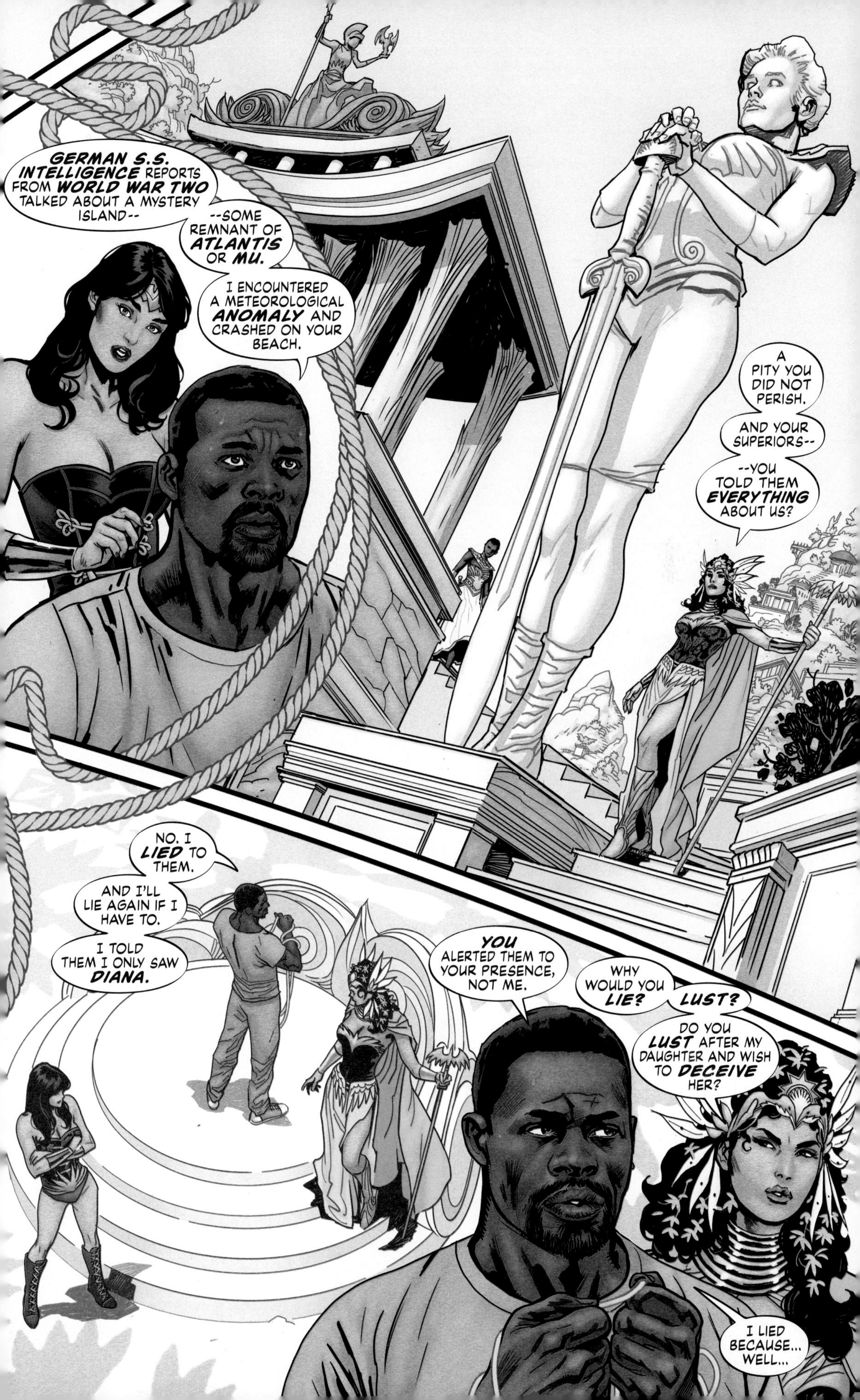
GERMAN S.S. INTELLIGENCE REPORTS FROM WORLD WAR TWO TALKED ABOUT A MYSTERY ISLAND--
--SOME REMNANT OF ATLANTIS OR MU.
I ENCOUNTERED A METEOROLOGICAL ANOMALY AND CRASHED ON YOUR BEACH.
A PITY YOU DID NOT PERISH.
AND YOUR SUPERIORS--
--YOU TOLD THEM EVERYTHING ABOUT US?
NO. I LIED TO THEM.
AND I'LL LIE AGAIN IF I HAVE TO.
I TOLD THEM I ONLY SAW DIANA.
YOU ALERTED THEM TO YOUR PRESENCE, NOT ME.
WHY WOULD YOU LIE?
LUST?
DO YOU LUST AFTER MY DAUGHTER AND WISH TO DECEIVE HER?
I LIED BECAUSE... WELL...

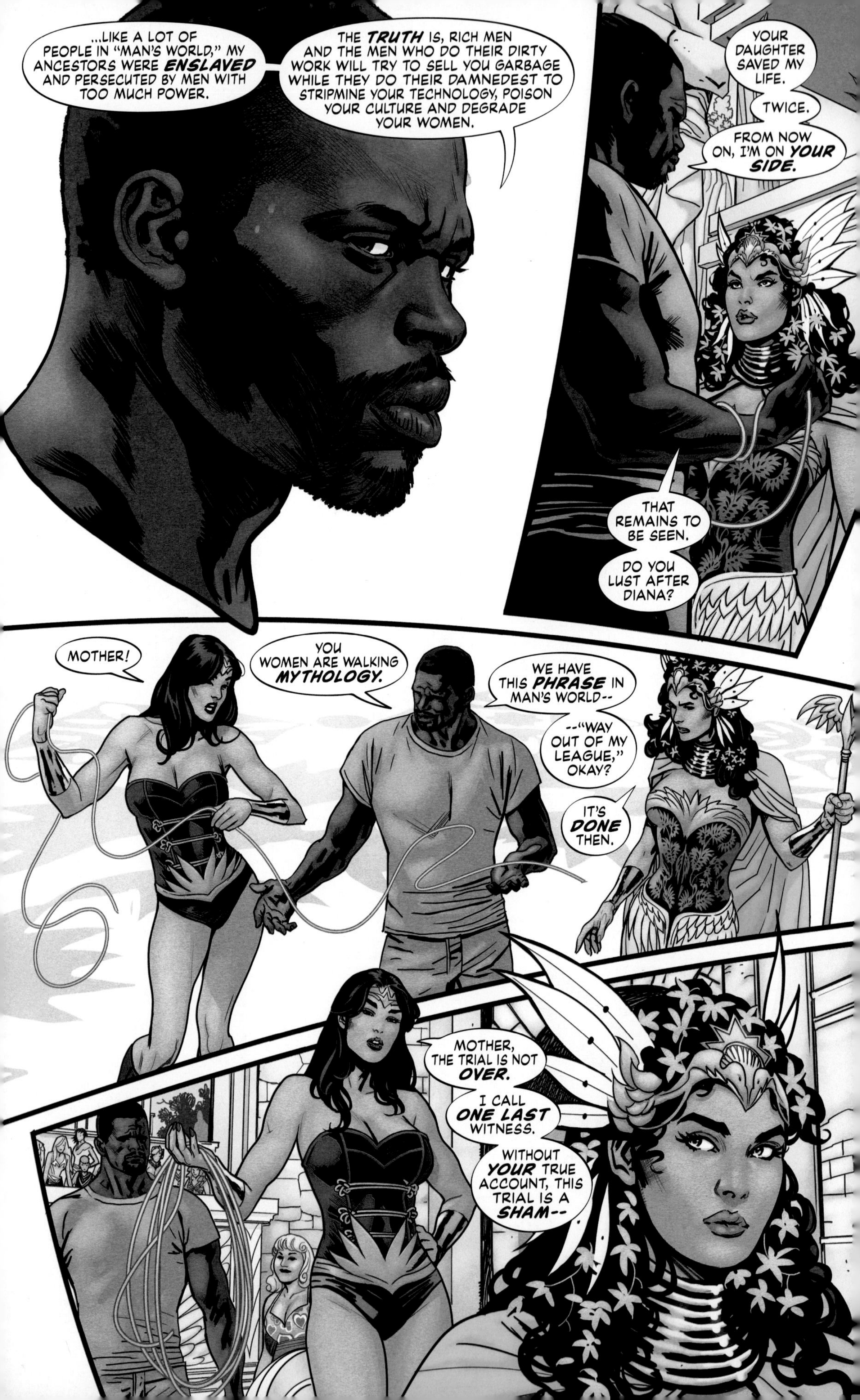
...LIKE A LOT OF PEOPLE IN "MAN'S WORLD," MY ANCESTORS WERE ENSLAVED AND PERSECUTED BY MEN WITH TOO MUCH POWER.
THE TRUTH IS, RICH MEN AND THE MEN WHO DO THEIR DIRTY WORK WILL TRY TO SELL YOU GARBAGE WHILE THEY DO THEIR DAMNEDEST TO STRIPMINE YOUR TECHNOLOGY, POISON YOUR CULTURE AND DEGRADE YOUR WOMEN.
YOUR DAUGHTER SAVED MY LIFE.
TWICE.
FROM NOW ON, I'M ON YOUR SIDE.
THAT REMAINS TO BE SEEN.
DO YOU LUST AFTER DIANA?
MOTHER!
YOU WOMEN ARE WALKING MYTHOLOGY.
WE HAVE THIS PHRASE IN MAN'S WORLD--
--"WAY OUT OF MY LEAGUE," OKAY?
IT'S DONE THEN.
MOTHER, THE TRIAL IS NOT OVER.
I CALL ONE LAST WITNESS.
WITHOUT YOUR TRUE ACCOUNT, THIS TRIAL IS A SHAM--

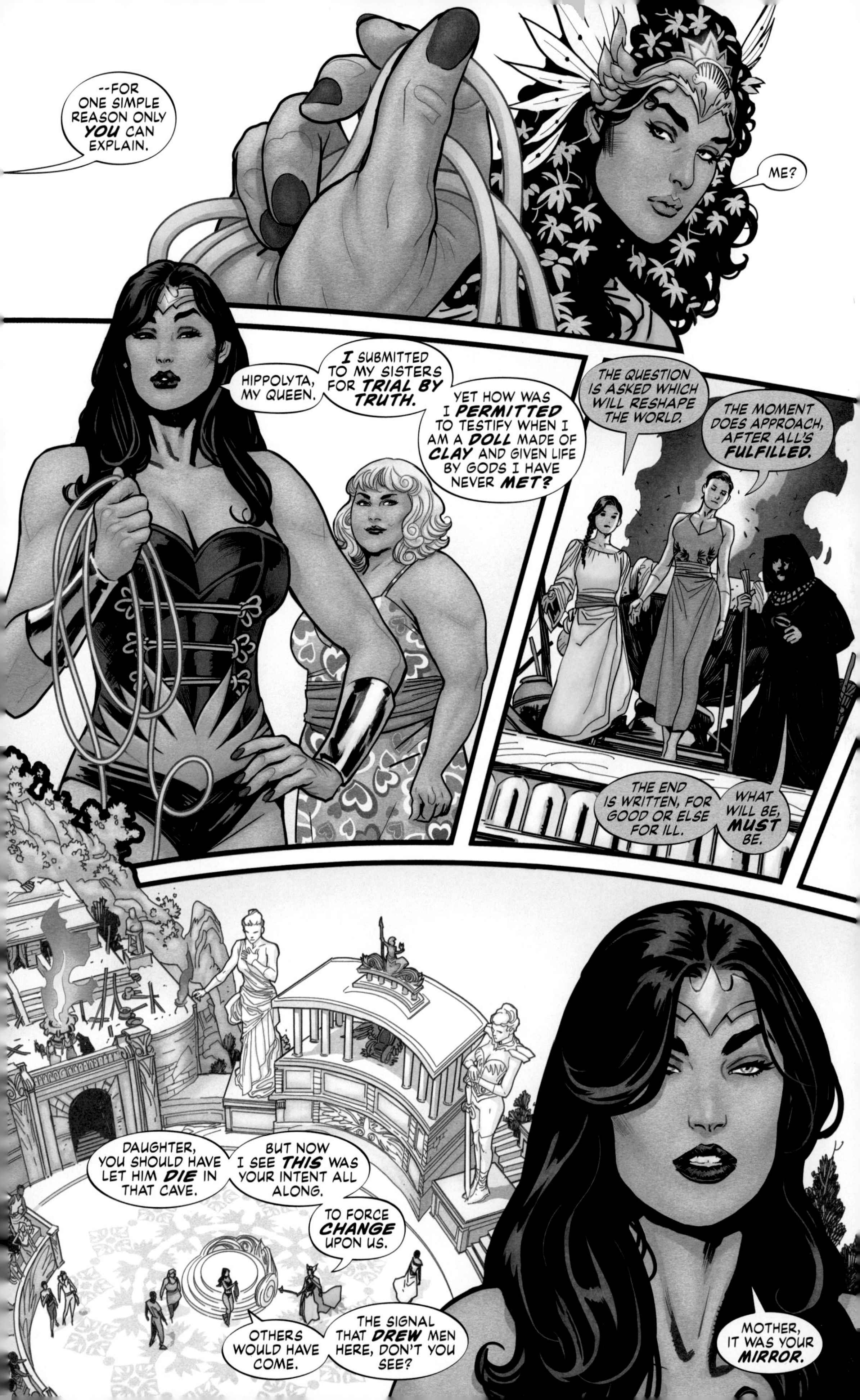
--FOR ONE SIMPLE REASON ONLY YOU CAN EXPLAIN.
ME?
HIPPOLYTA, MY QUEEN.
I SUBMITTED TO MY SISTERS FOR TRIAL BY TRUTH.
YET HOW WAS I PERMITTED TO TESTIFY WHEN I AM A DOLL MADE OF CLAY AND GIVEN LIFE BY GODS I HAVE NEVER MET?
THE QUESTION IS ASKED WHICH WILL RESHAPE THE WORLD.
THE MOMENT DOES APPROACH, AFTER ALL'S FULFILLED.
THE END IS WRITTEN, FOR GOOD OR ELSE FOR ILL.
WHAT WILL BE, MUST BE.
DAUGHTER, YOU SHOULD HAVE LET HIM DIE IN THAT CAVE.
BUT NOW I SEE THIS WAS YOUR INTENT ALL ALONG.
TO FORCE CHANGE UPON US.
OTHERS WOULD HAVE COME.
THE SIGNAL THAT DREW MEN HERE, DON'T YOU SEE?
MOTHER, IT WAS YOUR MIRROR.

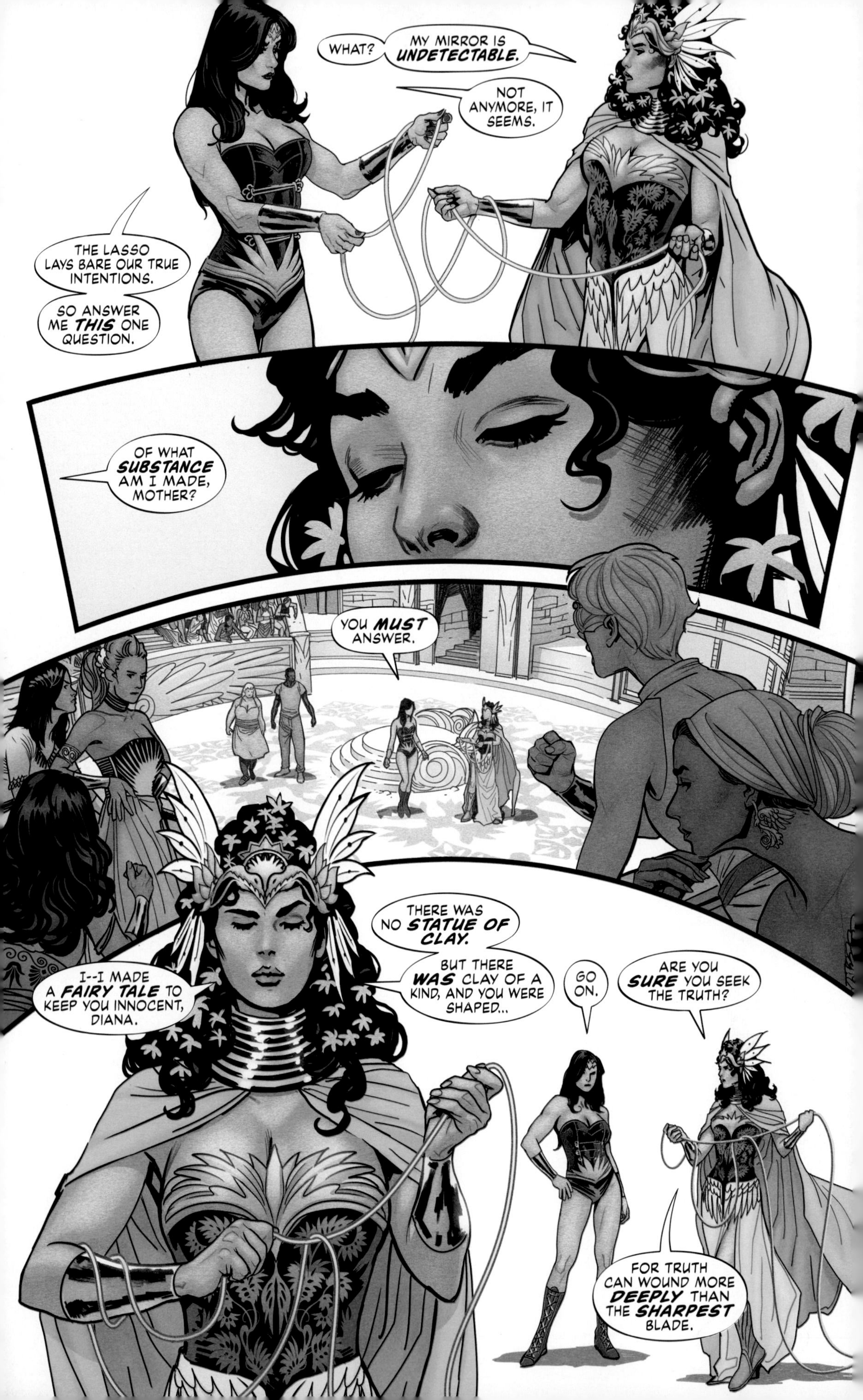
WHAT?
MY MIRROR IS UNDETECTABLE.
NOT ANYMORE, IT SEEMS.
THE LASSO LAYS BARE OUR TRUE INTENTIONS.
SO ANSWER ME THIS ONE QUESTION.
OF WHAT SUBSTANCE AM I MADE, MOTHER?
YOU MUST ANSWER.
I--I MADE A FAIRY TALE TO KEEP YOU INNOCENT, DIANA.
THERE WAS NO STATUE OF CLAY.
BUT THERE WAS CLAY OF A KIND, AND YOU WERE SHAPED...
GO ON.
ARE YOU SURE YOU SEEK THE TRUTH?
FOR TRUTH CAN WOUND MORE DEEPLY THAN THE SHARPEST BLADE.

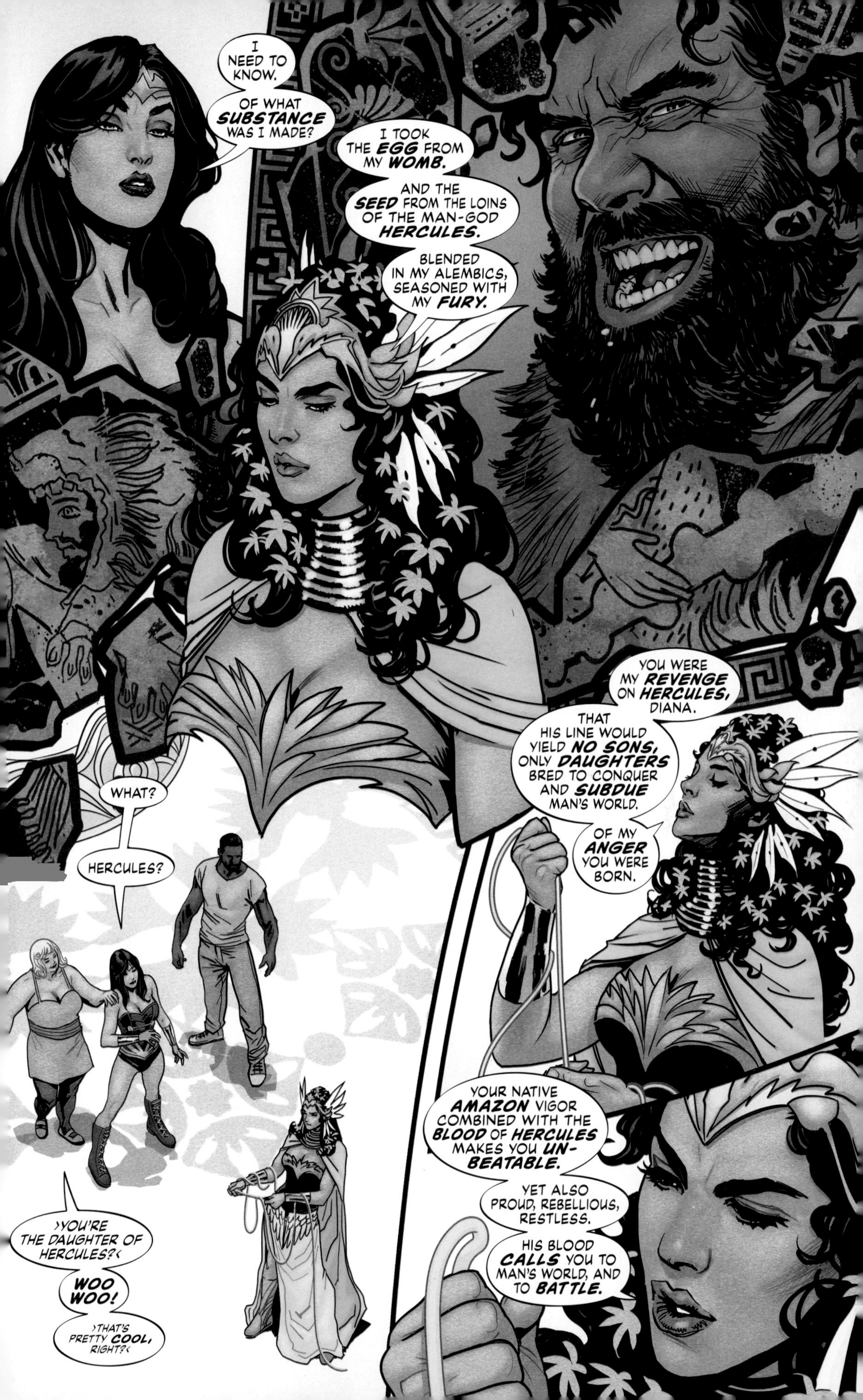
I NEED TO KNOW.
OF WHAT SUBSTANCE WAS I MADE?
I TOOK THE EGG FROM MY WOMB.
AND THE SEED FROM THE LOINS OF THE MAN-GOD HERCULES.
BLENDED IN MY ALEMBICS, SEASONED WITH MY FURY.
YOU WERE MY REVENGE ON HERCULES, DIANA.
THAT HIS LINE WOULD YIELD NO SONS, ONLY DAUGHTERS BRED TO CONQUER AND SUBDUE MAN'S WORLD.
OF MY ANGER YOU WERE BORN.
WHAT?
HERCULES?
›YOU'RE THE DAUGHTER OF HERCULES?‹
WOO WOO!
›THAT'S PRETTY COOL, RIGHT?‹
YOUR NATIVE AMAZON VIGOR COMBINED WITH THE BLOOD OF HERCULES MAKES YOU UN-BEATABLE.
YET ALSO PROUD, REBELLIOUS, RESTLESS.
HIS BLOOD CALLS YOU TO MAN'S WORLD, AND TO BATTLE.

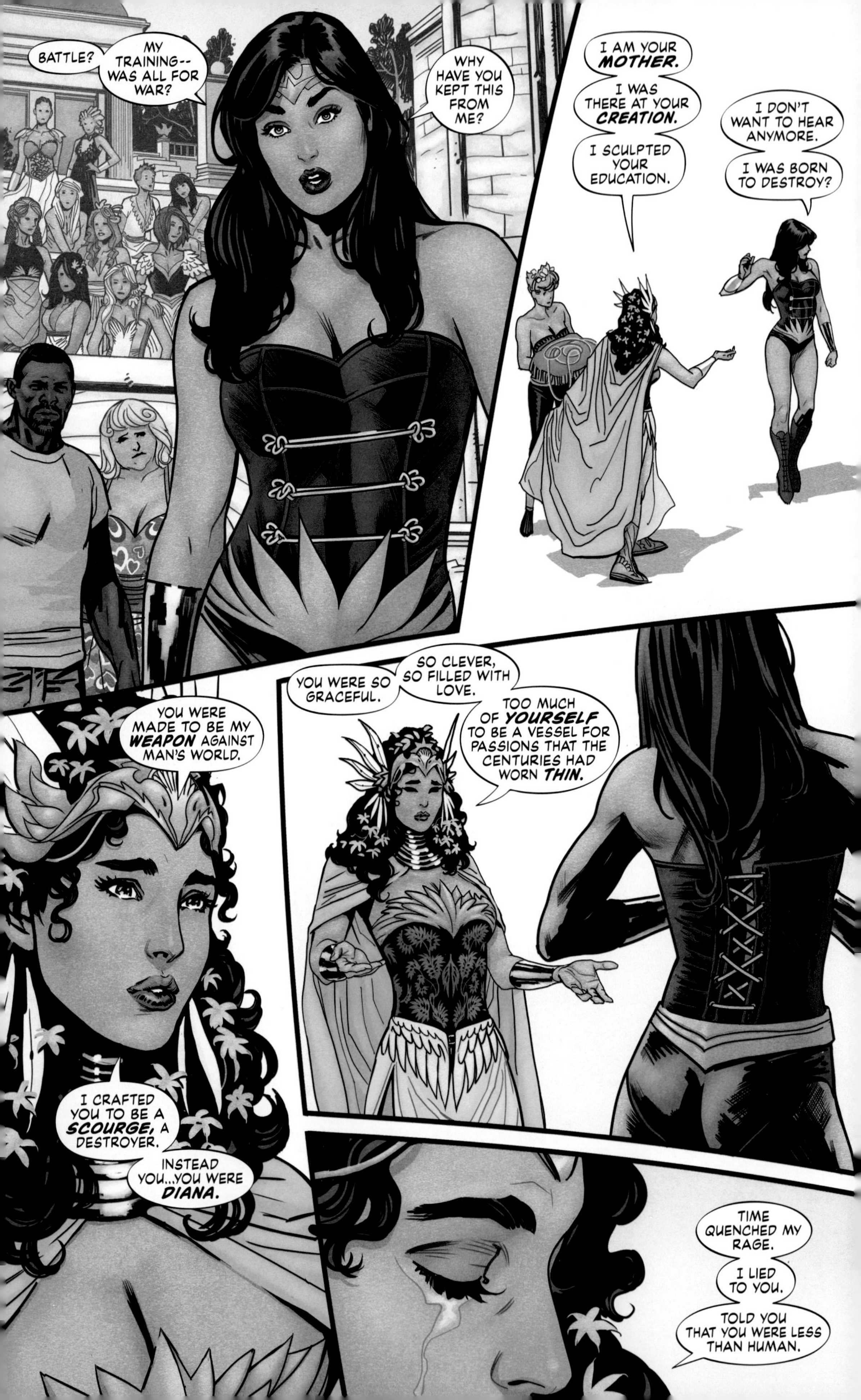
BATTLE?
MY TRAINING-- WAS ALL FOR WAR?
WHY HAVE YOU KEPT THIS FROM ME?
I AM YOUR MOTHER.
I WAS THERE AT YOUR CREATION.
I SCULPTED YOUR EDUCATION.
I DON'T WANT TO HEAR ANYMORE.
I WAS BORN TO DESTROY?
YOU WERE MADE TO BE MY WEAPON AGAINST MAN'S WORLD.
I CRAFTED YOU TO BE A SCOURGE, A DESTROYER.
INSTEAD YOU...YOU WERE DIANA.
YOU WERE SO GRACEFUL.
SO CLEVER, SO FILLED WITH LOVE.
TOO MUCH OF YOURSELF TO BE A VESSEL FOR PASSIONS THAT THE CENTURIES HAD WORN THIN.
TIME QUENCHED MY RAGE.
I LIED TO YOU.
TOLD YOU THAT YOU WERE LESS THAN HUMAN.

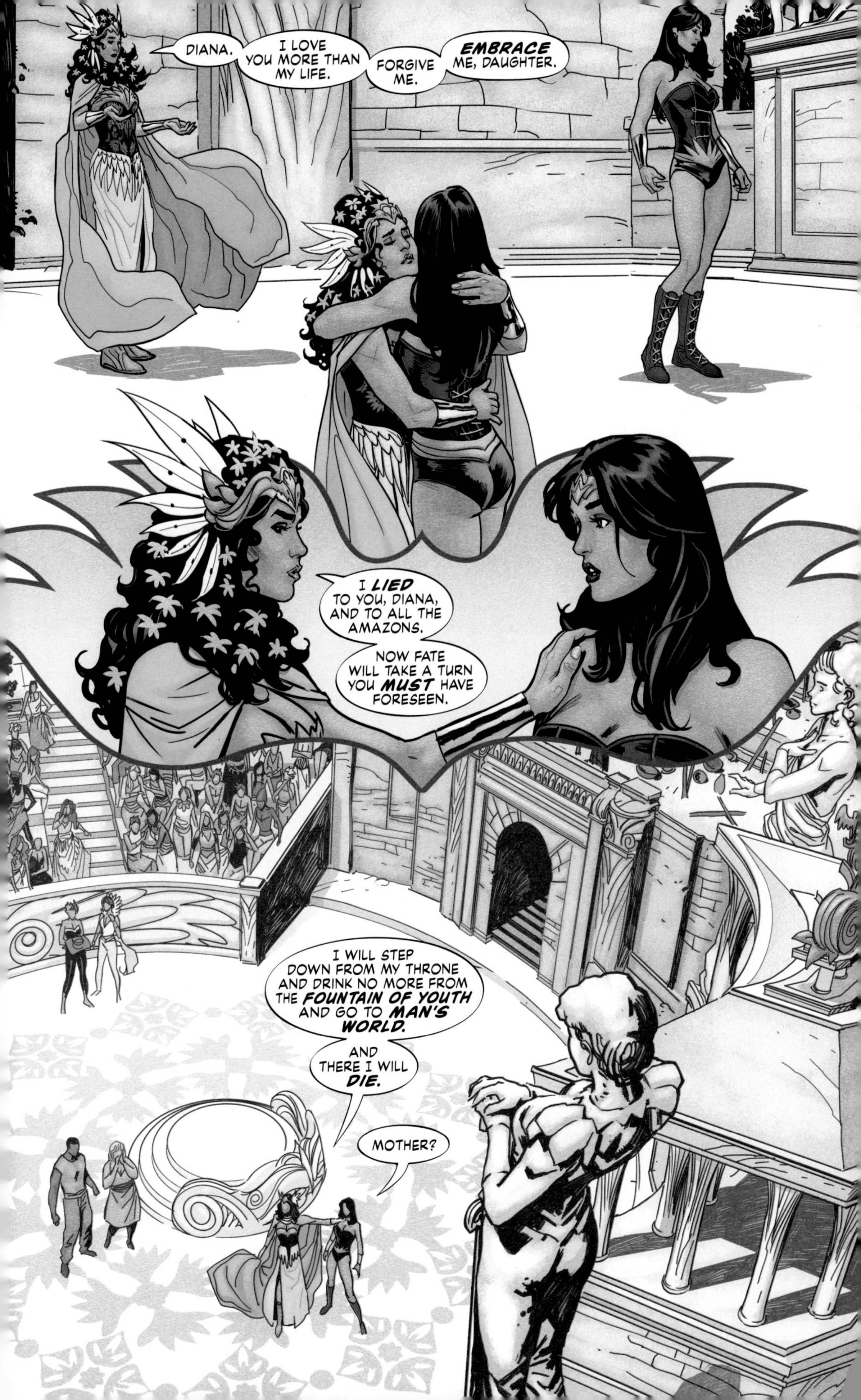
DIANA.
I LOVE YOU MORE THAN MY LIFE.
FORGIVE ME.
EMBRACE ME, DAUGHTER.
I LIED TO YOU, DIANA, AND TO ALL THE AMAZONS.
NOW FATE WILL TAKE A TURN YOU MUST HAVE FORESEEN.
I WILL STEP DOWN FROM MY THRONE AND DRINK NO MORE FROM THE FOUNTAIN OF YOUTH AND GO TO MAN'S WORLD.
AND THERE I WILL DIE.
MOTHER?

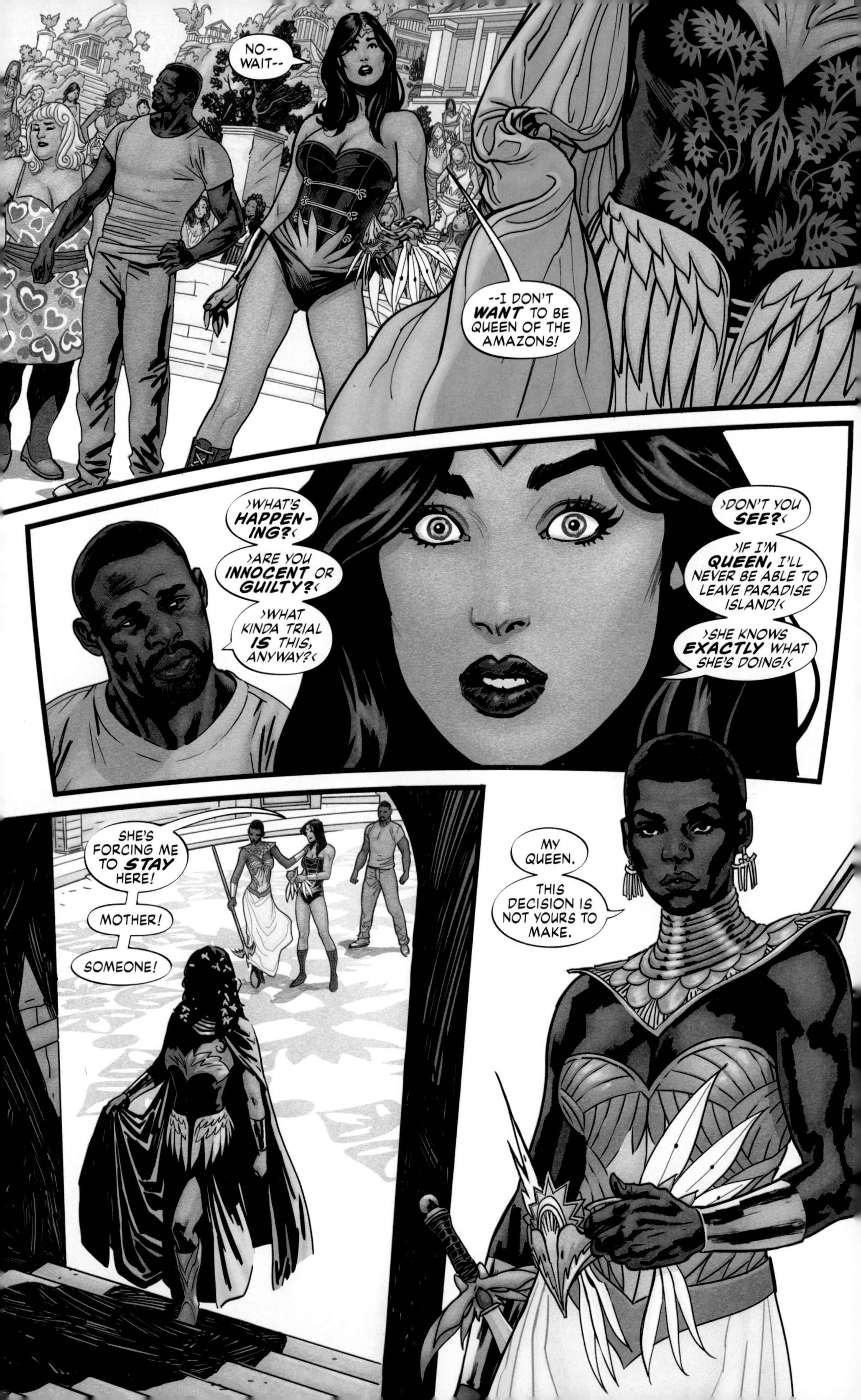
NO-- WAIT--
--I DON'T WANT TO BE QUEEN OF THE AMAZONS!
›WHAT'S HAPPENING?‹
›ARE YOU INNOCENT OR GUILTY?‹
›WHAT KINDA TRIAL IS THIS, ANYWAY?‹
›DON'T YOU SEE?‹
›IF I'M QUEEN, I'LL NEVER BE ABLE TO LEAVE PARADISE ISLAND!‹
›SHE KNOWS EXACTLY WHAT SHE'S DOING!‹
SHE'S FORCING ME TO STAY HERE!
MOTHER!
SOMEONE!
MY QUEEN.
THIS DECISION IS NOT YOURS TO MAKE.

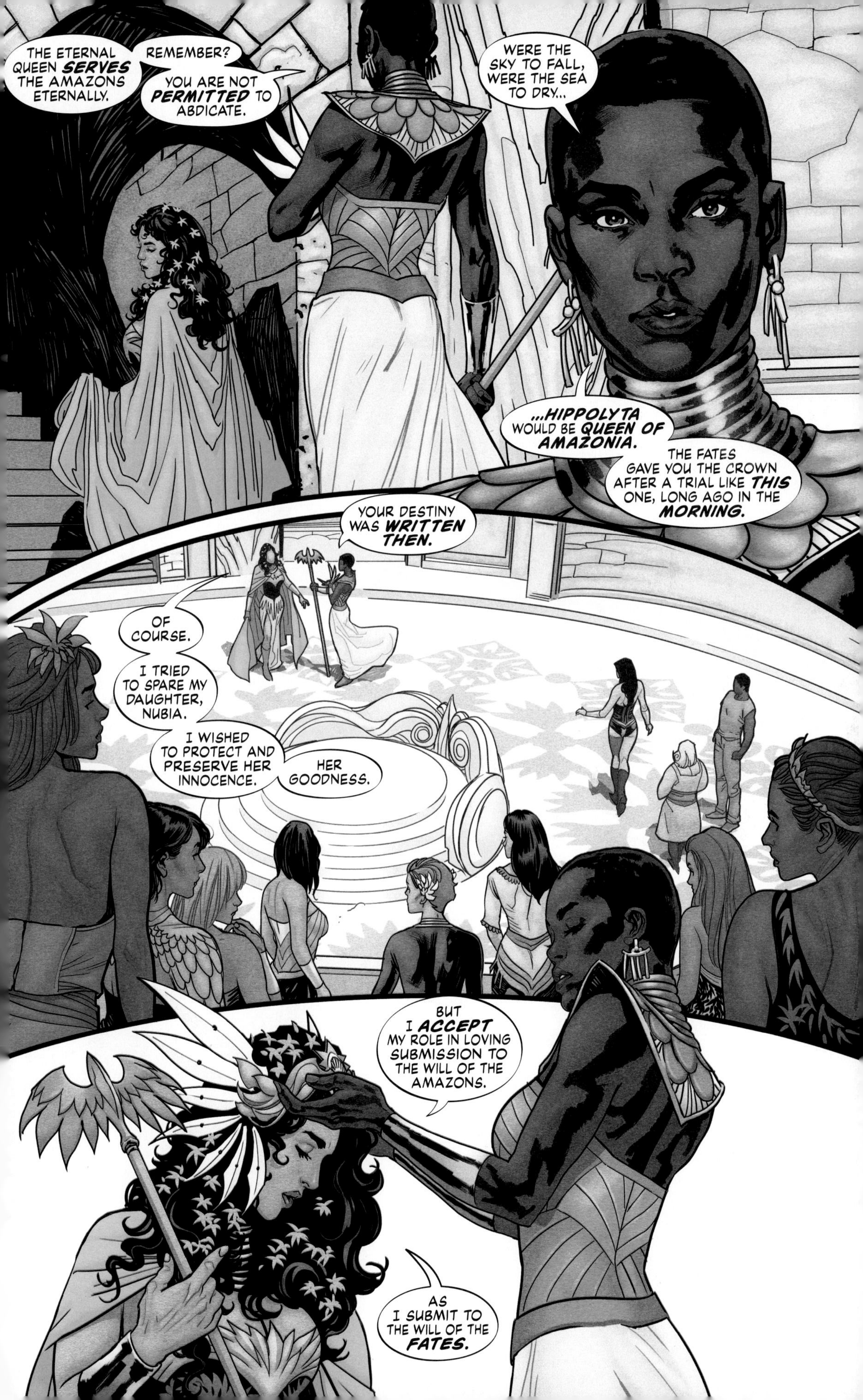
THE ETERNAL QUEEN SERVES THE AMAZONS ETERNALLY.
REMEMBER?
YOU ARE NOT PERMITTED TO ABDICATE.
WERE THE SKY TO FALL, WERE THE SEA TO DRY...
...HIPPOLYTA WOULD BE QUEEN OF AMAZONIA.
THE FATES GAVE YOU THE CROWN AFTER A TRIAL LIKE THIS ONE, LONG AGO IN THE MORNING.
YOUR DESTINY WAS WRITTEN THEN.
OF COURSE.
I TRIED TO SPARE MY DAUGHTER, NUBIA.
I WISHED TO PROTECT AND PRESERVE HER INNOCENCE.
HER GOODNESS.
BUT I ACCEPT MY ROLE IN LOVING SUBMISSION TO THE WILL OF THE AMAZONS.
AS I SUBMIT TO THE WILL OF THE FATES.

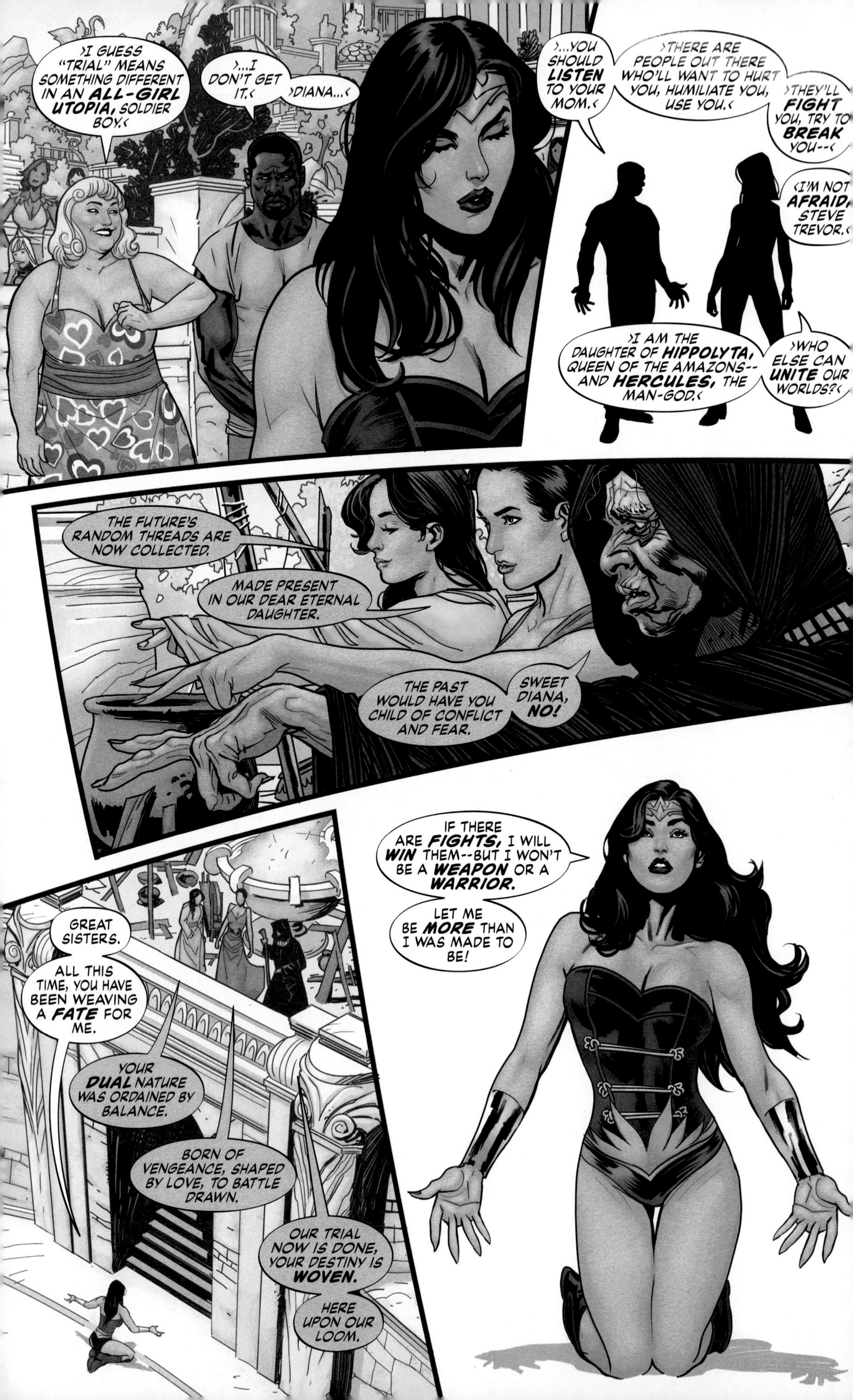
›I GUESS "TRIAL" MEANS SOMETHING DIFFERENT IN AN ALL-GIRL UTOPIA, SOLDIER BOY.‹
›...I DON'T GET IT.‹
›DIANA...‹
›...YOU SHOULD LISTEN TO YOUR MOM.‹
›THERE ARE PEOPLE OUT THERE WHO'LL WANT TO HURT YOU, HUMILIATE YOU, USE YOU.‹
›THEY'LL FIGHT YOU, TRY TO BREAK YOU--‹
‹I'M NOT AFRAID, STEVE TREVOR.‹
›I AM THE DAUGHTER OF HIPPOLYTA, QUEEN OF THE AMAZONS--AND HERCULES, THE MAN-GOD.‹
›WHO ELSE CAN UNITE OUR WORLDS?‹
THE FUTURE'S RANDOM THREADS ARE NOW COLLECTED.
MADE PRESENT IN OUR DEAR ETERNAL DAUGHTER.
THE PAST WOULD HAVE YOU CHILD OF CONFLICT AND FEAR.
SWEET DIANA, NO!
GREAT SISTERS.
ALL THIS TIME, YOU HAVE BEEN WEAVING A FATE FOR ME.
YOUR DUAL NATURE WAS ORDAINED BY BALANCE.
BORN OF VENGEANCE, SHAPED BY LOVE, TO BATTLE DRAWN.
OUR TRIAL NOW IS DONE, YOUR DESTINY IS WOVEN.
HERE UPON OUR LOOM.
IF THERE ARE FIGHTS, I WILL WIN THEM--BUT I WON'T BE A WEAPON OR A WARRIOR.
LET ME BE MORE THAN I WAS MADE TO BE!

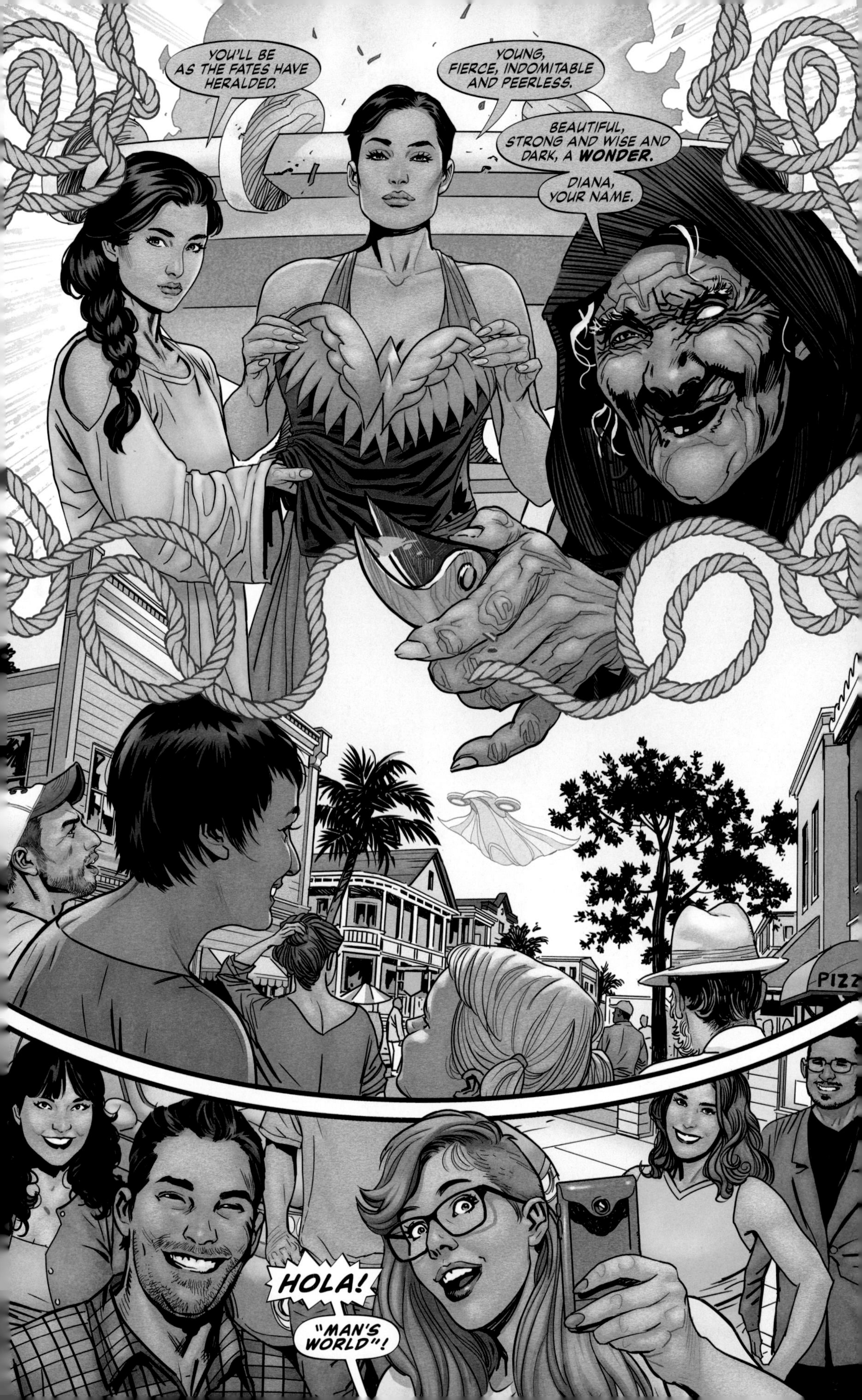
YOU'LL BE AS THE FATES HAVE HERALDED.
YOUNG, FIERCE, INDOMITABLE AND PEERLESS.
BEAUTIFUL, STRONG AND WISE AND DARK, A **WONDER.**
DIANA, YOUR NAME.
PIZZ
HOLA!
"MAN'S WORLD"!

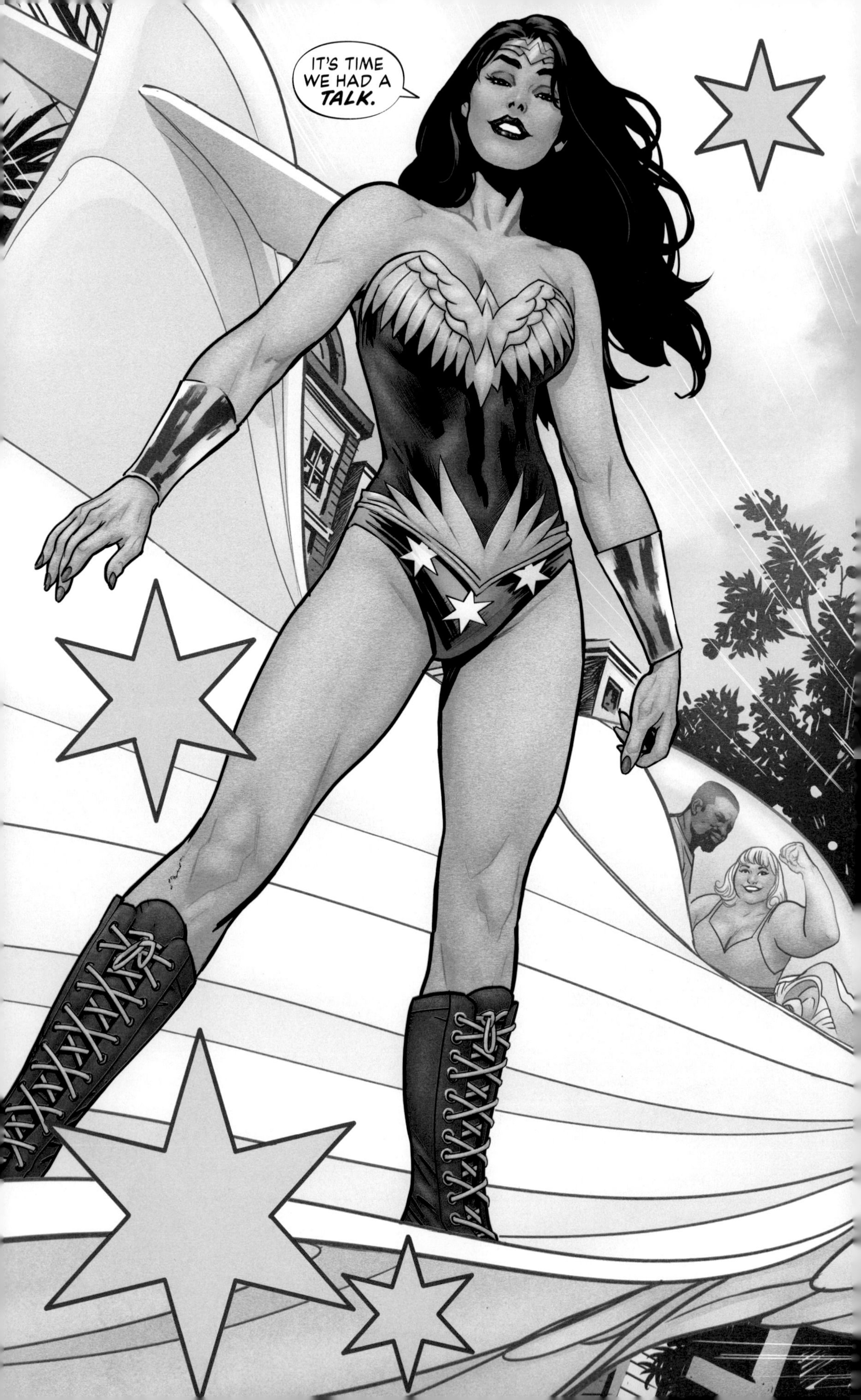
IT'S TIME WE HAD A *TALK.*

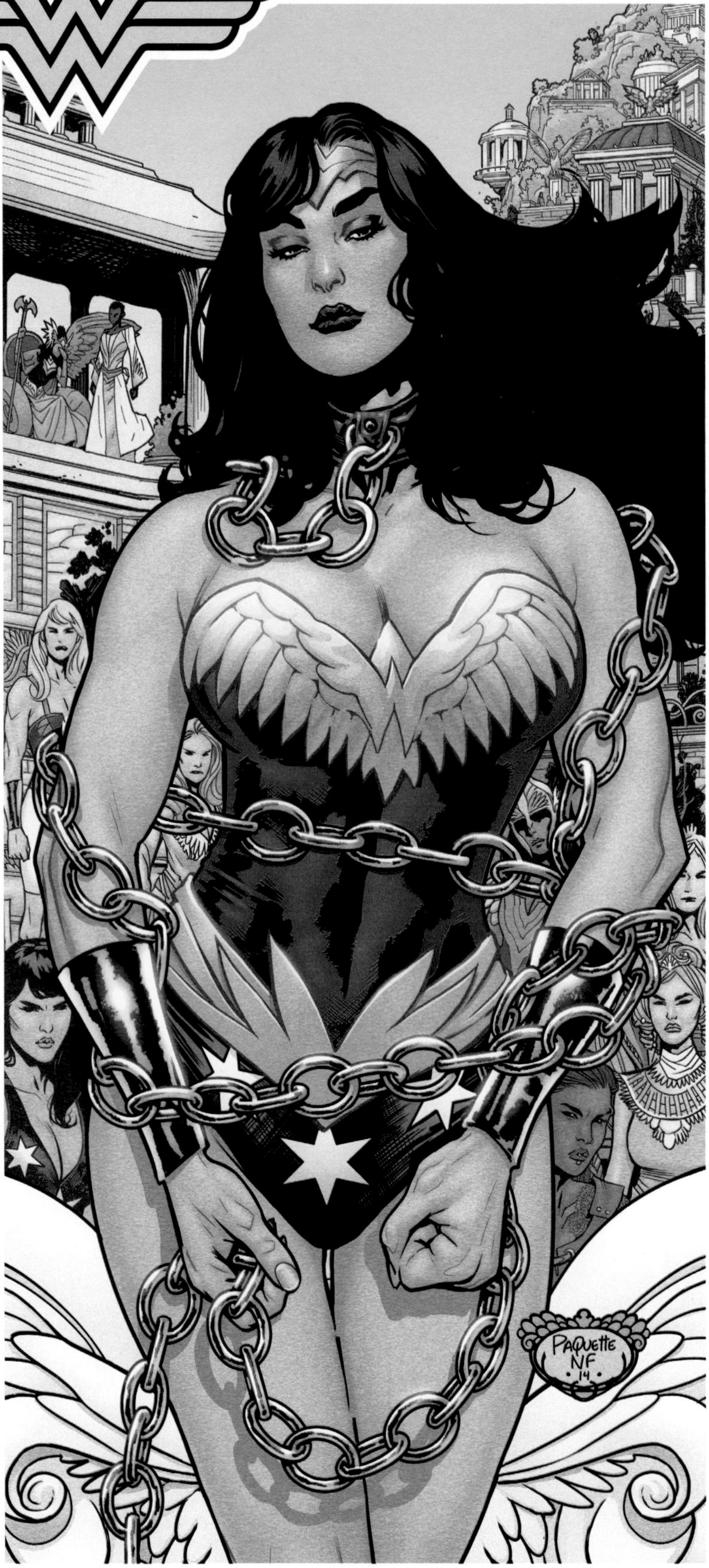
PAQUETTE
NF
'14

Earth One Sketchbook

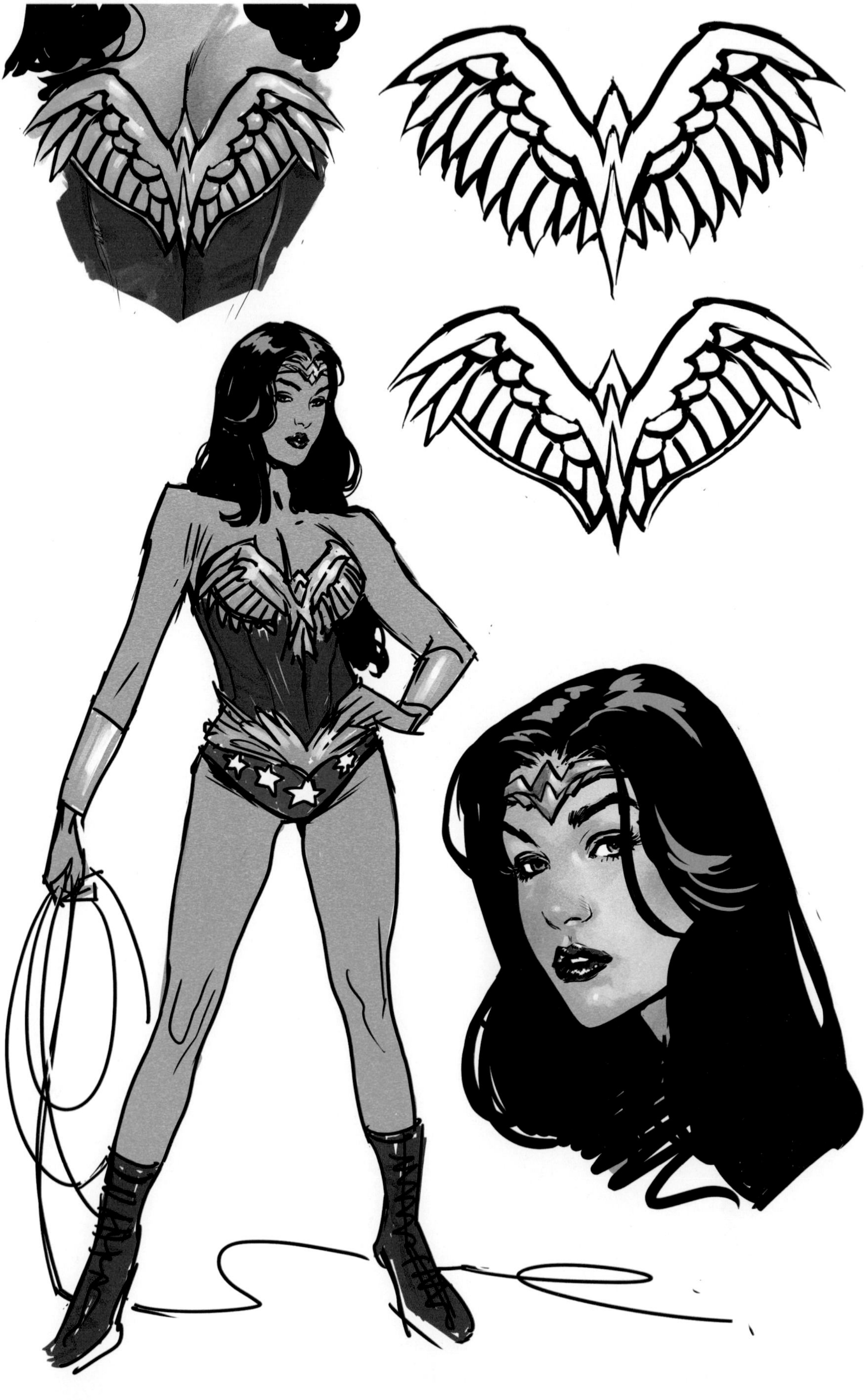

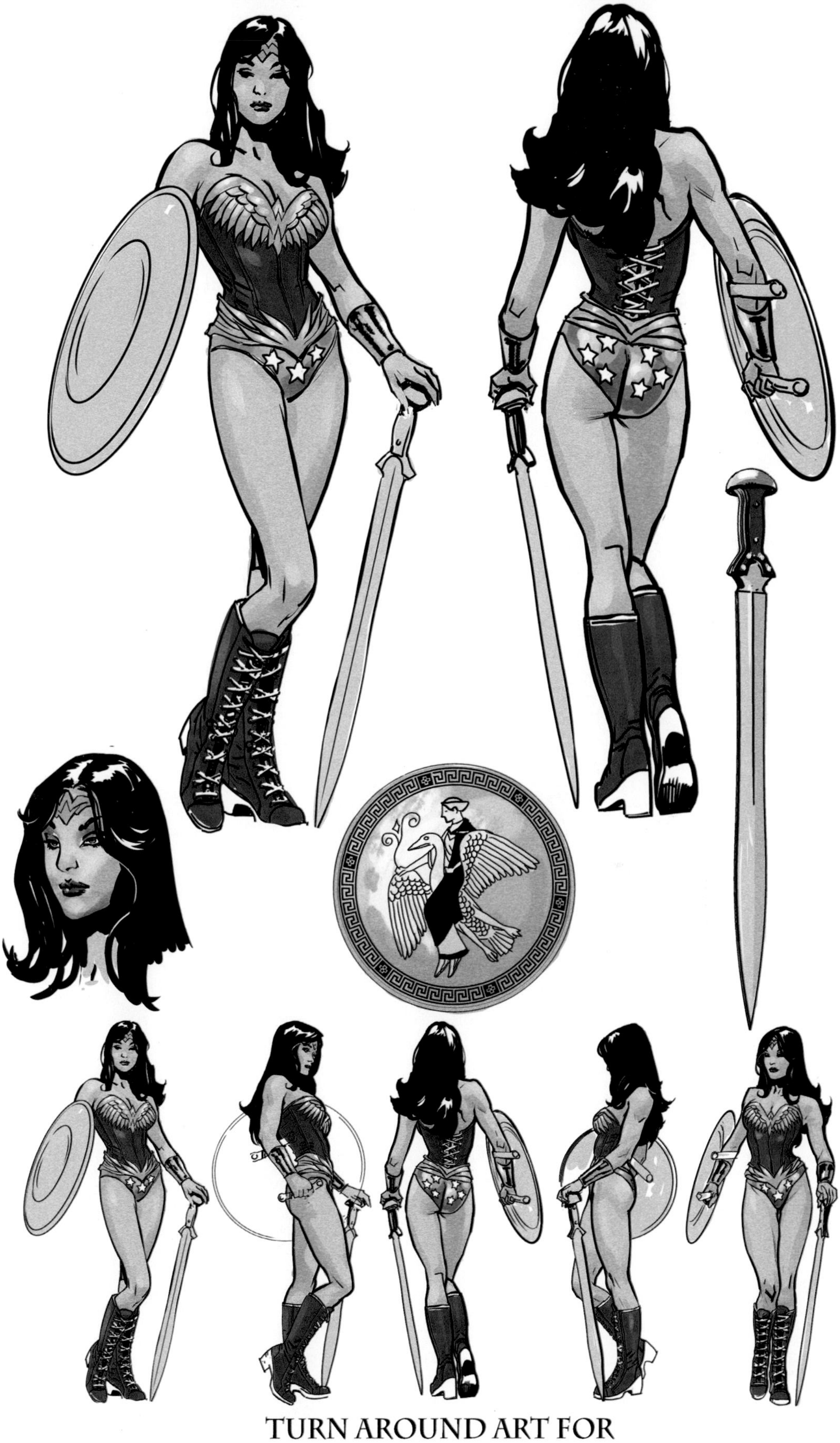

TURN AROUND ART FOR
DC COLLECTIBLES WONDER WOMAN:
ART OF WAR STATUE BY YANICK PAQUETTE

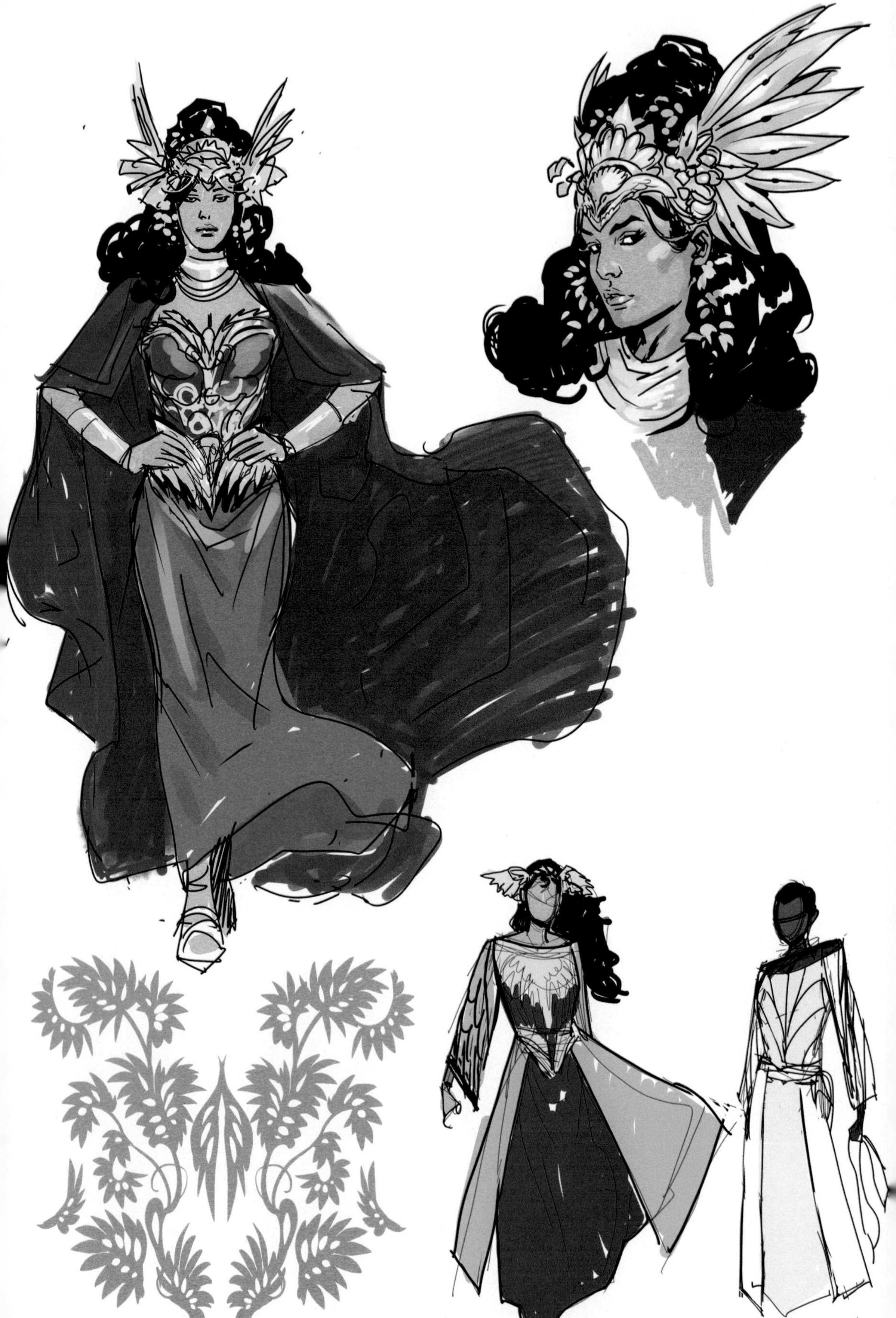

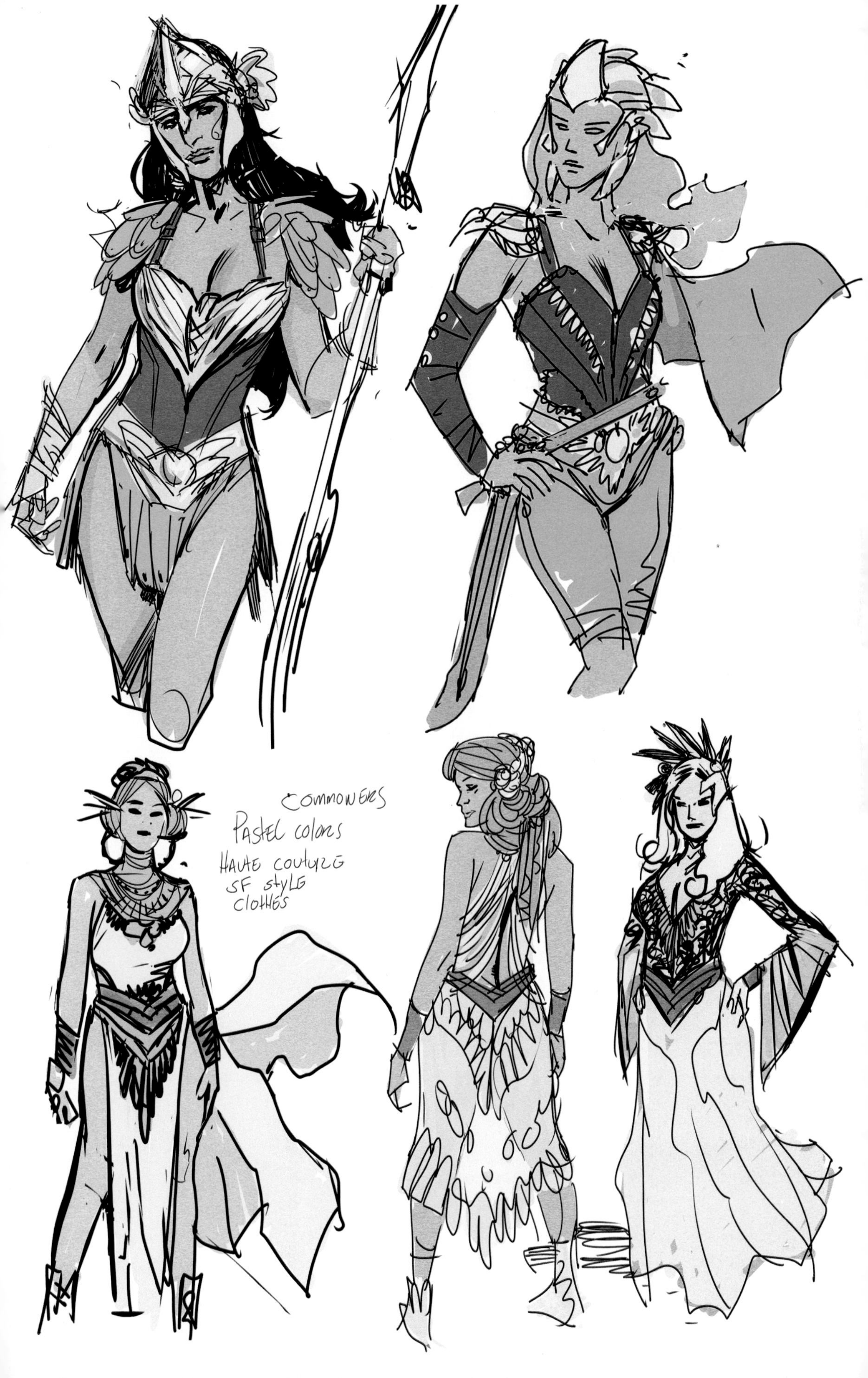
COMMONERS
PASTEL colors
HAUTE COUTURE
SF STYLE
CLOTHES

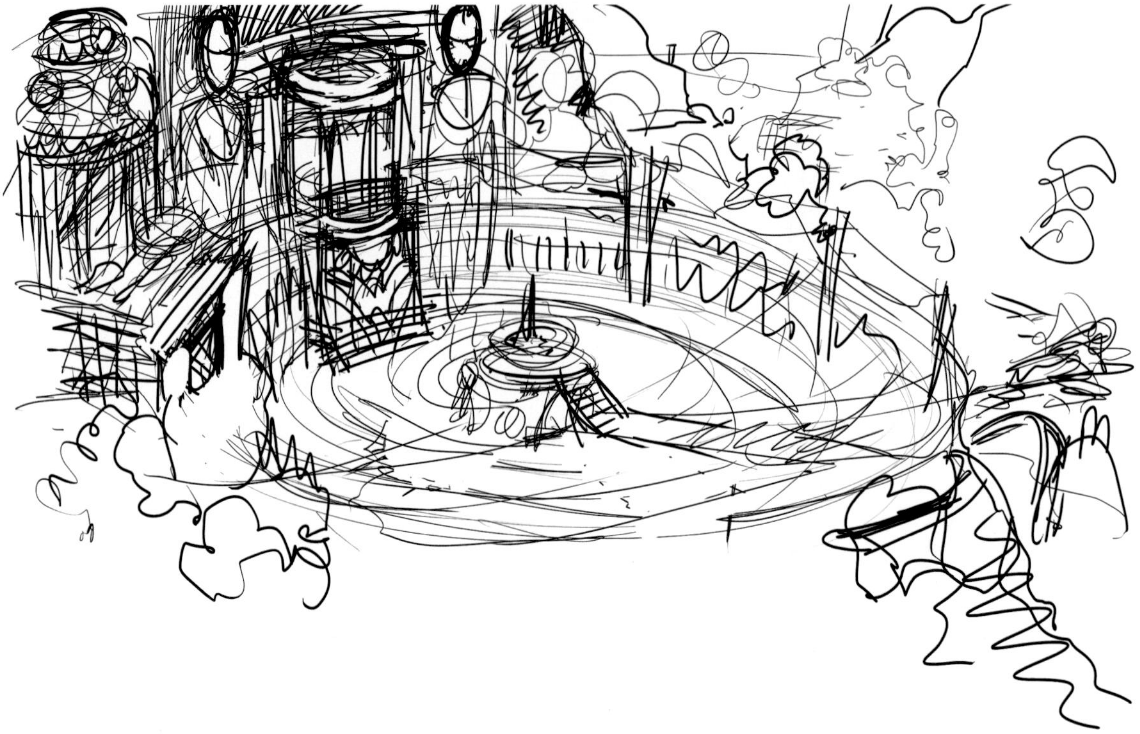

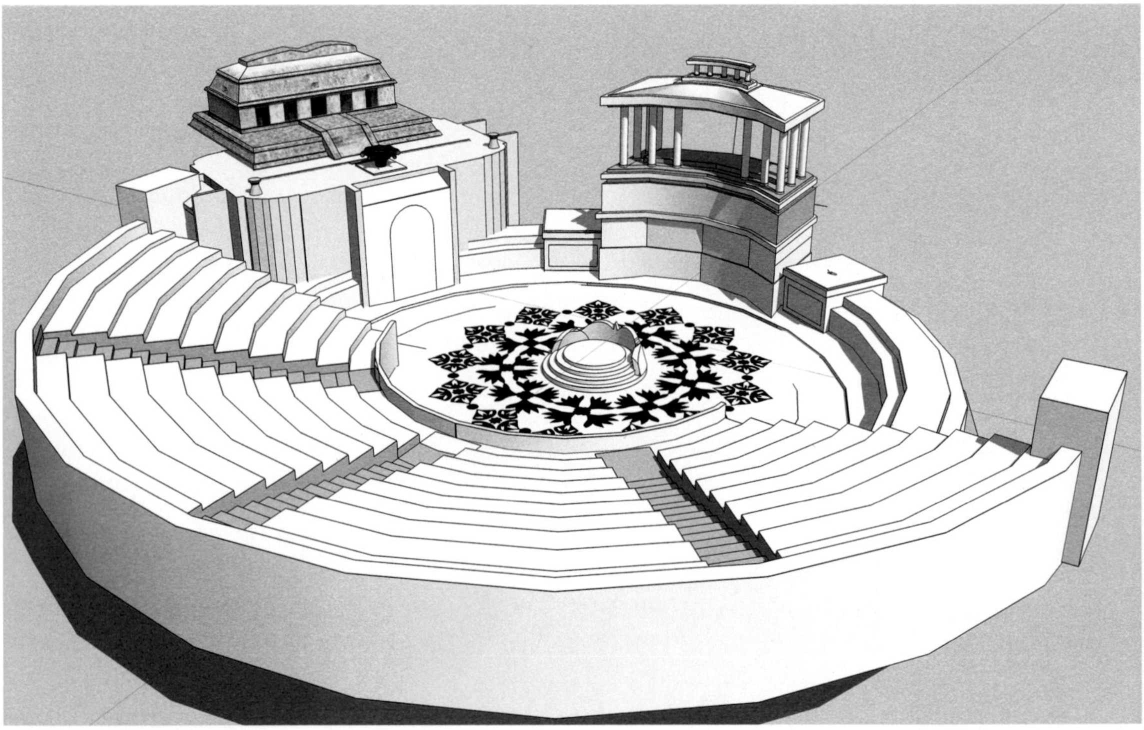

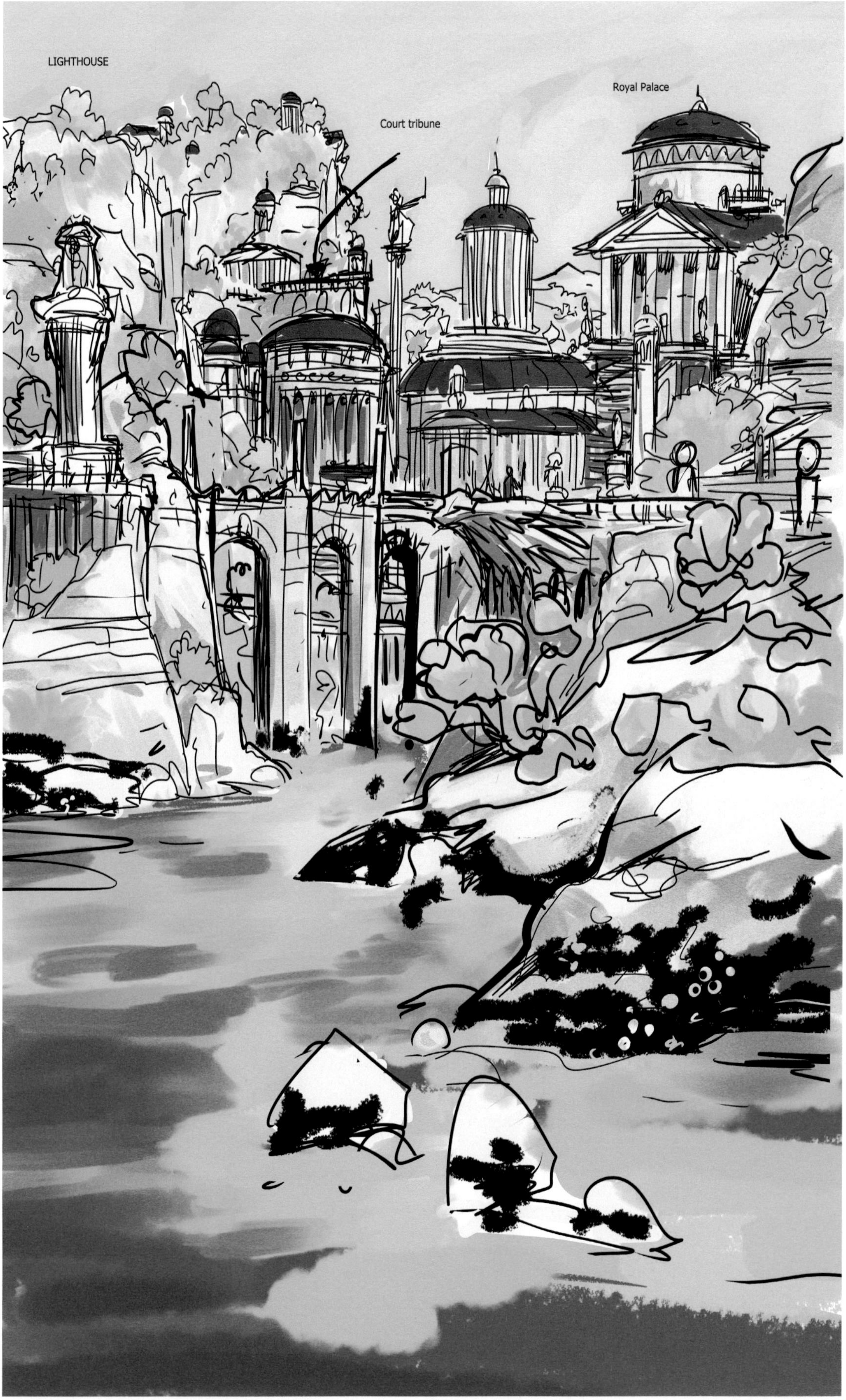
LIGHTHOUSE
Court tribune
Royal Palace

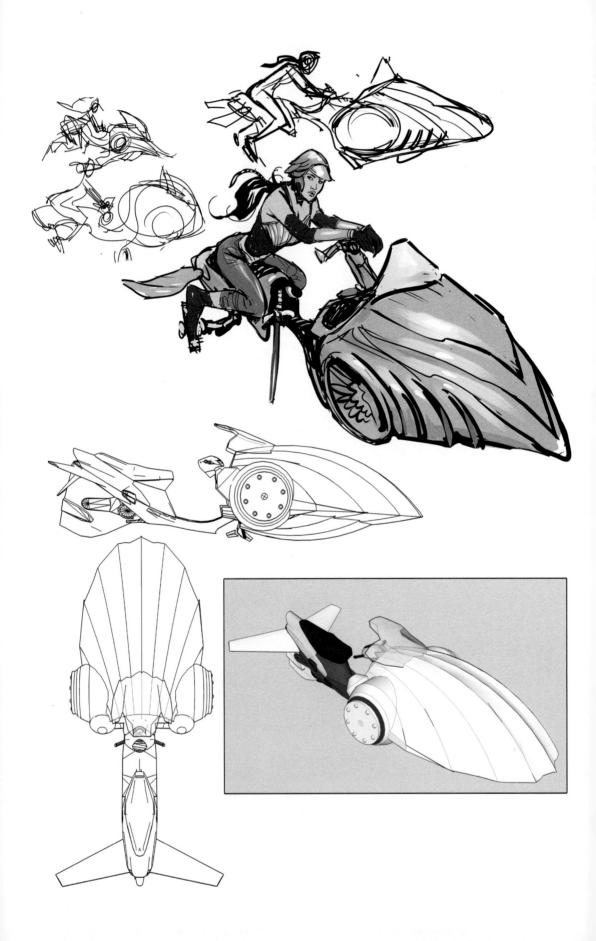

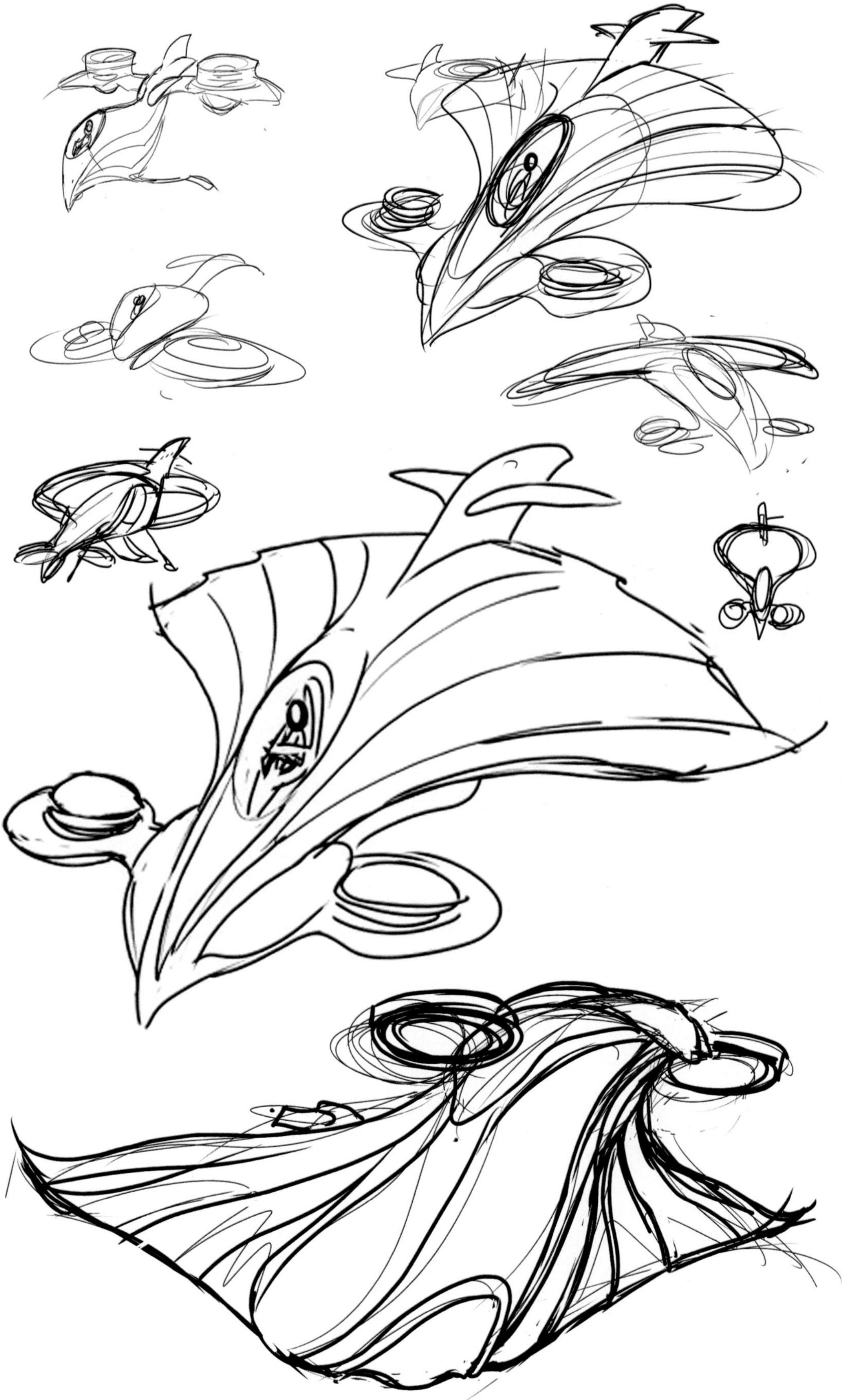

EARTH ONE

GRANT
MORRISON

Yanick Paquette

DC
COMICS™

EARTH
ONE

GRANT
MORRISON

Yanick paquette

DC COMICS™

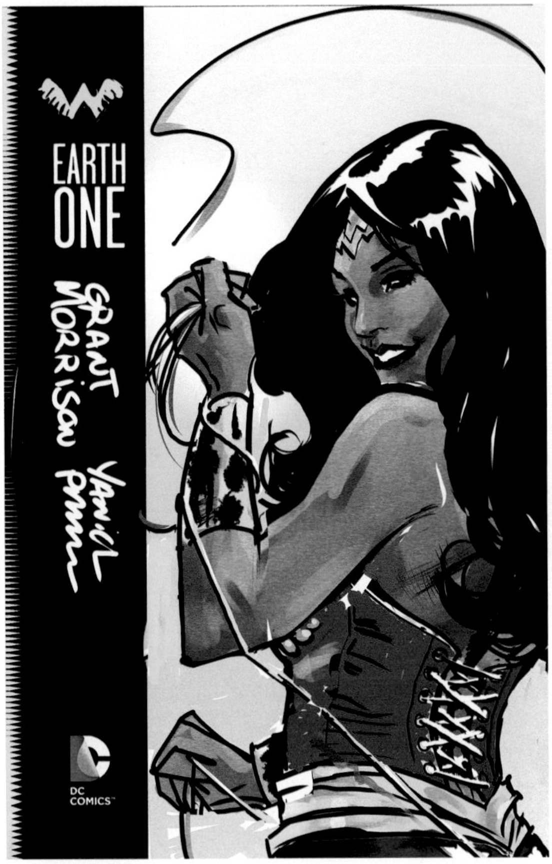
EARTH
ONE
GRANT MORRISON
DC COMICS

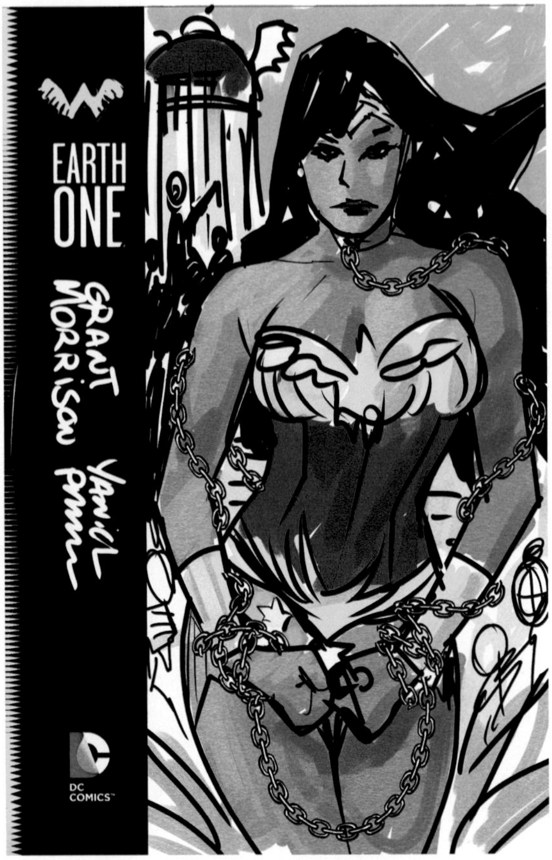
EARTH
ONE
GRANT MORRISON
DC COMICS

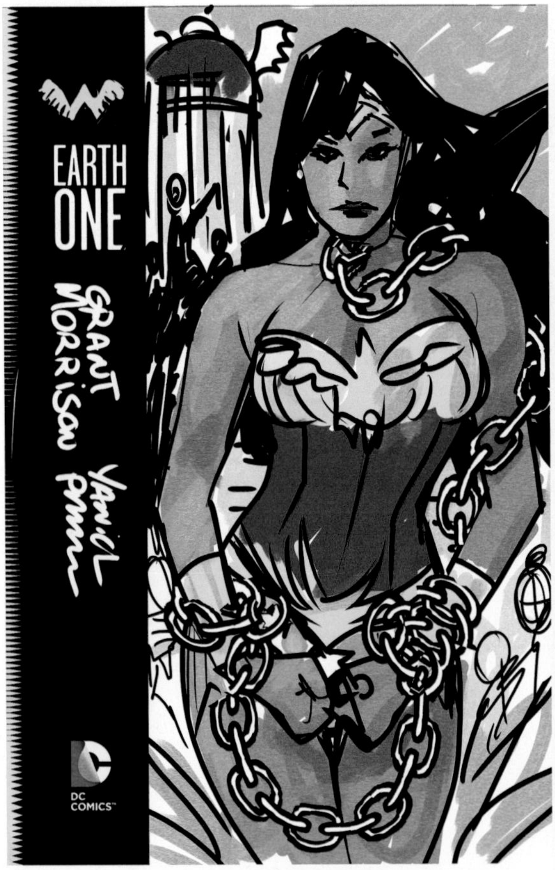
EARTH
ONE
GRANT MORRISON
DC COMICS

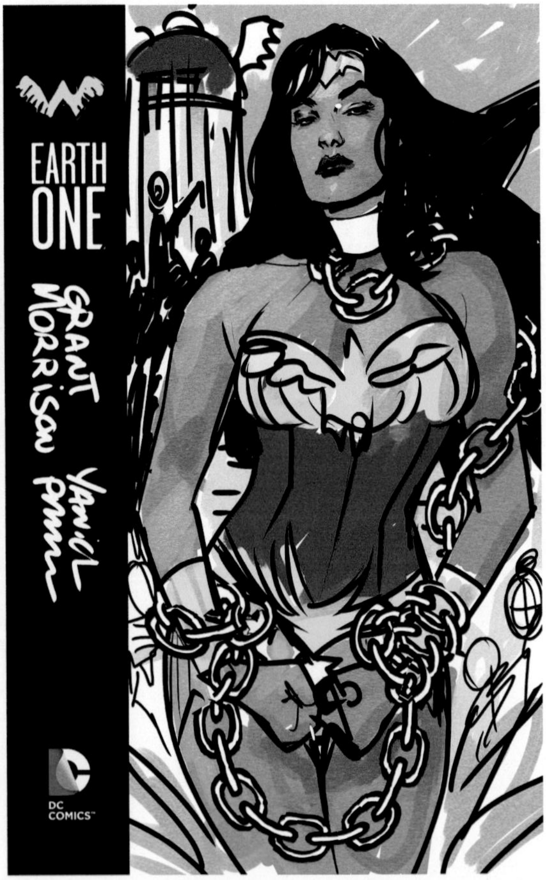
EARTH
ONE
GRANT MORRISON
DC COMICS

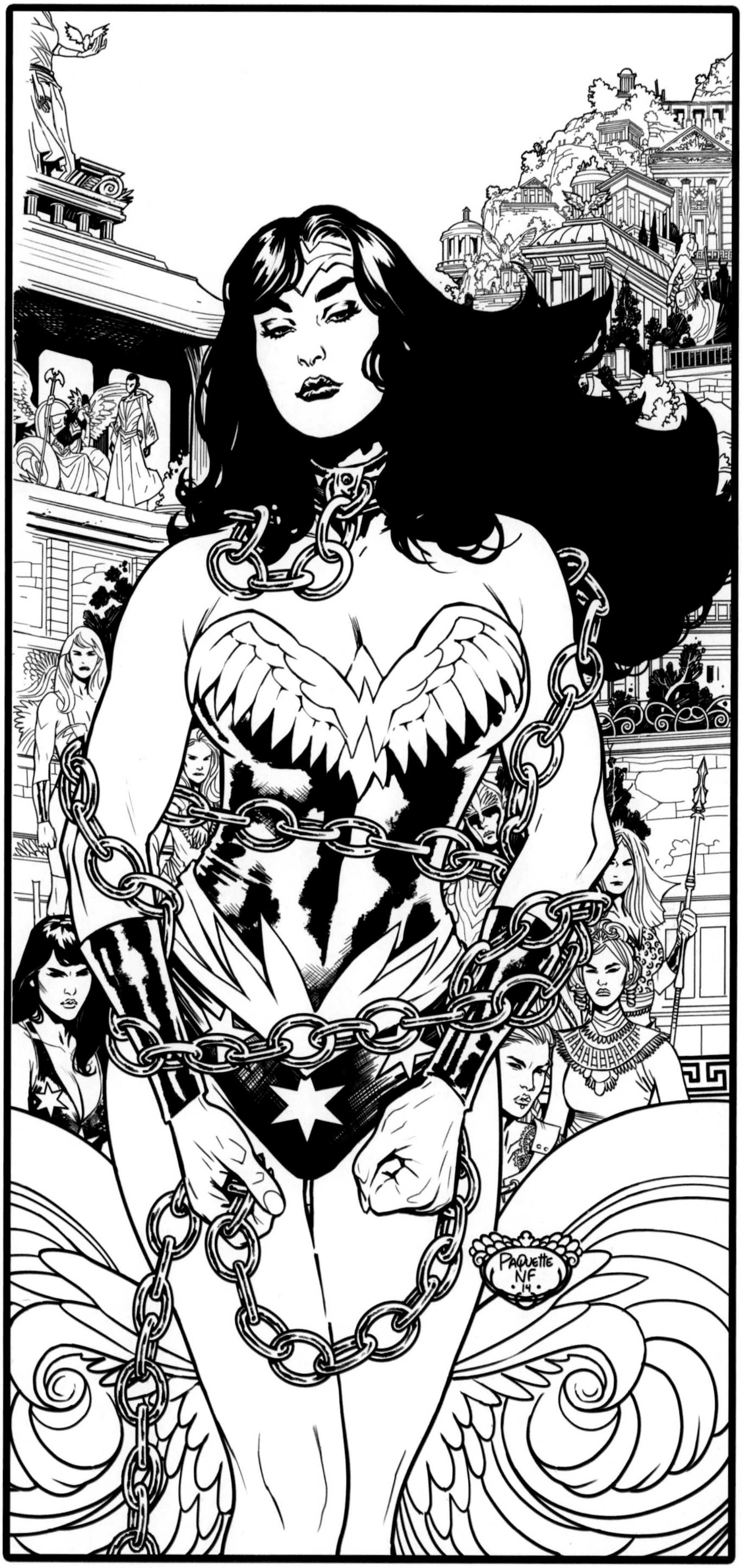
PAQUETTE
NF
'14

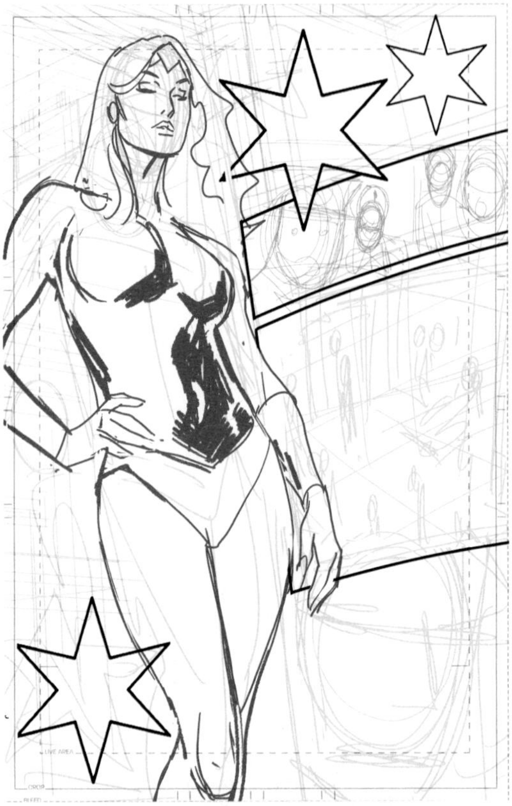

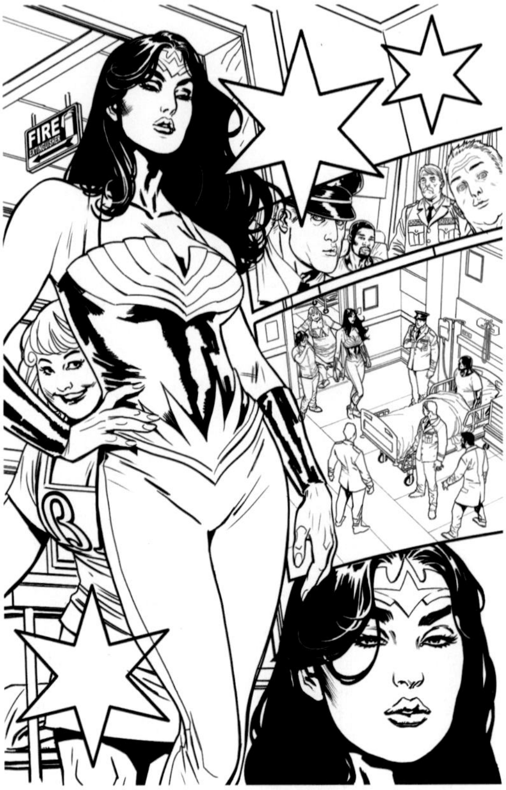
FIRE

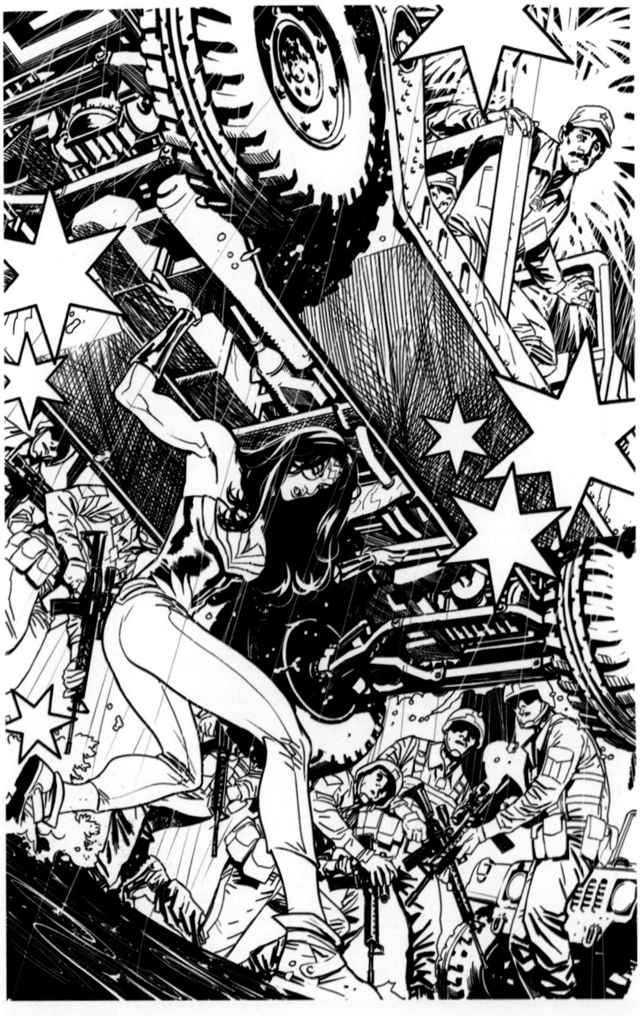

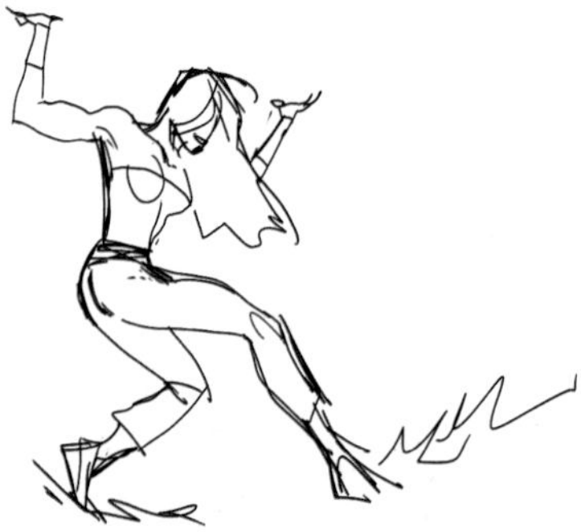

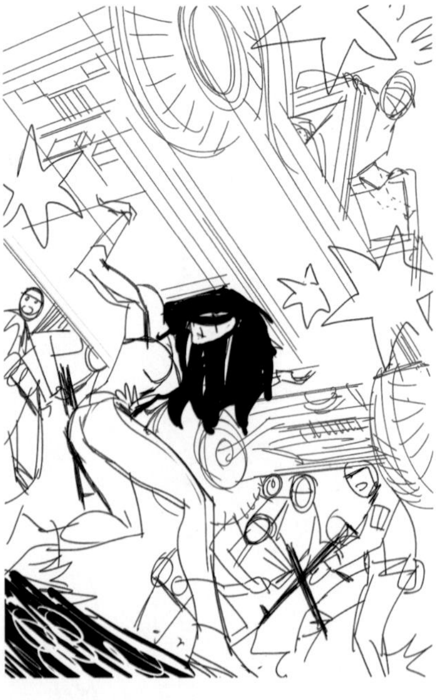

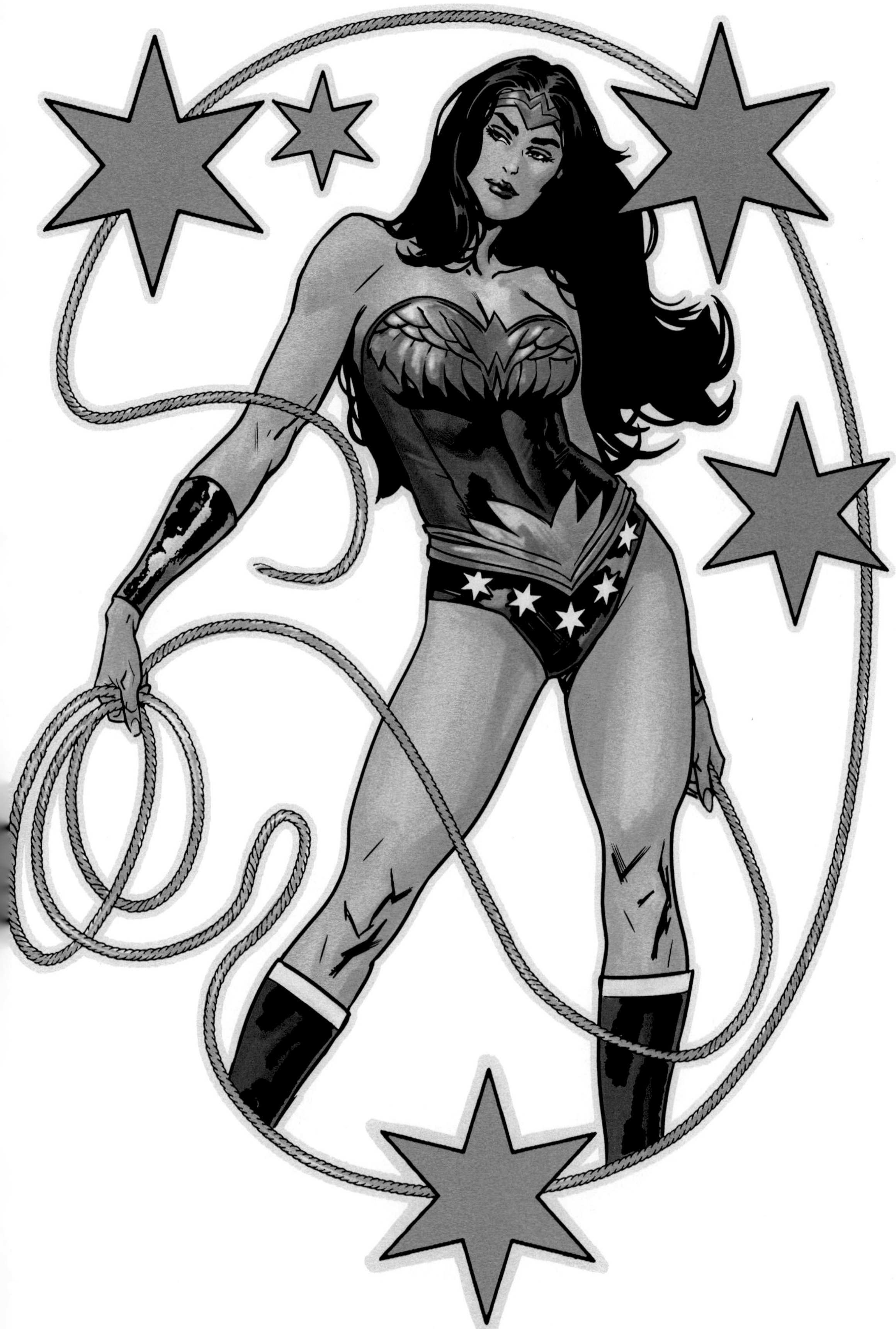

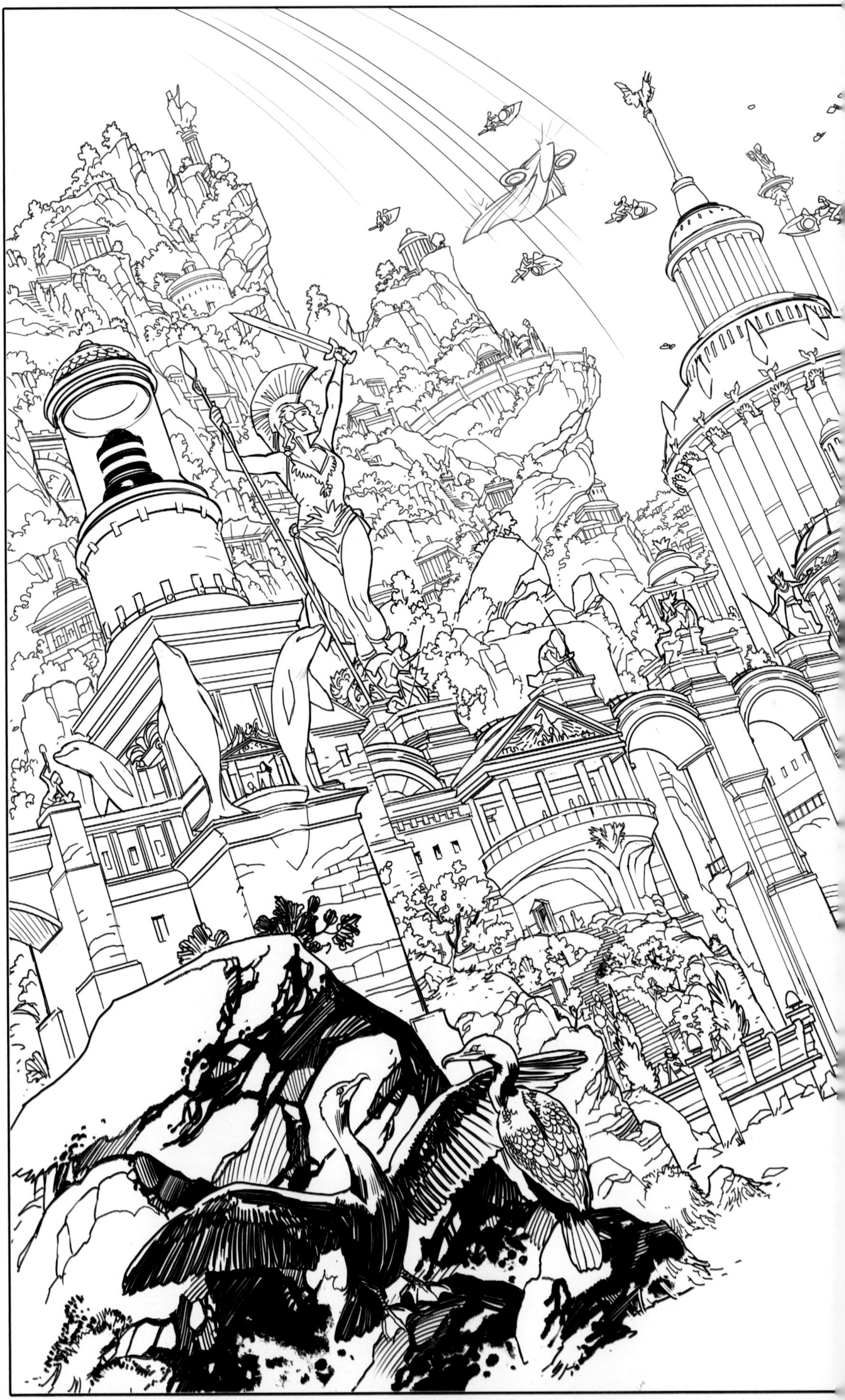

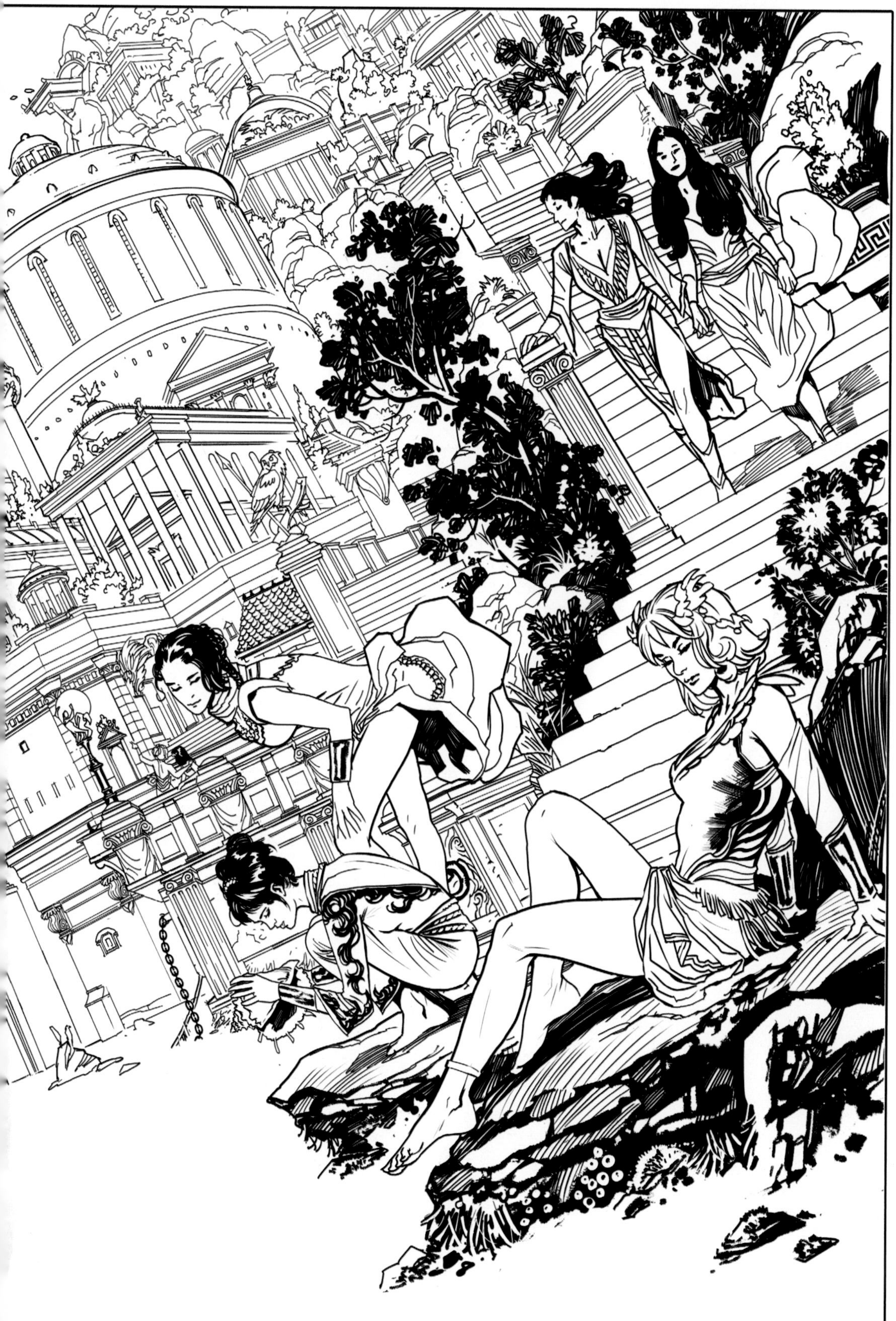

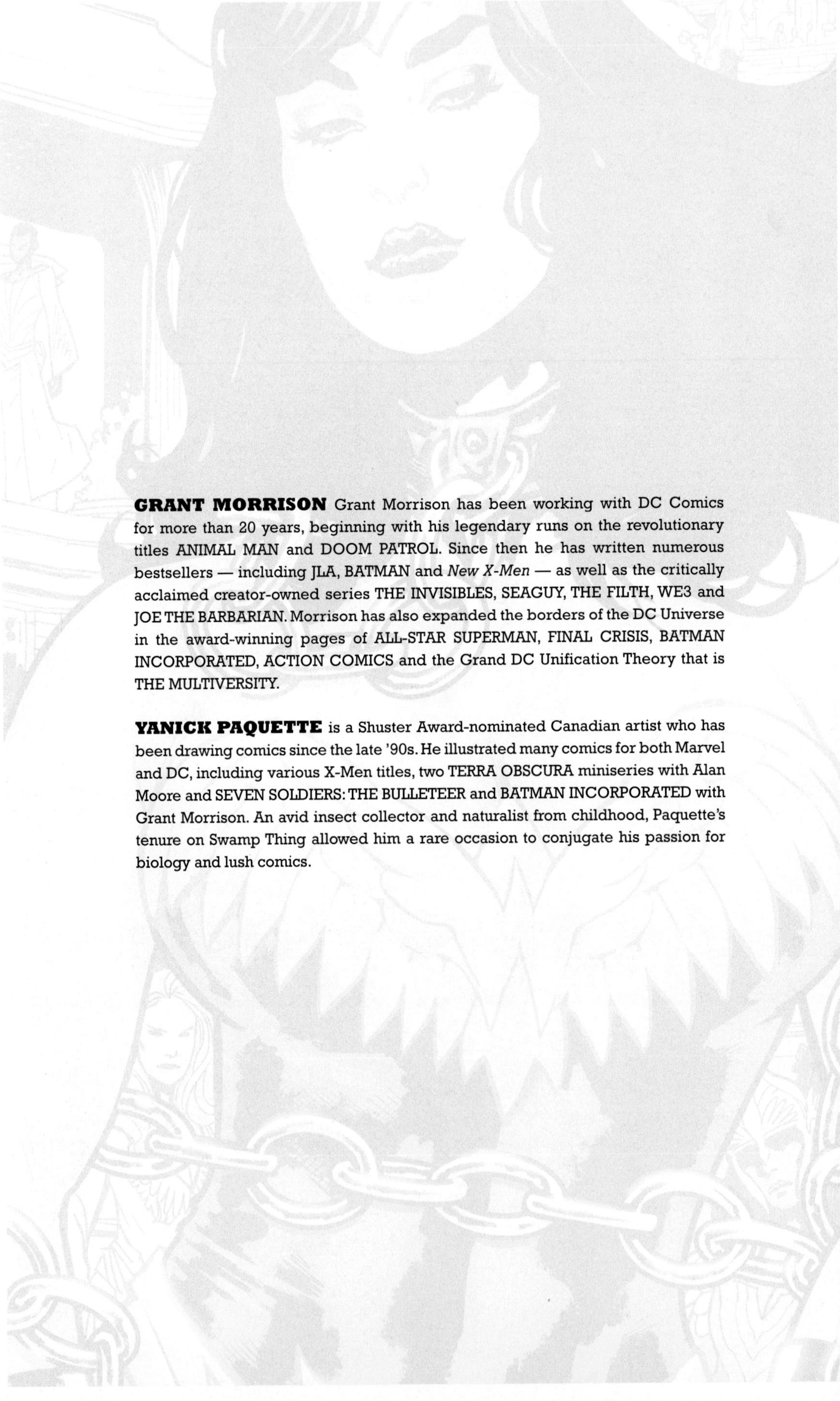

GRANT MORRISON Grant Morrison has been working with DC Comics for more than 20 years, beginning with his legendary runs on the revolutionary titles ANIMAL MAN and DOOM PATROL. Since then he has written numerous bestsellers — including JLA, BATMAN and *New X-Men* — as well as the critically acclaimed creator-owned series THE INVISIBLES, SEAGUY, THE FILTH, WE3 and JOE THE BARBARIAN. Morrison has also expanded the borders of the DC Universe in the award-winning pages of ALL-STAR SUPERMAN, FINAL CRISIS, BATMAN INCORPORATED, ACTION COMICS and the Grand DC Unification Theory that is THE MULTIVERSITY.

YANICK PAQUETTE is a Shuster Award-nominated Canadian artist who has been drawing comics since the late '90s. He illustrated many comics for both Marvel and DC, including various X-Men titles, two TERRA OBSCURA miniseries with Alan Moore and SEVEN SOLDIERS: THE BULLETEER and BATMAN INCORPORATED with Grant Morrison. An avid insect collector and naturalist from childhood, Paquette's tenure on Swamp Thing allowed him a rare occasion to conjugate his passion for biology and lush comics.